CRYPTS

 OF

LONDON

MALCOLM JOHNSON

The
History
Press

For Dr Julian Litten and Professor Arthur Burns.
With thanks and respect.

Cover illustration: Westminster Abbey.
Thomas Rowlandson (1757-1827)
Death and the Antiquaries, 1816, aquatint
(reproduced by kind permission of Derrick Chivers FSA).
The drawing recalls the opening of Edward I's coffin by antiquaries
in 1744 in the Abbey. It accompanied a poem by William
Combe in his English Dance of Death: 'A curious wish their
fancies tickled / To know how royal folk were pickled.' Death's
dart is aimed at one of the antiquaries disturbing the dead.

First published 2013

The History Press
The Mill, Brimscombe Port
Stroud, Gloucestershire, GL5 2QG
www.thehistorypress.co.uk

British Library Cataloguing in Publication Data.
A catalogue record for this book is available from the British Library.

ISBN 978 1 86077 672 4

Typesetting and origination by The History Press
Printed in Great Britain

☠ CONTENTS ☠

 Foreword

Christian faith emerged from the empty tomb and the early Christians, in great cities like Rome, often chose to hold their services in the catacombs. Most religions have offered an approach to the mystery of death, and part of what signals the evolution of human beings in the earliest times is evidence of care in the disposal of human remains.

Against this background, Malcolm Johnson has amassed some fascinating material on the 'eternal bedchambers'; the crypts of the churches of the Cities of London and Westminster.

I vividly remember conducting a requiem at St Andrew's Holborn on the occasion, described in this book, when the remains of centuries were reverently transferred from the crypt of the church to the City of London Cemetery. Despite visits over the past twenty years to many of the places described in this book, I learnt a very great deal that was new to me, and I imagine that Dr Johnson's work will prove a goldmine to local historians and the organisers of ghost tours for many years to come.

Our ancestors practised contemplation of their own mortality as a fruitful spiritual discipline and while *Crypts of London* is a significant contribution to social history, it is also a reminder that 'here we have no abiding city'. Instead we look for 'The life of the world to come'.

Richard Londin,
Bishop of London
2013

💀 Acknowledgements 💀

My grateful thanks to Richard, Bishop of London, for taking the time in the midst of his busy life to write the Foreword.

I owe a debt of gratitude to the late Miss Isobel Thornley's Bequest to the University of London which helped me financially to publish this book based on my PhD for King's College, London. The photographs enhance it greatly, and I thank my friends Paul Thurtle, Kevin Kelly and Ian Brown for climbing over gravestones in cemeteries to take them. David Hoffman, a professional photographer, whose work for my homeless centre at Aldgate attracted much attention (and money), spent a day in the vaults of St Clement, King Square (by kind permission of Fr David Allen), and I find it difficult to thank him enough for some superb illustrations.

Dr Tony Trowles, Head of the Abbey Collection and Librarian, and Mr Jo Wisdom have kindly checked chapters 4 and 5 for me. My editors, Cate Ludlow and Ruth Boyes, have been supportive and patient with me and Stephen Green checked my grammar so I am grateful.

This book is dedicated to Professor Arthur Burns (my PhD supervisor) and to Dr Julian Litten. Both have guided and helped my research.

List of Illustrations

St Andrew Holborn crypt (photos by Russell Bowes, courtesy of the Venerable Lyle Dennen and Dan Gallagher)
Anthropoid coffin.
Jumbled coffins.
Lead coffin.
Steps from the church surrounded by coffins.
Two skeletons share a coffin.

St Luke, Old Street (courtesy of Oxford Archaeology)
Coffin in crypt vault before clearance, 2001.

St James Garlickhythe (by permission of the rector and PCC; photos by Ellis Charles Pike)
The desiccated seventeenth-century corpse 'Jimmy', still resident in the church.

St Dunstan in the West crypt
(by permission of the Revd William Gulliford; photos by Ian Brown)
Gate to north catacombs.
Inside catacombs.
Hoare family vault.
Central vault.
Staircase to crypt.

All Hallows Lombard Street (by courtesy of the vicar and PCC, All Hallows Twickenham; photos by Joe Pendock)
Father Time and the Grim Reaper.
Father Time.

St Clement Danes (photos by Alan Taylor)
West end of crypt, *c.*1956.
The crypt chapel today.
Blocked crypt door.
Sunlight in crypt.
Uncovered entrance.

St John Smith Square
Today's crypt restaurant (Helen Bartosinski).

Holy Trinity Minories (by permission of the rector of St Botolph Aldgate; David Hoffman Photo Library)
Six depositum plates taken from the Dartmouth family coffins in the crypt. Notes by
  Dr Julian Litten.

💀 ABBREVIATIONS 💀

Repositories etc.
- BL   British Library
- GL   Guildhall Library
- HS   Harleian Society
- LDF   London Diocesan Fund Archives
- LMA   London Metropolitan Archives
- LPL   Lambeth Palace Library
- ODNB   Oxford Dictionary of National Biography
- PP   Parliamentary Papers
- TNA   The National Archives
- UCL   University College London Library
- WCA   Westminster City Archives

Source types
- Br   Burial register
- Ca   Churchwardens' accounts
- Tf   Table of burial fees
- Vm   Vestry minutes

Unless otherwise stated the place of publication is London.

Key
- [*]   Church still standing
- [T]   Tower still stands

N.B.   Church or tower without symbol has been demolished

1

INTRODUCTION

The two cities of London and Westminster stank in the eighteenth and early nineteenth centuries. The Thames, full of sewage, flowed past streets covered in human and animal filth. Smoke from chimneys made the air more putrid. The word 'effluvium', a noxious exhalation affecting the sense of smell, appears regularly in the early nineteenth century when a few Londoners began to suspect that there might be a link between disease, destitution and foul smells. One of these was the smell of death, almost unknown in Britain today, since corpses are embalmed soon after death. Such a smell inevitably led back to the Anglican burial places of the two cities, which were either crypts full of rotting coffins or graveyards, where bones were dug up after twenty or more years. Worshippers knew that beneath their feet as they walked into church or sat in their pews lay the decomposing bodies of their forebears, but, unlike in France, no one proposed changes until the 1830s.

In the early eighteenth century the City of London possessed seventy churches with crypts, thirty-one of which no longer survive. Westminster has had twenty-five churches with crypts since 1666, and only six have been demolished or leased after the human remains have been removed. Rarely do the published histories of these buildings mention these undercrofts. Two exceptions are Westminster Abbey, whose tombs are described in chapter 4, and St Paul's Cathedral, whose crypt is described in chapter 5 (this relies heavily on a recent scholarly book).[1] Obviously it is possible to visit the churches that have survived and establish precise details of their crypt; where it is not possible to enter, burial registers can give details of size and layout. For the churches that have not survived, the best descriptions of their undercrofts are often found in the faculties that authorised their destruction, and in vestry minutes recording the process of emptying the human remains and transferring them to a cemetery. Written accounts are rare, because few people visited these dark, dismal places apart from the sexton. However, an account by Frank Buckland of the undercroft at St Martin-in-the-Fields in 1859 has survived, and is contained in chapter 2.[2] Two churches over the borders of the two cities – Christ Church Spitalfields and St Luke Old Street – are included because both have had the contents of their crypt removed, and thus provide valuable information. St Clement King Square is described because the incumbent has allowed me access.

Before proceeding it is necessary to clarify matters of terminology. Dr Julian Litten, a leading authority on funeral fashions and furnishings, describes a vault as 'The eternal bedchamber'. His *The English Way of Death* is a good starting point for anyone interested in this topic, covering as it does burial customs over a long period.[3] A burial vault, he says, is a subterranean chamber of stone or brick capable of housing a minimum of two coffins side by side and with an internal height of at least 5½ft. Anything narrower is best understood as a brick-lined grave. A crypt is a semi-subterranean copy of the floor plan of the building. The bays below a church's side aisles were often private freehold vaults, partitioned, whereas under the nave was one large space for parish or public interments. Clerical corpses were usually placed under the chancel in open or closed vaults. Family brick graves or single brick graves covered with a ledger stone differed only slightly from vaults, and the incumbent decided where they should be – perhaps under a particular pew.[4] Earth graves were often unmarked. The vaults could not be emptied or sold, so if a family moved away the space became unproductive; but in the City all this changed when the Great Fire destroyed many churches, and in the rebuilding programme vaults were cleared.[5] The new crypts were open plan and space was easily available, although private vaults were soon located behind grilles in the bays around the walls. When a death occurred, families could ask the sexton to find where their forebears lay, so that they might be interred there too. Rarely did mourners enter a crypt, because the committal was said at its door or in church.

Until 1666 only the royal family and the aristocracy were interred in vaults, usually beneath a cathedral. Medieval monarchs were laid in tomb chests above ground, but Henry VII built a chapel at the east end of Westminster Abbey with chambers underneath, in which the Tudor and Stuart sovereigns still lie.[6]

After the Reformation, burial within a church was seen as a mark of social distinction. The nobility regarded it as their right, but by the mid-seventeenth century the professional classes were also seeing it as a sign of a successful career. Over the next century doctors, solicitors, high-ranking soldiers and 'gentlefolk' frequently left instructions in their wills for intramural burial, although some cautioned prudence and economy in arranging it because fees could be high. By law, according to the Revd William Watson, an eighteenth-century canonist,[7] the incumbent alone decided who should be interred in the crypt:

Because the Soil and Freehold of the Church is in the Parson alone, and that the Church is not, as the Churchyard is, a common Burial-place for all the Parishioners, the Church-wardens, or Ordinary himself, cannot grant Licence of Burying to any Person within the Church but only the Rector, or Incumbent thereof … yet the Church-wardens by Custom may have a Fee for every Burial within the Church, by reason the parish is at the Charge of repairing the Floor.[8]

Precise figures of intramural interments are hard to establish, because rarely are they recorded separately by the parish clerk. In the eighteenth century the percentage of burials in church varied from 3 per cent in the poor parish of St Botolph Bishopsgate to around 60 per cent in the wealthy parishes of St Margaret Pattens and St Stephen Walbrook. An examination of parochial records in the two cities suggest that an average for intramural interments was between 5 and 8 per cent.

Burial fees represented a high proportion of parish income. According to my research, until 1700 the City of London parishes could receive between 7 and 20 per cent of their non-poor rate annual income from burial dues. In the eighteenth century most received around 7 per cent of their income from interments, although at St James Garlickhythe the average was 26.9. By contrast, all the five Westminster parishes had a high burial income at the end of the eighteenth century: it was around 35 per cent of the wardens' income at St Martin-in-the-Fields and 25 per cent at St James Piccadilly. It thus made a significant contribution to the parish economy.

The cataclysmic Great Fire of 1666 had a profound impact on burial provision in the City of London: eighty-six churches were destroyed along with St Paul's Cathedral (where the congregation of St Faith, who met in the crypt's Jesus chapel, also lost their place of worship). Of these churches thirty-two were not rebuilt, although twenty-four in the east or north-east of the City were not affected. Crypts were destroyed with their buildings, so the space available for intramural burial declined.

During the next thirty years Wren, together with Robert Hooke, Peter Mills and Edward Jerman, designed and built St Paul's Cathedral and fifty-one replacement churches. Most of Wren's churches had vaults beneath them, and nearly all had burial grounds, which were well used because the population of the Square Mile was still large. Most of the sites of churches that were not rebuilt were now used as burial grounds.

During the next 150 years fourteen of these churches were rebuilt, either to enlarge them or because of dilapidation; all except St James, Duke's Place, had a crypt as spacious as the church above.[9] In Westminster the five churches in existence in 1600 all had undercrofts, and three of these retained them when rebuilt. Crypts were also given to the twenty additional churches built in Westminster before 1852.

The clergy, churchwardens and vestries[10] decided to use these spaces to earn money by interring wealthy parishioners in them, instead of using the space for other purposes. In doing so, however, they went against the advice and opinions of both architects and others. Some had always doubted the wisdom of burying the dead among the living. In 1552 Bishop Hugh Latimer thought it 'an unwholesome thing to bury within the city', considering that 'it is the occasion of great sickness and disease'.[11] Mainly for architectural reasons Wren was also opposed to burial in or close to the church, and his first designs for the rebuilding of the City contained no churchyards. Some years later he wrote to the commissioners responsible for building fifty new churches:

> I would wish that all burials in churches might be disallowed, which is not only unwholesome, but the pavements can never be kept even, nor pews upright: If the Churchyard be close upon the Church, this also is inconvenient, because the Ground being continually raised by the Graves, occasions in Time, a Descent by Steps into the Church, which renders it damp … It will be enquired, where then shall be Burials? I answer, in Cemeteries seated in the Outskirts of the Town … they will bound the excessive growth of the City with a graceful Border, which is now encircled with Scavengers Dung-stalls. The Cemeteries should be half a Mile, or more, distant from the Church, the Charge need be little or no more than usual; the Service may be first performed in the Church.[12]

Sir John Vanbrugh agreed with Wren, and suggested that suburban walled cemeteries should be opened.[13] When submitting his designs for fifty new churches in 1710, he described burial in churches as 'A Custome in which there is something so very barbarous in itself besides the many ill consequences that attend it; that one cannot enough wonder how it ever has prevail'd amongst the civiliz'd part of mankind …'

Although in 1711 the second New Churches in London and Westminster Act had stated that 'No Burial shall, at any Time hereafter, be in or under any of the Churches by this Act intended to be erected', this applied only to the fifty new churches that were to be built, so other churches continued to use their crypts to earn money. Moreover, only three vestries obeyed the commissioners (those of St George Hanover Square, St George Bloomsbury and St John Smith Square).[14] It soon became obvious that the ban on intramural burial was unenforceable, because the dues derived from interments were an important source of income for incumbents and their vestries.

Crypts could, however, have been put to other uses. After 1666 they might have been used for charity schools or perhaps rented to local merchants for storage. This would have been nothing new, because the crypt of the pre-fire St Mary-le-Bow had been leased for cellar storage, as had part of the crypt of All Hallows the Less.

In 1612 the authorities of All Hallows, Honey Lane had re-possessed their vaults from a neighbour, and beneath St Mary Colechurch were shops and part of the Mitre Tavern. In these cases coffins had to be placed between the floor of the church and the roof of the vaults.[15]

During the eighteenth century the vaults of St John Smith Square, Westminster, were let to various tenants, but despite the temptation of increasing their income, the churchwardens refused their incumbent's request to allow interments there. Early in the nineteenth century the vestry of St George Hanover Square also leased their vaults, which had never been used for interments, to a local wine merchant to lay down wine, but this was terminated after a while because the bishop objected.

Until the 1830s most people in England were buried in their local church or churchyard – 'God's acre'. Each knew their place in death as in life, with the wealthy coffined in the vaults below the building and everyone else buried in the churchyard – the poor, the unbaptised and social outcasts usually in the northern part, and the better-off in the sunny southern portion. Small city graveyards might not be able to make such distinctions, but their crypts were reserved for those who could pay substantial fees. Outside 'The mingled relics of the parish poor'[16] were jumbled namelessly together, possibly in pits, and pauper burial was feared by all. No member of the Established Church was refused burial; it was their right to be interred in their parish church or churchyard, although the unbaptised or those who had taken their own life had no such right. There is no record of a City church turning away plague victims in 1665, although pits rather than individual graves were used, the largest of which was in Aldgate, where 1,114 corpses were interred.[17]

In the early nineteenth century growing concern about the capital's poor sanitary conditions and the need to improve burial provision coincided with the opening of new cemeteries beyond the City boundaries. Ten of the first thirteen successful cemetery companies in England were opened by nonconformists, who objected to the established Church's privileges in burial provision. A few privately owned burial grounds already existed in the metropolis, mainly used by dissenters, such as Bunhill Fields, a short distance north of the City.

The first joint-stock cemetery in London was established at Kensal Green.[18] George Carden, a London barrister and philanthropist, had visited Paris in 1821 and been impressed by the Cimetière du Père-Lachaise, which had opened in 1804.[19] On his return he invited influential friends to consider whether the Parisian model might be copied. By 1830 he had assembled a provisional committee chaired by Andrew Spottiswoode, MP for Colchester, which resolved that 'The present condition of the places of interment within the Metropolis' was 'offensive to public decency and injurious to public health' and 'afforded no security against the frequent removal of the dead'. This was an important consideration, because the trade in cadavers was lucrative: the demands for dissection were increasing.

The General Cemetery Company was established, and in May 1830 a petition for a new cemetery was presented to the House of Commons by Spottiswoode, who mumbled so badly that at first members thought that a new road was being proposed.[20] Land was purchased at Kensal Green in December 1831, and after negotiations with Blomfield, Bishop of London, about clergy fees, he consecrated it on 24 January 1833. Over the next twelve years a further seven joint-stock cemeteries opened, forming 'a jet necklace around the throat of London'.[21] They offered families a freehold tenancy for their deceased members that churches could not – unless interment was in a crypt.

The vestries responded in different ways to these challenges. Jealous of their rights but loath to authorise any expenditure, they needed to be encouraged by legislation to make changes. Fortunately another key player was now the local secular state: the minutes of the City Corporation, for example, show that on 23 September 1847 the City of London Court of Common Council 'carried by acclamation' a motion asking Parliament 'to prohibit interment of the dead in the churches and churchyards of the City and other large towns'. Notably absent from the discussion until then was the government, whose members considered that this was the concern of local vestries. Now they were forced to take action.

The government was influenced by two important reports – *a Report from the Select Committee on Improvement of The Health of Towns together with the Minutes of Evidence. Effect of Interment of Bodies in Towns* (1842), and Edwin Chadwick's *Supplementary Report on the Results of a Special Inquiry into the Practice of Interment in Towns* (1843). Chadwick was one of the men who most influenced Parliament and public opinion concerning sanitation and the undesirability of burials in urban areas.[22] Formerly Jeremy Bentham's literary secretary and playing a decisive role in Poor Law, policing and factory legislation, by the late 1830s he developed from his experience what he called 'The sanitary idea'.[23] At Bentham's house in Queen Square, Chadwick met doctors, political economists and lawyers, who informed and helped his work on public health. Not only do the two reports illuminate the contemporary culture of interments in London, but the minuted evidence given by clergy, undertakers and others is detailed and important, making it evident that legislation was necessary.

Vestry minutes show the frustrations felt by congregations at the delays in setting up alternative burial arrangements, but only two vestries decided to open their own cemeteries. In 1854 St George Hanover Square Burial Board purchased 12 acres in Hanwell, and in the same year the St Marylebone Board founded the St Marylebone Cemetery, with 47 acres in East End Road. Why did others refuse to make what would almost certainly be a good investment? The response of St Anne Soho's vestry was typical: 'it would be a very great expense to buy a piece of land and build two chapels as required by law and maintain it'.[24] Instead several vestries decided to buy land at Brookwood.

An 'Act to make Better Provision for the Interment of the Dead in and near the Metropolis' was passed by Parliament without a division on 20 June 1850, but had to be abandoned two years later since there were financial problems;[25] it was difficult to implement; no mortuaries had been built; no cemeteries purchased; and no Officers of Health appointed. It was replaced by the 1852 Metropolitan Burial Act, which contained many of the earlier Act's provisions. Parochial Burial Boards were to be set up, and the Commissioners of Sewers became the Board for the City of London and its Liberties. This was a severe blow to the incumbents and vestries of the Square Mile. Not only would their parishes lose considerable income, but also, unlike their Westminster counterparts, the incumbents, despite being compensated, would not be members of a Burial Board. Their influence over burial provision had ended, and although the archdeacon of London, William Hale, complained, it was obvious that the City Corporation had no intention of involving the clergy in the work of the Commissioners of Sewers. Hale disagreed with his friend Blomfield on intramural burial, but did not say so until his lectures and Charge to the clergy of 1855.[26] It occasioned a rare joke from the bishop: 'I have two archdeacons with different tastes: Sinclair is addicted to composition and Hale to decomposition.'

The 1852 Act allowed the Parochial Boards to raise money from the Poor Rate to buy land for new cemeteries, and confirmed that the sovereign could, by an order-in-Council, close urban crypts and churchyards; this began to happen over the next few years. An exception was made for Westminster Abbey and St Paul's, some private freehold vaults and for Quaker and Jewish burial grounds if they were not injurious to health. The Queen could also make specific exceptions – the only example traced being that of St Stephen, Rochester Row for Baroness Burdett-Coutts and her friends Dr William Brown[27] and his wife Hannah, the baroness's adored governess and later companion. The baroness had prepared her own tomb there in 1850, but when she died on 30 December 1906 she was buried in the Abbey, after a dispute with the Chapter who would only accept her cremated remains.[28] They eventually changed their minds, and so her body was buried close to the memorial of her friend Shaftesbury on 5 January 1907.

Over the next few years all the vaults and churchyards in the two cities were closed. In consequence the clergy lost influence, and contact with their parishioners began to wane as families opted to use the new cemeteries, realising that they would no longer be able to 'lay their bones beside those of their relatives'.

Sextons and clerks, unlike incumbents, received no compensation for their lost burial fees. Furthermore the parishes themselves lost considerable income. My research suggests that in the City of London the ten parishes with a population over 3,000 lost an annual income of between £30 (today £3,420) and £70 (£7,980). The monetary loss in the twelve Westminster parishes was much greater, because all except St Mary-le-Strand had large populations with a large number of interments.

The annual parish burial income, which now ended, would have varied from around £6,000 (£684,000) at St Margaret Westminster, £2,500 (£285,000) at St Marylebone and £378 (£43,092) at St James, Piccadilly.

What happened to the crypts and churchyards now that they were closed? Over the next 150 years many churches were demolished for road widening, to construct new buildings such as the Royal Exchange, or to raise funds. Sales were obviously a lucrative source of revenue, and parishes, diocese and Church Commissioners (after 1836) shared the proceeds. In the City of London since 1666 there have been ninety-seven separate sales and one long lease of churches and/or churchyards. Obviously much depended on the size of the site, but where a church and church-yard were sold the sum received varied from £2 million to £13.5 million in 2012 values. In Westminster, where there have been thirteen sales of burial grounds and nine sales of churches with crypts, the sum paid for a church and churchyard varied from £3 million to £12½ million in today's terms.

In Westminster there have only been eighteen sales of Anglican burial grounds and four of churches with crypts, with one still to be sold, but the sum paid for only nine is known.[29] It is unlikely that more will be found because, although the London Diocesan Fund Archives revealed some sums, the Church Commissioners informed me that the files relating to post-war sales of burial grounds were 'destroyed as part of a departmental appraisal of records a number of years ago'.[30] It is also unlikely that there will be further sales because the local authority would almost certainly not give permission.

Today fifty-nine of the churches in the two cities have a crypt the same size as the church floor, of which ten are fully cleared and in use, five are cleared but empty, and five are in part use. Three crypts that have never been used for interments are also in use. It could be argued that this is a surprisingly small percentage of cleared space, not least because in central London meeting rooms are much sought after. Before 1852 these undercrofts contributed significant income to the parishes. Until a survey is conducted of the thirty-three uncleared crypts it is impossible to decide if they could be cleared and used.

The removal of human remains has always been a complicated business, involving the parish, diocese, Church Commissioners, the local authority (after 1881), Home Office, undertakers, architects and builders. The costs were and are considerable, but if the reason for clearance was sanitation, or what today would be called 'health and safety', a charge could be made on the rates. If a building including the undercroft was demolished in order for the site to be sold, then the cost was taken from accrued profits. If the building remained and a new use for the crypt was found, then an appeal for funds was made, such as at St Bride Fleet Street in the 1950s, when its museum was equipped from the gifts of nearby publishing firms. Other churches have attracted grants from the Lottery fund, statutory bodies, charitable foundations, business houses or individual donors.

After 1852 there were three possible functions for a cleared crypt – to be of service to the community, which might include the congregation of the church, to earn money for the church, or a combination of both. The space might be used for worship, social service, parish space, restaurants or museums, and these are described in the chapters that follow. The first time a crypt cleared of human remains was used for a purpose other than storage was in 1915, when the vicar of St Martin-in-the-Fields, Dick Sheppard, set up a canteen to welcome men returning from the Front (see chapter 2). Crypts were also used during the Second World War as air-raid shelters. Geoffrey Fisher, Bishop of London, was scandalised that an incumbent was considering applying for £100 (£4,740) compensation, so on 16 February 1940 he told Prebendary Eley of the London Diocesan Fund, who had described them as 'lumber-holes', that 'a vicar or parish should not try to profiteer over its use as an air raid shelter'.[31] Eventually the rent was fixed at £1 pa Another possible use is the interment of ashes, but at present only eight churches have a columbarium.

Three parishes have demonstrated that their crypt can produce a good income to fund their work and worship; forty-four crypts in the two cities produce no revenue for their church; and six only a small income. However, before starting a project the incumbent and the Parochial Church Council should have a clear aim and vision of what the use will be, obtain the approval of the diocesan authorities, draw up a business plan and consider how the necessary funds can be raised.

Finally, this book poses several questions:

HOW LONG IS IT BEFORE A BODY AND COFFIN DISINTEGRATE?

Interment in a crypt obviously preserves a corpse and coffin longer than if it was buried in a churchyard. Even so, at the exhumation of 983 bodies, dating from the eighteenth and early nineteenth centuries, from the crypt of Christ Church Spitalfields in the 1980s the state of preservation of those in coffins varied from virtually complete, including skin, hair and internal organs, to a sediment of crystal debris, being all that remained of the bones. If lead had been used, as it was in this crypt after 1813, this preserved the cadaver longer, but if air or water was allowed to penetrate then decomposition became quicker.

There are, however, stories of completely sealed coffins exploding, which is why sextons often pierced the lead. The 1842 Select Committee examined an undertaker, George Whittaker, who told them that gas can escape from a lead coffin: 'Some drill a hole, put a pipe in, and then [...] set the gas alight. It burns for 20 minutes.' The 1843 Supplementary Report contained evidence from Mr Barrett, a surgeon and Medical Officer of the Stepney Union, who observed that he knew of a coffin which had exploded in a vault with 'so loud a report that hundreds had flocked to the place', and a great number were attacked with sudden sickness and fainting.

The speed of decay of vault-deposited cadavers depended on a number of factors: age and weight at death, what the individual died of, how soon after death the body was encased, and the weather conditions at the time of death. Crypt coffins were often covered with charcoal, which absorbs the smells, and quicklime, which acts as a disinfectant, although insects might bore into and weaken wooden coffins. After a while the coffins were occasionally removed elsewhere, as at St Martin Ludgate, but most remained *in situ*, although the sexton might re-stack them if more space was needed. At Spitalfields coffins were often stacked up to seven high, which meant that the lowest could have a quarter of a ton pressing on it, so even lead caskets might be flattened, particularly if the atmosphere was damp.

Water from the body is sufficient for the formation of adipocere (a chalky wax-like substance generated from fat deposits). If the lead coffin was standing at an angle then the part of the corpse soaked in body liquor often showed signs of preservation, while the part of the corpse above the liquor was skeletonised. Coffins containing sawdust packing yielded clean, dry bones.[32]

Decomposition is much quicker in soil. A body decomposes faster than its coffin. After two years in soil the coffin remains (unless the soil is very damp), but inside the coffin only bones, hair and skin tissues are left. Wet soil means everything rots quickly, although a chipboard coffin could be intact after sixteen years because it contains resin.[33] The survival of bones depends on the acidity of the soil; chalk preserves them, but acid gravel dissolves them quickly.[34] Bones will disappear eventually, but how long will that take? Remains in graves from Neolithic cultures (at least 6,000 years ago) are still being found.

HAS ANYONE CONTRACTED A DISEASE
AS THE RESULT OF VAULT CLEARANCES?

Dr Julian Litten knows of one. In October 1902 part of T.G. Jackson's scheme for re-ordering the church of St Thomas, Portsmouth (now Portsmouth Cathedral), included transferring the remains from all of the brick graves in the main body of the church to a new purpose-built vault in the north-east corner of the building. 'The work had only gone on for two days when the stench from the open vaults, polluted soil and decomposing remains became so overpowering that the Medical Officer of Health, Dr A. Mearns Fraser, inspected the works and ordered the closure of the church.[35] In mid-December the Revd Charles Darnell, vicar of St Thomas, was taken ill with typhoid fever, with septicaemia intervening. All efforts to save his life were fruitless and he died on 6 January 1903.'[36] Regulations for the exhumation of human remains are very strict today, and are described in the section on Spitalfields in chapter 3.

WHAT IS TODAY'S VALUE OF THE SUMS GIVEN FOR FEES AND SALES?

To calculate this I have used the Bank of England's Inflation Calculator (1750–2012), and the 2012 value has been put in brackets after the sum quoted. The sums paid for church sites are listed in the Appendix.

WHERE WERE THE HUMAN REMAINS REMOVED TO?

A minority went to the East London Cemetery, Plaistow, or to the Great Northern London (now New Southgate) Cemetery. Some relatives were allowed to take the coffin of a family member to a burial ground of their choice, but most were taken to Brookwood or Ilford.

Brookwood, Surrey

At the end of 1849 Richard Sprye and Sir Richard Broun decided to provide a 'City for the Dead' at such a distance from the metropolis that it would never be part of the capital. Edwin Chadwick was not enthusiastic, and in an undated

A coffin being loaded into a hearse van on the train to Brookwood, c.1905. The funeral party has probably just emerged from a private waiting room on the left.

angry letter to Blomfield referred to 'a large new trading job, the Woking scheme, vulgar projections, a vulgar architect trying to get a Bill for the purpose and to make a market with the parishes'.[37] Some 2,200 acres of land owned by Lord Onslow on Woking Common at Brookwood were duly purchased by the newly formed London Necropolis and National Mausoleum Company.

The Necropolis train en route to Brookwood, passing Wimbledon, on 25 June 1902. The hearse vans are the third and last coaches.

Despite opposition Royal Assent was given to the London Necropolis Bill on 30 June 1852, but the first funeral was not held there until 13 November 1854. Soon afterwards several Westminster parishes, including St Anne Soho, St Giles-in-the-Fields and St Margaret Westminster, reserved plots there. Unusually, interments at Brookwood could take place on Sundays, which was an added advantage.

St Magnus the Martyr. Fallen obelisk 1893–94 at Brookwood. (The plot contains 534 cases of remains.)

Coffins and mourners were transported by special trains from a private terminus near Waterloo to the cemetery's two stations, one for Anglicans and one for others.[38] Addressing the 1842 Select Committee, the bishop had already suggested that a railway should not be used to transport the funeral party because few were used to it, and the 'hurry and bustle' was 'inconsistent with the solemnity of a Christian funeral'. He also found the idea of assembling a number of funerals from widely social backgrounds in the same conveyance 'offensive'. 'It might sometimes happen,' he told members, 'that the body of some profligate spendthrift might be placed in a conveyance with the body of some respectable member of the church, which would shock the feelings of his friends.'[39] The bishop would certainly not have approved of the notice in the station refreshment room at Brookwood: 'Spirits served here'.[40]

It was originally thought that the cemetery would be sufficiently large to contain all London's dead forever, and Dr Sutherland of the Home Office estimated that the 60,000 who died each year in the 1850s could be accommodated in separate graves in perpetuity. It is estimated that 80 per cent of the Brookwood interments were of paupers, and each year Necropolis tendered for the burial of the poor from London parishes who often, as at St Giles-in-the-Fields, left the location to be decided by Necropolis.[41] This meant that most of the middle classes were not attracted to Brookwood, and Necropolis succeeded in attracting only a small proportion of metropolitan burials: in the twenty years after consecration the average annual number of interments there never exceeded 4,100.[42]

Sadly the plots purchased by the City and Westminster parishes at Brookwood are now an overgrown wilderness, with the memorials in a parlous condition. Fortunately in the last ten years the picture has begun to change thanks to the formation of a Friends organisation, and priority is being given to green areas.[43]

City of London Cemetery, Ilford

In 1848 the City Corporation appointed Sir John Simon as its first Medical Officer of Health, and he persuaded the corporation to purchase their own burial ground. In 1853 he recommended that 'a very eligible site' of 200 acres at Aldersbrook Farm near Ilford be acquired.[44] Opened in 1856 and approximately 8 miles north-east of the City, this cemetery was used by nearly all the City parishes once the Corporation's Commissioners of Sewers became the Burial Board for the Square Mile under the 1852 Burial Act. Recompense was agreed with the incumbents and a chaplain appointed. This did, however, mean that the City vestries, unlike those in Westminster, lost control of burial provision. Since then over forty City parishes have removed crypt remains to Ilford, which is today one of the most beautiful cemeteries in Great Britain.[45]

Holy Trinity the Less. City of London Cemetery. House Tomb with decorated tracery, 1872. (The plot contains remains from the churchyard.)

IS THERE A MORAL DILEMMA IN EXHUMING BODIES?

Can the Church justify clearing the remains of those whose relatives paid dearly for a place of 'perpetual' deposit in the vaults? In taking money a contract was established, so what restitution, if any, should descendants of the deceased expect? Burial in a churchyard or municipal cemetery was precisely what these relatives were trying to avoid through purchasing a vault. Should human remains be disturbed? In the Middle Ages the Church often had no compunction in disturbing burials and putting bones in a charnel house, and this continued into the eighteenth century. Parish councils planning a clearance might consider cremating the remains and placing the ashes below the crypt floor, as happened at St Clement Danes and St Mary-le-Bow, or they might stack coffins in one area and wall them up.

2

WORSHIP  AND SERVICE

Three parishes, thanks to entrepreneurial incumbents and parish councils, have a splendid record of serving the community.

[*] ST MARYLEBONE, MARYLEBONE ROAD

'I warn you,' said the rector in February 1983 as he took a *Standard* reporter into the crypt, 'that the sight is horrifying.' He shone a torch into the darkness to reveal scores of coffins that had been tossed about the vaults so that some stood on end, others had crashed together and a few had cracked open. 'It is a mystery. Surely they could not have been thrown in here when they were buried 150 years ago? Perhaps it was a heavy bomb nearby during the war that did it?'[46]

Four years earlier, in July 1979 soon after his arrival as rector, Christopher Hamel Cooke had approached the Chancellor of the London Diocese, who said that he might agree that the crypt be cleared and the coffins perhaps stacked behind a wall. The church's surveyor, architect and Westminster Environmental Health Department were then consulted, as was Frank Harvey, Archdeacon of London, who asked if any famous people were buried there. The burial registers for 1817–50, when the coffins were interred, were consulted by the staff of the Museum of London, who failed to find anyone of interest.

A church has existed in this area since the thirteenth century, when it stood in what is now Oxford Street and was dedicated to St John. Large numbers of bones were found at the bottom of Marylebone Lane, near Stratford Place, so this may have been the churchyard.[47] In 1400 a church was built on the present site, St Mary by the Bourne – the Bourne being the River Tyburn – and it was rebuilt in 1740 in Marylebone High Street. In July 1804 an angry parishioner wrote to the *Gentleman's Magazine* complaining that the populous parish of Marylebone only had a small church to serve it, and that when he visited the building 'there were no fewer than five corpses laid out in the pews, eight children with their sponsors to be christened and five women to be churched'.[48] Vestry members were already studying plans for a chapel of ease, and this was built a few yards to the north between 1813 and 1817 by the architect Thomas Hardwick. While it was being built the vestry decided to make it the parish church, and demote the old building to a chapel.

In 1834 the St Marylebone vestry appointed a committee to revise the parish burial fees and they reported on 24 January 1835. Interment in the parish church vaults was very popular, but not in the three daughter churches – the vaults of Holy Trinity were almost unoccupied: 'A considerable diminution in fees is recommended in the fees of the district churches.'[49] In the parish church the committee considered that the placing of coffins in the 'Public Vaults ... is unseemly', and that the area should be re-ordered with walls and doors. This was accepted by the vestry.

The Marylebone vestry met seventeen years later on 10 November 1852 to discuss the new Interment Act, which had closed their vaults and burial grounds. The following year the members through their Burial Board purchased the Newmarket Farm, and founded the 47-acre St Marylebone Cemetery in East End Road, which was consecrated by Blomfield on 13 March 1855. This was one of only two new burial grounds opened by parishes of the Cities of London and Westminster.

The old chapel behind the parish church was later badly damaged in the Second World War and demolished in 1949. Burials here were exhumed in 2004 by Toop Ltd, in order that the St Marylebone Secondary School could be extended. A total of 348 complete or truncated burials in wooden coffins were recovered, with a further twenty-one lead coffins and two wood coffins from the three vaults and one lead coffin outside the vaults. The soil also contained a quantity of disarticulated human bone; 107 bodies were identified, with that of Lady Elizabeth Worsley 95 per cent complete.

Before the alterations in the 1980s the crypt consisted of three groin-vaulted passages running north-south intersected by barrel vaults. The entrance was and still is by small stone staircases at the north-east and north-west corners of the building. Many of the vaults were behind 3ft brick walls surmounted by railings, and some vaults were bricked up completely. In the mid-nineteenth century, probably when interments ceased, the coffins in each recess were placed on the floor, covered with a

St Marylebone. The Revd Christopher Hamel Cooke in the crypt.
The Standard, 7 February 1983.

mixture of soil and charcoal and bricked in. A concrete 'lid' was placed over them. A decision was made to clear the crypt and not stack the coffins in part of it, but a warning note was sounded when Biscoe and Stanton, the church surveyors, wrote to the rector:

> There are a large number of vaults under the arches which despite the presence of iron grilles across the openings are nevertheless completely bricked in. A structural engineer should be consulted on the removal of the brick columns supporting the arches on which the church floor is carried. Steel columns would be needed to support the floor.

This was agreed, and a faculty was issued by the chancellor on 23 October 1980, but this had to be extended by two years as preparations proved lengthy.

In February 1982 it was decided to build a slope on the eastern side of the church down to a new opening in the crypt outer wall, so that the builders could drive a small dumper truck down it and get through the 6ft-wide vaults opposite the opening.

Father Christopher was quite clear how the crypt space should be used. Having a great interest in the relationship of religion and medicine in his previous parish of St Mary, Bedford, he had worked closely with local doctors and social workers, and had been chairman of the Samaritans. As his new parish had Harley Street consulting rooms and seven hospitals nearby, he was convinced that a healing centre should be established to address the physical, mental, social and spiritual needs of men and women, and where stress and loneliness would be the concern of trained counsellors.

The work began in late 1982, but most of the clearance of over 850 coffins took place in 1983. They were transported to Brookwood Cemetery, where they now rest in plot 77 between St Edmund's Avenue and Cemetery Pales. A large stone cross, still in good condition, has been erected there and a plaque was placed in the north-west corner of the building commemorating the move; but when he granted the Faculty in June 1983 Chancellor George Newsome objected to '1982–3', saying that this was a tax year and not a year of Our Lord.

Not everyone approved of the rector's plans. One objector wrote to Archdeacon Harvey to point out that good money had been paid to place the coffins in the crypt and he had heard that all the bones were being jumbled together. What was happening to the jewellery, such as wedding rings, on the corpses? Was a priest

St Marylebone Memorial at Brookwood Cemetery.

supervising the work? Having consulted the rector, the archdeacon, who described himself as 'A thug who says his prayers', gently replied on 24 February 1983 saying that when discovered the coffins had been thrown in a heap and not decently interred. Now they were reverently being placed in separate wooden coffins and reburied in a garden cemetery. No jewellery or artefacts had been found, and the clergy were not able to supervise as their first duty was to the living, not the dead.

After only a few weeks everyone was surprised when four more vaults were discovered behind a brick wall at the southern end. The vault under the portico had been cleared and it seems that the poorer parishioners had been buried there. Dr Julian Litten visited regularly, and describes the coffin of a 2-year-old boy who had been interred soon after the crypt was opened in 1817:

> Once the lids of the outer case and the leaden shell had been removed, the workman prised off the lid of the inner coffin; the slightly yellowed silk sheets were drawn back and there lay the body of the child, looking as if he had gone off to sleep but a few minutes before. This child had not been embalmed and his preservation was due to nothing more than the construction of the coffin, for the wood was no less thick – 1½ inches – than that of an adult's coffin, and the lead was likewise no different in gauge. The thickness of the wood gave a quality of robustness to the small coffin, whilst the lead made it airtight.[50]

Dr Litten noted that the majority of the coffin furniture was of the usual sub-seventeenth-century baroque type, though the furniture on the Beverley family coffins was of very high quality and included both relief and three-dimensional coronets. Some Egyptian revival plates were also seen, and one is now in the Victoria and Albert Museum.

> We saw one man of the 1830s, skeletal but for an auburn wig and gold/ivory dentures. Another couple, husband and wife, of the 1840s were well preserved and probably underwent Hunter's embalming process of evisceration. Another had an arm amputated at the elbow with the lower arm laid in place and the hand strung up in a bottle. Of interest was the exceedingly good state of preservation of the grave clothes and coffin linings. All, regardless of rank, were in shrouds.[51]

One man was dressed in military uniform and another, an octogenarian, was laid out in a *macaroni* outfit more suited to a man sixty years his junior.

The work was undertaken by local builders who were, perhaps, cavalier in their handling of the clearance. One witness described to me how he saw a dog making off with a femur, while another told me that during a visit he saw two workmen playing football with a skull, and a well-preserved skeleton with a cigarette in his mouth.

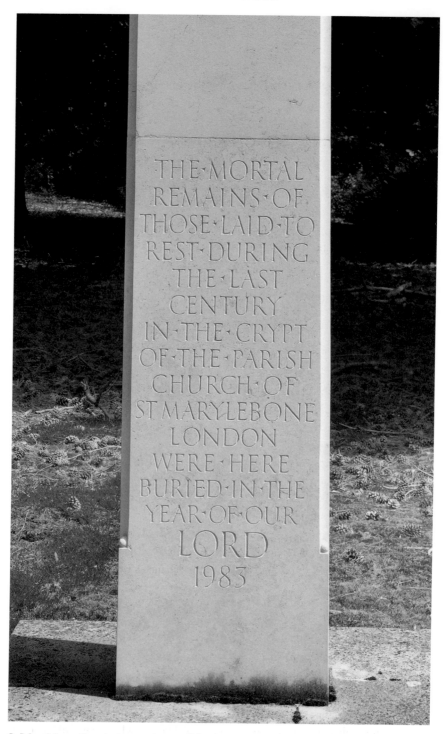

St Marylebone. Inscription on the 1983 Memorial at Brookwood Cemetery.

The crypt floor had to be lowered by 2ft and the walls sandblasted, which caused a few dust problems in the church upstairs. The cost of the project rose to over £2 million over the next few years, and by October 1985 £700,000 (£1,796,141) had been given or covenanted. The Prince of Wales performed the opening ceremony on 24 July 1987. Today the centre is staffed by GPs and ancillary staff, who pay an economic rent for over half the crypt area. It also offers alternative complementary therapy and is linked with Westminster University. The crypt was extended to the west under the car park to house an MRI scanning service for patients.

The St Marylebone Healing and Counselling Centre, whose full-time director is the Revd Chris MacKenna, a trained psychotherapist, is also located in the crypt. It is staffed by fourteen counsellors and psychotherapists and six spiritual directors, who work on a part-time basis with clients who pay according to their means. Lectures, seminars and meditation groups are offered, and Services of Healing and prayer groups are regularly held. As well as the counselling rooms the crypt has a chapel, a restaurant under the portico, a spacious meeting room, offices and lavatories. A columbarium has been created in the crypt's north-east corner.

Christopher Hamel Cooke considered that the London Diocesan authorities did not give sufficient support to his imaginative plans. In a statement sent to the author on 7 March 1989 he said that he had asked Graham Leonard, Bishop of London, why he had written to the Prince of Wales telling him that the coffins had been removed without faculty and that the diocese had other plans for the crypt. What were these plans? The bishop did not reply. George Cassidy, who had become Archdeacon of London on the untimely death of Frank Harvey, was also less than helpful. He declined to meet the rector and wardens informally to discuss granting temporary licences to the doctors so that they could begin work before faculties were issued. When a Consistory Court was convened, the archdeacon intervened to oppose the grant of the licences. These were eventually granted, but by then legal costs had soared and the parish was ordered to pay the archdeacon's costs of over £5,000 (£12,829). 'The whole tenor of the consistory court was unnecessarily legalistic and adversarial,' said the rector. 'Generally the parish appears to be considered by the Diocese as a nuisance.' The episode left a great deal of bitterness at Marylebone, whose clergy and laity had shown so much initiative and enthusiasm to create a centre that is now an important resource for London life. Not only that, it provides the church with useful revenue: for the year ending 31 December 2009 the PCC received £150,711 from the Marylebone Health Centre: around £20,000 was the service charge, and the remainder was rent.[52]

[*] ST MARTIN-IN-THE-FIELDS, TRAFALGAR SQUARE

Sir Simon Jenkins has described this famous building as 'England's most loved, most photographed and most imitated church'. Designed by James Gibbs, it was consecrated in 1726, when it was surrounded by seventy-six shops and over 3,000 houses, all of which pressed closely against the splendid new structure, which was to be copied on both sides of the Atlantic. However, the smells and sounds of the countryside were still present, as sheep and cows grazed in Green Park, and fields, farms and woods lay between the church and the village of Chelsea.

'The church and burial place of St Martin' was first mentioned when the Bishop of London was having a quarrel with the Abbot of Westminster about territorial rights. However, parish status was not granted until 1536 when King Henry VIII grew tired of seeing coffins carried past his palace in Whitehall for burial at St Margaret, Westminster. There was a risk of infection from plague victims, and so it was better that they be buried at St Martin's. In fact this was already happening, because in 1525 the accounts show a payment of 2*d*: 'For the paper book for the clerk to write in buryall'.

The parish grew in importance and size, so that when King James I arrived from Scotland in 1603 many of his courtiers built and bought houses nearby. The church was enlarged, and the King by Letters Patent of 28 October 1607 gave an acre of land (where the National Portrait Gallery now stands) for a burial ground. At the end of the seventeenth century St Martin's had 15,856 burials in eleven years, an annual average of over 1,400.[53]

Bodies were still buried beneath the church, including that of Nell Gwynne, who was interred in the vicar's vault in 1687. When the building was demolished in 1721 a gruesome poem appeared:

> The Pews pale squares in their whole lengthened row
> Gave way, and opened a sad scene below!
> Beauty, youth, wealth, and power reduced to clay,
> Larded with bones, yet moist, unsheltered lay:
> Remnants of eyeless skulls, with hollow stare,
> Mocked the proud looks, which living charms wear,
> Coffins rose, broke, unfaithful to their trust!
> And flesh flew round me in unjointed dust,
> Scarce a short span beneath that opening floor,
> Where kneeling charmers prayed a week before.

Gibbs's new building had extensive vaults beneath it, stretching out to the north and east. The churchwardens realised that these and the space under the vestry House would provide a sizeable income from parishioners who did not want to be interred in the churchyard or cemetery on the other side of St Martin's Lane. The most sought-after place was under the church and portico, which cost £3 10s (today £654; the pall could be used free), while a burial under the vestry was £2 (£375). By 1801 charges had increased, and Mr Young Thomas was charged £42 (£7,886) for a middle vault under the church. In 1748 the fabric of the building was threatened by all the burials beneath the floor of the crypt, so the sexton was instructed to

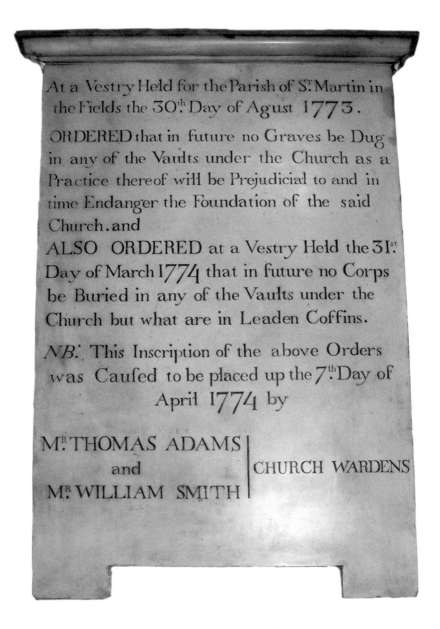

At a Vestry Held for the Parish of S. Martin in the Fields the 30th Day of Agust 1773.

ORDERED that in future no Graves be Dug in any of the Vaults under the Church as a Practice thereof will be Prejudicial to and in time Endanger the Foundation of the said Church. and

ALSO ORDERED at a Vestry Held the 31st Day of March 1774 that in future no Corps be Buried in any of the Vaults under the Church but what are in Leaden Coffins.

NB: This Inscription of the above Orders was Caufed to be placed up the 7th Day of April 1774 by

Mr THOMAS ADAMS
and   CHURCH WARDENS
Mr WILLIAM SMITH

St Martin-in-the-Fields. Plaque on south-west stairs to the crypt.

stop digging. However, he obviously took no notice: another order was made by wardens Thomas Adams and William Smith and the vestry on 30 August 1773 that 'No Graves be dug in any of the vaults under the Church as a Practice thereof will be Prejudicial to and in time Endanger the Foundation of the said Church'.

The following year on 31 March the vestry ordered that 'No Corps be Buried in any of the Vaults under the Church but those who are in Leaden Coffins'. We know that the sexton was a busy man, because in 1792 the vicar, Dr Anthony Hamilton, told vestry members that he had buried 4,544 parishioners in sixteen years.

By the early nineteenth century the crypt was crowded with coffins and in 1817 the wardens paid £68 3s 11d (£4,993) for a clean-up and re-stacking. The following year a gun was purchased for the watchman who patrolled the graveyard at night to deter bodys-natchers. By an Act of Parliament a new 4-acre burial ground was purchased in 1804 for £2,000 in Pratt Street, Camden Town, 2 miles from the church, and consecrated two years later. In 1842 Mr Le Breton, clerk to the guardians, reported that 10,982 people had been buried there, 1,987 of whom were non-parishioners and 4,624 were paupers.[54]

In the 1820s the area around St Martin's began to change. A road was built to connect Pall Mall with the Strand, and the churchyard to the south of the church was compulsorily purchased in 1826 to create Duncannon Street. The bodies, some recently interred, were removed to Camden Town or placed in the vaults. It was a costly business, as the Commissioners of Woods and Forests had also to pay for catacombs to be built for 3,300 coffins to the north and east of the church. These were consecrated on 7 June 1831 by Charles Blomfield, Bishop of London. It was agreed that lead coffins should weigh 6lb to the foot, and that the burial fee would vary from £1 16s 4d (£152) for a child parishioner to £7 0s 10d (£614) for an adult non-parishioner.

When the new catacombs opened in 1831 the *Sunday Times* reported that they were:

> The most capacious structure of the sort in London. They consist of a series of vaults, running out of one another in various directions. They are lofty … and of a comfortable appearance. Crowds of ladies perambulated the vaults for some time, and the whole had more the appearance of a fashionable promenade than a grim depositary of decomposing mortals.[55]

The parish also had a cemetery in Drury Lane, which still exists with its mortuary house and keeper's lodge. Approximately ¼ acre, it was purchased in 1762 for an annual rent of £6 (£1,044) and used to bury paupers; in the early 1840s it had forty burials each year.

The coffins in St Martin's crypt had to be re-stacked in 1841, then twelve years later Parliament forbade further burials in London's church vaults. St Martin's already had 3,250 coffins in residence and the churchwardens decided to have another tidy-up. They advertised to ask families whether they wanted their ancestors moved to Camden Town or bricked up in the catacombs to the east of the church. In May 1859 Mr Burstall, the vestry's surveyor, reported that approximately 1,857 coffins had been transferred to join those already in the new vaults. All the bodies except 246 were listed by name. They included those of a former vicar, Dr George Richards, who had died twenty-two years earlier, and his wife, Hannah.[56]

In 1858 Frank Buckland, a famous naturalist, had spent sixteen days trying to find the remains of Dr John Hunter (1728–93), who is known as the father of scientific surgery. He eventually found the coffin, and has left this account of his search:

> On going down below the church we found ourselves in the crypt. This crypt is supported by massive pillars, and the spaces between some of them are bricked up so as to form vaults, some large and some small. There are the rector's vault, the portico vault and the steeple vault, as well as several smaller vaults taken by private families. The larger vaults were guarded by strong iron gates, through which the coffins could be seen from the outside. Mr Burstall having unlocked the ponderous oak door of the vault No. 3, we threw the light of our bull's-eye lanterns into the vault, and then I beheld a sight I shall never forget. After our eyes had got accustomed to the light, we perceived that this vault was a good sized room, as full as it ever could hold with coffins, piled one over the other, from the very top to the bottom. Many coffins were even piled up crosswise in front of the door, so that no entry could be obtained except by moving them, and others were jammed up together in all possible positions, without the least attempt at order, reminding one much of books packed in a box to be sent away. To the left of this vault there began another, in which there was a great mass of wooden coffins of persons buried anterior to the Act which ordered that no person should be buried there except in lead. The faint and sickly effluvia which emanated from these was truly overpowering and poisonous.[57]

On 28 March 1859 the Royal College of Surgeons took Dr Hunter's coffin in procession to Westminster Abbey and buried it on the north side of the nave next to Ben Jonson, who had been educated at St Martin's School and achieved the distinction of being the only person interred at the Abbey standing up: 'He couldn't afford the price of a plot six feet by two feet so bought a two-feet-by-two-feet one instead, and went to his reward like a tent peg.'[58]

The Office of Works in 1866 compulsorily purchased the land given by King James I for a burial ground to the west of St Martin's to extend the National Gallery. Another re-interment took place, this time to Brookwood Cemetery, Woking. No record was kept of the names on the graves.

St Martin's crypt has a brick-groined barrel-vaulted ceiling springing from square piers, which are governed by the positions of the columns to the main body of the church above. The floor to the southern bays is paved with old gravestones, and these and those erected against the walls are listed in the Survey of London.[59] Fragments of monuments from the earlier church are also preserved, and these are also mentioned together with a list of famous people buried here in McMaster's 1916 *History of St Martin-in-the-Fields*.[60]

Social service is always associated with St Martin-in-the-Fields, and this parish was the first to use a crypt space for a project other than storage. In 1915 Dick Sheppard became vicar, and on his arrival he found that a large area in the space under the church was unused. Sheppard decided to use this to provide hospitality for soldiers arriving at Charing Cross station from the Front, and volunteers provided a warm atmosphere where the men could have a meal and sleep.

After 1918 the undercroft became a centre for the homeless, the first time such a project had been undertaken. Sheppard's successor, Pat McCormick, Miss Whitmore, the social worker, and their volunteers felt challenged by the scale of the problem. In the tax year ending March 1933 workers interviewed 854 homeless people and 606 others; 5,281 meal tickets and 433 bed/food vouchers were distributed; 717 received clothing and 48,555 men, 6,395 women and 41 children slept in the crypt during the year.[61] McCormick and his Parochial Church Council realised more room was obviously needed for the work, so the diocesan chancellor, Dr Errington, was asked to visit. He subsequently described the vaults under the school playground to the east of the church as 'simply a mass of skulls and bones', and issued a faculty on 2 July 1938 for Necropolis Ltd to remove around 3,000 lead coffins and a large quantity of human remains from the vaults to Brookwood.

St Martins. Case of bones ready to go to Brookwood Cemetery, 1938.

St Martins. A vault before clearance, 1938.

Above and previous page: St Martins. Crypt before clearance, 1938.

The six vaults, measuring 140 x 70ft provided further meeting rooms and two offices. A million shilling fund had been launched by Pat McCormick to pay for it all, and he was photographed beaming benignly beside a pile of bones.

Thousands of needy people continued to visit the crypt, which was staffed by full-time workers, and today the Connection at St Martin's continues the work by providing a day and night centre, outreach for rough sleepers and specialist support and advice to over 200 people every day.[62]

The new space was needed in 1940 not for the homeless but as an air-raid shelter, in which the dormitories each had 100 bunks arranged in tiers of three. Mattresses and blankets were supplied, and a special area at the other end of the building under the portico was reserved for mothers and small children. Numbers were large, and often 1,950 people crowded into the crypt by 7 p.m. One lady arrived asking what time the next air raid would be, and another said that she was frightened by the 'insanitary bombs'. Westminster City Council soon became alarmed at the overcrowding, and after a while restricted the numbers each evening to 550.[63]

After 1945 the homeless work continued in part of the crypt, and services, concerts and meetings were held in the main area, but by 1985 it was obvious to everyone that the parish finances needed addressing. As the previous vicar, Austen Williams, had pointed out, they survive because of the Angel of Death – but legacies and the huge sum recently raised for the building could not finance everything over the next decade. Bankruptcy loomed unless something drastic was done – and the

St Martins. The Revd Canon Pat McCormick, vicar, views one of the vaults to be emptied, 1938.

newly formed St Martin's Players presented *Doomsday*, which must have sent a chill down the congregational spine. The new vicar, Geoffrey Brown, and his parish council decided to plunge into the world of business and make the crypt earn money. The space there was an important resource, a large loan was negotiated and the Enterprise was launched on 1 December 1987, when the press was shown the new 200-seat crypt restaurant (open from 10 a.m. until midnight), bookshop, brass rubbing centre, visitors' centre and exhibition space. Not all the congregation was impressed by these daring decisions, believing that the

St Martins. Crypt air-raid centre, 1940.

Left: St Martins. Eileen Joyce plays to the Darby and Joan Club in the crypt, *c.* 1953.

Below: St Martins. The homeless centre in the crypt, *c.* 1980.

homeless had been marginalised by the new venture. Some wanted a revitalised church but on the old, much-loved model. Was there now a Berlin Wall between the rich in the café and the poor in the Unit? Some worshippers needed to be reminded that profits are not wicked, and, as Richard Rouse, chairman of the enterprise, pointed out, God loves the poor but he also loves accountants, stockbrokers and the stinking rich.

Early in 1989 the Bishop of London decided that there should be an Episcopal Visitation. This was understandable, because the diocese was apprehensive that it might be financially liable if the church went into liquidation. Three wise men – a priest and two laymen – were appointed to do this, and after a careful study of accounts and a full enquiry into all other matters they gave St Martin's a clean bill of health, and said that the new crypt plans should be supported and affirmed. By the end of the year it was reported that the Enterprise was making a profit, but that the bank loan would not be discharged until 1992. Until then the parish would receive a licence fee – £82,000 in 1989. It was estimated that without this funding all the assets would be gone by 1995.[64] From then on the project went from strength to strength.

In 2004 the vicar, Nicholas Holtam, and his Parochial Church Council launched the most exciting and ambitious plans in St Martin's 800-year history. Eric Parry Architects created a contemporary design that made many underground areas accessible for the first time. The damp eastern vault has been modernised to provide rehearsal rooms for visiting choirs and musicians, and a sequence of beautiful, practical and inspirational spaces provide meeting and exhibition areas beneath the church. A new lightwell enables the crypt to be bright and airy. Gibbs's church has been redecorated, and modern care facilities for the homeless fill the buildings to the north. These exciting facilities opened in 2008 so St Martin's tradition of worship, music-making, commerce and social care was greatly enhanced.[65]

[*] ST MARY-LE-BOW, CHEAPSIDE

The three-aisle Bow crypt which dates back to c.1090 is one of the most historic places in London, having survived the Great Fire and the Blitz. As Betjeman wrote, it is 'a pleasant amalgam of slate-and-stone floors, old brick and stone and modern concrete supports'.[66] St Mary's was a busy City parish in medieval London, and 'le Bow' derives from the arches or bows of the crypt. First mentioned in 1091, when its roof blew off in a storm, the church lost its tower in 1271 when it collapsed, killing twenty-nine people. Pantomime tradition says that the great bell of Bow was heard by Sir Richard Whittington, who was born in about 1350 and came from Pauntley, Gloucestershire, to London to seek his fortune. He is meant to have lost heart at Highgate and made for home, but the bell told him and his cat to 'turn again'. He did, and became a mercer dealing in cloth. Whittington was Lord Mayor four times, dying in 1423 and leaving charities which still exist today, administered by the Mercers' Company.

Between 1670 and 1683 Sir Christopher Wren rebuilt the church after it had been destroyed in the Great Fire. The bodies under the central area must have been disturbed, and were probably taken to Bunhill Fields. Wren had hoped to keep the tower, but decided to demolish it and replace it with a tower that had 'The most perfect Renaissance steeple'.[67] This meant the final bill of £15,421 made it the costliest of the new churches, with St Lawrence Jewry coming next at £11,870. Bow bells have also achieved fame because the traditional definition for Cockneys refers to those who are born within their sound. Wren made room for twelve bells, but only eight were hung. By 1881, however, there was a peal of twelve, which melted in the hideous fire during the air raid of 10 May 1941. Fortunately on 11 June 1964 a new peal sounded over the City, when the church was re-consecrated.

At the Old Bailey on 14 January 1732 Thomas Middleton, under gravedigger at Aldgate and a bearer at St Mary-le-Bow, was accused of stealing two lead coffins from Bow vaults on 3 and 8 January. The first belonged to a Mr de Boyville's son Rene, aged 16, who had been interred in the vaults in February 1721. The second coffin belonged to Nathaniel Garland's brother, interred on 30 March 1726. Middleton had obtained the key of the vaults from Mary Robinson, the sexton's daughter, who let him have it any time because he gave her 'a penny or two'. Middleton threw the bodies on the floor and took 200lb of lead from the coffins to a Mr Robert Moore in King Street, who bought it, believing Middleton's story that the churchwardens had given it to him 'as a perquisite to make the best on't'. He had promised also to bring some coffin handles, and Moore deducted a shilling until they were brought. Moore, who paid 9s 4d per cwt, sold it to Seth Williamson for 11s per cwt. Williamson, who kept an old-iron shop in Chissel Street, sold it on the same day for 13s per cwt to John Newton, although one of his men said 'this Lead smells so strong of dead Corps that it almost chokes me'.

Francis Warner, who helped Middleton, testified that on the second occasion they:

Went into the Vault with this Mallet and Chissel. He broke the Wooden Coffin, and then cut the Sides of the Leaden one, and tumbled the Corps out upon the Ground, and cover'd it with the Saw-Dust that came out of the Coffin. 'Says I, this Corps will soon be discover'd by the smell if ye leave it here, and then I shall come into a scrape, and my Master may lose his place: No, says he, it has been Buried so long that there's no fear of smelling.'

The corpse was identified by Garland because one leg was shorter than the other, 'and after his Death his Body was open'd for the Satisfaction of his Friends to know what Distemper he dy'd of'.[68] Middleton was found guilty and sentenced to transportation.

George Gwilt the younger, when he altered the church in 1820, cleared some 800 coffins from the centre vault and bricked them up in the south aisle. He gives the dimensions of the crypt as 78ft by 60ft. 'On either side extends an aisle or corridor the same length as the nave by 14ft 5ins wide. Connections between each of the aisles and the nave are obtained by four lofty doorways on each side 4ft wide and the walls are 5ft thick.'

St Mary-le-Bow. Sketch by Frederick Nash, 1818, of the crypt during the restoration by George Gwilt.

On 16 June 1859 the vestry appointed a committee to supervise work in the vaults, which had been closed by an Order in Council on 15 August 1853. Relatives were told by newspaper adverts that they could remove their family coffins and the rest would be stacked in the south crypt. 'A Citizen' told Mr Lott, the vestry clerk, that there would be great anguish of mind at a death bed to think that someone would 'be prohibited from being laid by the side of them who was there [sic] great comfort in this life of probation'. Tenders for the work, which began the following March, varied from £115 (£11,841 today) to Mr Brown's £57 (£5,920), which was accepted. In three weeks all was tidy, and John Martin, the sexton and clerk of works, was given an extra £5 (£537) gift for never being absent 'when the vaults were scarcely endurable from the effluvia'.[69] He had stacked the coffins 'with decorum and decency' in consultation with the Medical Officer of Health, placing 12in of earth and 4in of powdered charcoal on top of the coffins in their new position. All openings had been blocked up, including the south-west staircase down which the coffins had been carried.

Gwilt built another staircase, which today comes down from the vestibule in the north-west corner of the church. He did not want to disturb those renting the north aisle, so he built a diagonal wall to preserve privacy, and they continued to use their own entrance in Bow Lane, probably where the car showroom now stands. The wall was removed in August 1907. The vestry minutes record that the vault below the vestry was rented in the 1860s to Messrs Copestake as a carpenter's shop. Relations with the firm were not easy, and they were upbraided for leaving the gas on at night. The firm left on 14 June 1865, having been told that the space could only be used as a store.

Laurence King, who between 1956 and 1964 restored this building to its former Wren glory after the Luftwaffe had gutted it in 1941, described the crypt as 'A precious relic of medieval London. It is a particularly fine and at the same time a somewhat unusual example of late eleventh-century architecture.' He considered that:

> Wren showed little regard for it, the nave of which he ruined by the erection of two large piers to support his columns for the main church above. On account of the scientific advance in building methods and the use of new materials, it will now be possible through the use of reinforced concrete construction to transmit the weight of the upper columns so that the brick piers in the underground nave can be dispensed with. This means that the crypt can be brought back to its former appearance.[70]

Unfortunately two huge piers remain.

There was, however, one snag: 1,000 coffins, some 150 years old, which were stacked from floor to ceiling in the south crypt aisle, would have to be moved. William George, general foreman of Dove Brothers, the builders undertaking the restoration, told Mrs Henrey that 'about half the bodies were in lead coffins' which his workmen had to cut open.[71] 'They look almost lifelike! Well, no that is not quite true. I mean they are all in one piece, with hair and teeth, and I think one might be able to recognise a face, though the features are sallow and ghoulish.' Some of the wooden coffins had already disintegrated, leaving only the metal name plates, and he thought that some had been brought to Bow from other churchyards. The Revd Frederick Baker, the rector, and his nine church-wardens, representing the now vanished churches that had been merged with

St Mary-le-Bow. Vicar General's court meeting in crypt *c.*1970.

St Mary-le-Bow. 'The Place' – today's crypt café.

St Mary, successfully petitioned the chancellor on 7 January 1954 to have the remains cremated. Any lead or jewellery was to be sold to pay for the project. The ashes were brought back to the crypt and placed beneath the floor of its south aisle, which is now a chapel with its own outside entrance in the south-west corner of the church.

Bow Church was one of the Archbishop of Canterbury's thirteen Peculiars in the City, which is why Wren built the vestry to house the Court of Arches. After the Second World War it met in the crypt but today it is held in the church. The court, which dates from the thirteenth century, is the archbishop's Court of Appeal, and during its history has heard a catalogue of human misfortune including matrimonial cases, questions concerning the manners and morals of the clergy and parochial disputes.

Most newly appointed diocesan bishops in the southern province come here to the court of the Vicar-General of the Province of Canterbury to have their so-called election confirmed, and then take the Oath of Allegiance in the presence of the archbishop. The ceremony was removed to Lambeth by Archbishop Carey, but today it is back in Bow, where it takes place in church with a party afterwards in the crypt.

After the war the crypt's north aisle was not let commercially but used to provide refreshments after services. Known as the Refectory, it became a commercial venture in 1989. Today the Café Below, begun by Bill Sewell, is a warm friendly place that opens early on a weekday morning to greet City workers and closes at 9 p.m. It makes a handsome profit for the church – over £25,000 pa in 2010.

The church is known for its ministry to City workers and the high standard of its worship. Rector George Bush has changed the format of the dialogues that were started by the Revd Joe McCulloch in the late 1960s. They are now debates, which he sees 'as an approach to ministry with the City, the world and other faiths'.

3

MUSEUMS AND RESEARCH

The works undertaken in these three churches have greatly increased our knowledge of intramural burials.

[*] CHRIST CHURCH, SPITALFIELDS

It was depressing and deeply disturbing. When I entered the derelict Christ Church in 1975 I was horrified – could it be possible that Nicholas Hawksmoor's masterpiece, a supreme expression of English baroque, had been left to decay for so long? The building's exterior still looked superb as it gazed loftily down on the busy fruit, flower and vegetable market opposite, but the interior was forlorn and crumbling fast. It was now technically a dangerous structure. The vicar, Eddy Stride, presided over his congregation not in the church but in the nearby parish hall. Quite properly his first priority was the care of his parishioners, many of whom were poor and homeless, and a hostel had been opened in 1965 for nineteen vagrant alcoholics in the eastern end of the crypt, which had been cleared some years earlier.

When I visited it never crossed my mind to ask what lay behind the brick walls of the crypt. I had no idea that hundreds of coffins were within a few feet of me. Facing so many social problems there was no way that Eddy and his people could find the resources to restore the building that had been closed for worship since 1956. It had already been vandalised a century earlier by the Victorians, led by Ewan Christian, the architect of the National Portrait Gallery, who had removed the box pews and galleries. In the 1960s, as part of the homeless programme, two flats had been shoehorned into the east end on either side and above the altar, and a Dickensian meeting room created above the derelict organ at the west end.

Help was fortunately at hand because parishioners, who included artists, craftsmen and businesspeople, joined others with vision and flair to form the

Friends of Christ Church Spitalfields in 1976. The following year the architect A.D. (Red) Mason arrived, and he stayed for nearly thirty years to advise the church council and guide the restoration, which eventually cost £10 million. When the church was opened in 1729 there were already nine French churches serving the mainly Huguenot population, and today the mosque, a former church then synagogue, at the other end of Fournier Street, is the area's busiest place of worship – because this part of Tower Hamlets now has many Bangladeshi residents.

Christ Church was built as a result of the Act for Fifty New Churches passed by Parliament in 1711. On 14 November the Commissioners made Christ Church a separate parish, and the foundation stone of Nicholas Hawksmoor's magnificent building was laid four years later by Commissioner Edward Peck, who in April 1727 was granted a family vault. It had been decided that all the new churches should be raised high above the street to reflect 'The awful majesty of God', so this meant that vaults could be built slightly below ground level, and they became obvious resting places for wealthy departed parishioners.[72]

The crypt extends beneath the entire area of Christ Church, including the front western steps that lead up to the portico of four Tuscan columns with its central barrel-vaulted arch, which is tied to the body of the church by the tower with its octagonal spire. The crypt was constructed in two phases; the tower foundation being erected before and separate from the main body of the building. The tower is supported by a brick pier, which is pierced by two tiers of vaulted tunnels, north, south and central along the east-west axis of the building. Each of the three upper and lower tunnels was probably secured with doors at the west end and shutters at the east end. The seven bays of the crypt correspond with those upstairs. The crypt has north and south aisles and a central section more than 16ft across, which corresponds to the nave. None of the separate vaults were purpose built but they were created by partitions.[73] There are two entrances – in the centre of the south wall and at the south-west corner, the latter used by the excavators.

By the time the church was consecrated by Edmund Gibson, Bishop of London, on 5 July 1729 the cost had escalated to £39,162, four times the original estimate and £6,000 more than the cost of St Martin-in-the-Fields, which the bishop had consecrated three years earlier. The first burial was on 3 August 1729 and the final interment was on 23 February 1859. An Order in Council forbade further burials, so the sextons rearranged and restacked the coffins that year, and again in 1867 when the eastern part of the crypt was cleared. Presumably there were other reshuffles, and some bodies have almost certainly been removed without record.

In 1843 the Revd William Stone, rector, wrote to Edwin Chadwick to tell him that the puritan jibe was true: 'The Established Church in burying the dead kills the living'. He had 'an interrable population of 23,642' and with only one church and one burial ground had to omit the service in church; otherwise the funerals would be 'overwhelmingly laborious, and absolutely impracticable and incompatible with our other professional engagements'. Thus because the wealthy had a funeral in church it was an invidious distinction between rich and poor, and he hints that they would probably prefer a cemetery at some distance where they would not have to wait in the rain. At the end of the service, having left the building, he had to force his way through 'a crowd of gossips and abusive, impertinent children' to get to the grave. 'My burial ground abuts Brick Lane at the east end where stands a public-house which of course is not without its attraction to all orders of street minstrels … so there is the most inappropriate musical accompaniment. I hardly witness in any of these crowds any indication of a religious sentiment.' When notorious criminals are interred, 'The vulgar excitement rises to an insufferable height'. The church is 'desecrated by the hurried intrusion of a squalid and irreverent mob. The mourners do not dislike the uproar, but congratulate themselves upon it as there is an éclat about it.'[74]

During the Blitz of 1940 some of the accessible parts of the western end of the crypt below the steps were used by Stepney Borough Council as an air-raid shelter. After two years the rector, George Bartle, decided to formalise the agreement and a faculty was issued on 22 May 1942 by which Christ Church was paid £40 pa (£1,596).[75] At the end of hostilities he reported that the alterations, which had been made at considerable cost to the council, were most valuable to the club he was organising, and hoped they would remain although the outside blast walls should be removed.

Christ Church. A family sheltering in the crypt during the Blitz, 1940.

Christ Church. Asleep in the crypt c. 1942.

In early 1983 it was decided to find out what lay below the floor of the church, so several keyholes were drilled through the brick linings of the vaults to see what was inside. Photographs and a video film were taken, and in May a proposal was made to excavate and scientifically examine the contents of the vaults. It would have been possible to employ a commercial firm to clear the vaults quickly, as has happened in other churches, but the Parochial Church Council, realising the archaeological and anthropological importance of the site, offered it for research, providing that funds could be found. They were, and, after the necessary permissions had been given, excavation began in November 1984. What happened has been documented in two scholarly reports on which this chapter has heavily relied.[76] By the end of the project 983 bodies were removed, together with parts (usually skulls) of approximately sixty individuals. This leaves some twenty or so bodies in the private vaults at the east end, under the altar, and there is no plan to remove these.

Many consultations were held with Health and Safety authorities before work commenced, as there was a risk that spores of viable smallpox might have survived in the human tissue to be exhumed. A code of practice was agreed whereby protective clothing would be worn – overalls, headgear including hard hats, steel toe-capped Wellington boots and surgical gloves. There were two sorts of protective respiratory masks, anti-dust and micro-biological, which were worn at all times. Excavated coffin wood was burnt, and human remains were examined in a laboratory on site, then taken to be cremated. Regular medical checks were held, and the morale and health of the staff, most of whom were women, were carefully monitored. Work had to stop for six and a half weeks in April 1985 when smallpox pustules were found on a semi-desiccated corpse. Fortunately all was well, but all workers were inoculated. When sealed lead coffins were opened on a daily basis, levels of lead in the blood of the staff rose, and some had to leave the site.[77] Lifting lead coffins was also a hazardous operation, as each one might weigh more than a quarter of a ton. It had not been realised how much rubble there would be: by completion 250 tons had been removed. This had probably been dumped when the vaults were sealed in 1867, and consisted of building materials, domestic rubbish and some of the church stone discarded during the restoration of 1866. Where textiles, including entire costumes, survived in a good state of preservation they were retained and sent to Bradford University, and when insects and parasites were found these were kept for analysis.

It was vital that all research data be recorded, but computer facilities had not been available when the excavation began. After two years the Friends of Christ Church provided an IBM PC: a simple card-type database was introduced and four databases were generated. Then in the summer of 1987 a more sophisticated relational database was introduced and the old databases were transferred into this system. A single data catalogue was generated, containing a comprehensive burial catalogue.

It is estimated from the church registers and from Bills of Mortality that there were about 68,000 interments during the 123 years that the crypt was in use, so the nearly 1,000 corpses discovered in the vaults represent only a very small percentage. The earliest date of death derived from the name plates in the crypt is 1729 (Thomas Hull), the year of the consecration of the building, and the latest plates are two burials in 1852.[78]

Those buried in the vaults, around 0.1 per cent of the total, were men and women whose families were wealthy enough to pay for the privilege. Some shrank from burial in earth, some wanted security of tenure and others were frightened of bodysnatchers. Above all it was warm and cosy inside, and you were near the worshipping community who might pray for you if asked. Of the 986 individuals exhumed, 312 were adult women, 311 adult males and 215 juveniles under 17. It was impossible to sex the others. Two whose plates said they were males proved to be female.[79]

Only 388 of the bodies had coffin plates giving details of name, age and date of death. Of these approximately 38 per cent lived in Spitalfields, 38 per cent nearby and the rest further away. Helena Shaw-Lefevre, who had died in Le Havre aged 81 in 1816, was the most travelled because her body was brought to London and interred in the crypt of St Martin-in-the-Fields; then a few months later she arrived at Christ Church to be placed near her father in the Lefevre family vault. The building had several such vaults, as 129 of the named corpses were related. There were four generations of the Pontardant family, and eleven individuals represented five generations of the Mesman family who were master weavers.[80] The Pontardant/Lemaistre vault was full shortly after 1795, and by about 1845 the second parochial vault was also full, so only the northern parochial vault and southern chasm were in use until interments ended.

Many of those buried in the vaults had French names and were of Huguenot descent. This is not surprising because many Protestant weavers had fled from France after the Revocation of the Edict of Nantes in 1685, and settled in Spitalfields near their friends who had arrived following earlier persecutions. They brought with them many skills and talents, among which was silk weaving, and soon their brocades, damasks and velvets were much in demand. The researchers studied wills, insurance policies, company records and land tax returns, and came to the conclusion that many of the crypt families were wealthy by the standards of the day. Few, however, owned the freehold of their property, although many held leases and several such as Charles Shaw Lefevre and Peter Ogier III owned country estates. William Harwood owned several houses in Brick Lane.[81] Entries in local marriage registers were found for 116 of the crypt sample, 44.8 per cent of these being married at Christ Church.

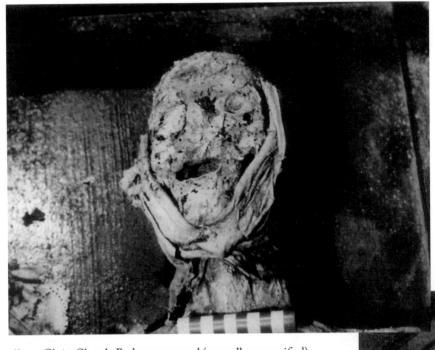

Above: Christ Church. Body as excavated (naturally mummified) showing textiles pinned around head and under chin.
Right: Christ Church. The northern parochial vault exposed for the first time in 140 years. It contained forty-eight interments.

Intermarriage between the families was common, because this meant that power and wealth were kept within their circle. The immigrant group preserved their identity by doing this, and a few of the families remained aloof from the host population for some years.

During the exhumations many oddities were discovered. Several coffins were empty, which might suggest a visit from the bodysnatchers. Perhaps this is why Mrs Mary Mason had three iron straps around her casket, and an undertaker, William Horne, who died in 1826 aged 68, was also taking no chances:

> The wooden lid of his inner coffin was supported by two iron bars running from the head to the foot end; the inner lead coffin had two iron straps nailed to the interior, which was placed inside the outer wooden coffin upside down, presumably concealing the soldered edges; the outer wooden coffin had two iron straps around it widthways, nailed into the wood.[82]

Four juvenile skeletons wrapped in cloth and separated by layers of ash were stuffed in one wooden container, and a double wooden casket contained only rubble. In some cases two cadavers were in a coffin made for one, and Master Thomas Williams had been forced to share his space with a friend. There were three prone burials, one with the skull placed between the feet, and one adult was discovered supine with a friend on his or her left side. Both were articulated. A skeleton, which had survived in good condition and appeared undisturbed, had no skull, and another tiny individual was in a very large coffin. Two caskets contained multiple burials; one had parts of at least nineteen people in it, and the other three adult bodies. Sixteen bodies were dressed in their own clothes and twelve were only wearing a shroud. Items worn included an eighteenth-century silk-faced gentleman's waistcoat and an early nineteenth-century lace-trimmed dress.[83]

Jewellery, dental prostheses and a medicine bottle were among the discoveries, together with a turned box-wood barrel containing a third party's extracted molars. Four burials had remains of wigs or hair pieces, three gentlemen were wearing

silk or woollen gloves and one old man wore slippers – of different sizes; was he suffering from gout? One stillbirth was found – Master Chauvet – and one suicide. William Leschallas, who had been suffering from severe depression, shot himself in 1852, and the rector, using his discretion, interred him.

The majority of containers in the crypt were flat-lidded single-break coffins, a familiar design that is still used today. These were constructed from a combination of elm, oak, conifer, lead and iron. In 1813 the vestry ordered that for hygienic reasons all further burials should be encased in lead, and in the eastern parochial vault 89.3 per cent of all interments complied to this rule. The wood/lead/wood triple caskets had a Russian doll effect, and the outer coffin was always covered with black or scarlet wool, baize or silk. Velvet was reserved for the aristocracy. This upholstery had various metal embellishments on it including handles for carrying – although these were only decorative on a lead container weighing a quarter of a ton. Details of the deceased were inscribed on a breastplate, the shape of which varied: a shield was used for a man, a lozenge for a spinster and an oval a married woman. A cartouche was used for men and women, and sometimes an end plate was affixed if the coffin was to be stacked. In 235 cases sawdust was used in the casket to stop the corpse moving around, the amount varying from a thin layer on the base to full to the brim. For readers with a strong stomach there is in the report a careful description of the body's putrefaction and its visiting insects.[84]

Christ Church. Skull and portrait of Peter Ogier, 1711-1775.

When Christ Church was consecrated in 1729 it cost 11s to be interred in the best part of the churchyard, but Philip Dutch paid £35 8s for his family vault six years later. It has been estimated that over the years a considerable sum in excess of £2,500 was received for the 1,000 interments in the church vaults.[85] Particularly welcome were non-parishioners who had to pay double fees. It was a lucrative business, but it had to end by law in 1852 by which time the annual income from crypt and churchyard was around £215 pa (£25,417).

Christ Church. Part of the eastern parochial area (from the west entrance) which contained a total of 181 coffins.

An excellent description of an 1839 funeral at Christ Church is given by William Hurlin,[86] who on 6 May attended his grandmother's interment. Writing on 30 September 1908 in Antrim, New Hampshire, he describes how the triple coffin, wood/metal/wood, was taken to the crypt:

On the day of the funeral, an hour before it occurred, the two men called 'mutes' took their places outside the front door, one on each side of it. They were dressed in black, and had a black silk sash over one shoulder and across the breast low down on the other side. Each had a broad black silk band on his hat with the ends of it, about 18 inches long, hanging down behind. In the hand farthest from the door, they each held a black staff about four and a half feet long, with a cross piece about a foot long on top of it, over which was laid a piece of black silk about eight feet long, which was bound close to the staff about two feet from the top, and its folds hung loose about two feet lower.

When the mourners were assembled, the undertaker dressed them; the men in long black cloth coats and black gloves, and a broad black crepe band around their hats, the ends of which hung down about eight inches, and the women in a long black scarf with a hood attached to it which covered their heads, and also with black gloves. When all were ready the procession started as follows:

First the undertaker in black with a black silk scarf and black silk hat band like the mutes.

Second, the mutes aside each other with their staves.

Third, a man in black with a black board about three by one and a half feet on his head, on which board were placed six groups of four or five large black ostrich feathers.

Fourth, the hearse covered with black cloth and drawn by two black horses, each having on his head a bunch of large black ostrich feathers; and eight groups of large black ostrich feathers on top of the hearse in which of course the coffin had been placed. The driver was dressed in a black cloak with silk hat band hanging down behind. An attendant in black with sash and hat band like the mutes, walked outside each horse, and each of them carried a small staff about 18 inches long which he grasped in the middle of it.

Fifth, two mourning coaches to accommodate six persons each, each horse having a plume of feathers on his head, the drivers being dressed as the driver of the hearse, and there being two attendants for each coach as in the case of the hearse.

After the prescribed portion of the Burial Service had been read in the church, the coffin was carried into the vault, and deposited in the place assigned it, and the remainder of the service was read. I think the attendants before spoken of acted as bearers.

The minister on this occasion entered the crypt to say the committal, but this was not always so. Presumably if the service was completed in the church the priest and mourners would not have to enter the vaults, which were not particularly pleasant. The sexton and the bearers were probably the only persons to penetrate the inner recesses of the interior, but a vault near the southern entrance may have been used as a vestibule where the final prayers could be said.

Spending months in the vaults was not pleasant for the researchers, but by 1986 after two years' hard labour there were only a few coffins left in the crypt. The team at Christ Church had done a remarkable job in the most trying conditions. In some cases bodies were so unpleasant or considered such a health risk that only a superficial recording of facts was possible before the corpse was sent for cremation. The state of preservation varied from virtually complete, including skin, hair and internal organs, to a sediment of crystal debris, being all that remained of the bones. There was no evidence that any of the bodies had been embalmed. The excavation represents the only large group of provenanced and closely dated human material and funereal artefacts from the eighteenth and nineteenth centuries.

Christ Church. Portrait of Louisa Courtauld (*née* Ogier), 1729–1807.

By that summer all the wood had been disposed of, and the lead stacked and hosed down with viricidal fluid, and so the Health and Safety authorities gave permission for the removal of the metalwork, fabrics and securely boxed skeletons, to the research laboratories for further study. Dr Tony Waldron, Margaret Cox, Dr David Whittaker and others continued their research. The chancellor's original faculty ordered that the remains be eventually cremated and the ashes returned to Christ Church, but since then it has been realised that the bones are an important resource for research so they will be preserved.[87] The bones which were reinterred are in Tower Hamlets Cemetery. The total cost of the operation was around £250,000.

The body of Louisa Perina Courtauld, *née* Ogier (1729–1807), was taken to Gosfield church, Essex, where seventy of her descendants, presided over by the Revd Christopher Courtauld and the Revd Anthony Salmon, attended a Service of Reburial in January 2002. She is honoured in the family because she provides the link between the two products for which they are best known – silver and silk. She successfully carried on her husband's silver business after his death, and made a connection with her father's silk trade when she apprenticed her son George to her cousin Merzeau, a silk-throwster in Spitalfields.[88]

After thirty-five years the homeless work closed in the crypt, because the accommodation of windowless dormitories was no longer suitable for a residential care home in the twenty-first century. The Spitalfields Crypt Trust moved a few yards northwards, and in May 2002 Princess Alexandra opened Acorn House, near St Leonard's Church, Shoreditch.

In 2011 there is a chapel in the crypt for church use only, and also two spaces, the east and middle crypts, available for private hire as a venue for choir rehearsals, music gigs, product/book launches, wine tasting and private parties. It is also used for art installations and exhibitions, which are curated by Lisa-Raine Hunt as part of the Public Programme – Arts, Education & Heritage. When there are large events in the nave the crypt is used by caterers or, if there is an orchestra performing, as a green room.[89]

[*] ST BRIDE, FLEET STREET

The crypt of this famous Fleet Street church attracts many visitors because it houses not only a medieval chapel but also a museum, which displays ancient archaeological remains found on the site and an exhibition, designed by John Lansdell, of 2,000 years of local history.

In the seventeenth century St Bride's was a busy, populous parish, and burials were in the crypt or churchyards. Samuel Pepys, who with his eight brothers and sisters was baptised at the church, had great difficulty finding room to bury his brother Tom in 1664. In his diary he notes on 18 March:

Above left: Christ Church. Skull of Louisa Courtauld. She was buried with her siblings rather than with her husband Samuel at Chelsea who had died forty-two years earlier.

Above right: Christ Church. Skulls found of the Ogier family. Top, left to right, three sisters, Louise Courtauld, 77, Frances Merzeau, 65, and Jane Julien, 78. Bottom row their brother Peter, 63, and Frances' son Peter Merzeau, 88.

> So to church, and with the grave-maker chose a place for my brother to lie in, just under my mother's pew. But to see how a man's tombes are at the mercy of such a fellow, that for sixpence he would, (as his owne words were), 'I will justle them together but I will make room for him;' speaking of the fullness of the middle aisle, where he was to lie; and that he would, for my father's sake, do my brother that is dead all the civility he can.

Later that day, at around 6 p.m., he and the 150 or so mourners, fortified by biscuits and burnt claret, attended the burial conducted by Dr Pierson, which was followed (for only a few invited guests) by wine and 'a barrel of oysters, cake and cheese'. The following year the churchyards were crammed with plague victims: Pepys notes that 238 people died in the parish in one week.

By 1830 the graveyard was almost full, so the vestry commissioned a report from a committee of fourteen men chaired by Mr Thomas Moores, who was asked on 6 January 1830 to make recommendations concerning burial provision at St Bride's. Three months later they told the vestry what they had discovered in the vaults:

> In the church the north aisle contains nine private graves and there is room for only one more. In front of the Communion table there is also room for one more but all the graves are of a very old date and probably might be recovered by the parish. The vaults are in good order except for one which is wet. The south-eastern vault is the most filled but there is room left in the five other vaults for 20–50 each. In future all coffins should be lead.

In June 1858, soon after the closure of the crypt, the Commissioners of Sewers prepared a plan of the vaults. A 120ft long vault 9ft high ran east-west, which was five-eighths full, three vaults were under the central aisle, one under the south aisle and two private vaults were at the south-west of the crypt.

Shortly after evening service on Sunday 29 December 1940 a fire bomb pierced St Bride's roof, and flames destroyed Wren's work. It was a devastating conflagration and the only good thing to come from this disaster was that at the end of the war archaeologists, led by Professor W.F. Grimes of the London Museum,[90] were able to excavate the site and make a study of the vaults. The bombs had hardly touched them, so the stone foundations of a Roman town house with a mosaic pavement were discovered, and they are on view today. Thanks to the work of Professor Grimes and his colleagues the origins of this site as a place of Christian worship could now be traced back to the sixth century, and it was realised that Wren had built his church on the foundations of six previous churches. Seven sealed vaults[91] were discovered, including two charnel houses – one containing approximately 300 skeletons piled to the roof, and another with skulls and bones laid out in squares like a chessboard. There was also a large eighteenth-century pillared vault, now the rector's study, and a well-built Stuart-period chamber. A fourteenth-century crypt with a chalk-block roof and hard sandstone ribs under the north-east corner of the church is now a chapel. It contains a half window and a lancet doorway or window.

In a letter of 27 August 1952 to the diocesan authorities the rector, Cyril Armitage, who had been appointed the year before, refers to 'a large quantity of lead coffins, many surrounded by earth and charcoal. In the nave of the crypt very few of the remains are in coffins – only three. These coffins are in a very bad state, battered and pierced. More seemly receptacles will be needed.'[92] He also mentions other finds, including 'a medieval altar tomb, an early lead coffin with the metal moulded to the corpse and a fully developed lead casement. In a Roman cess pit is a grave judged by experts as being unique in the Metropolis, showing a primitive mode of burial custom.' In addition to the 200 skeletons that were sent for study, nearly 5,000 human remains were found in the medieval charnel house, where all the bones have been put in their categories, thigh bone with thigh bone and so on. Armitage asked permission from Chancellor John Ashworth to send some of the disarticulated, unidentified skeletons to the laboratory of the Department of Physical Anthropology in the University of Cambridge to be measured and examined, 'as it is thought that they are of immense scientific value concerning the racial characteristics of the British race'. On 17 December 1953 the chancellor agreed to the plan, on the condition that the bones, which were of 500 individuals dating from 1600–1800, were not put on public display and were returned to St Bride's within two years. This was later extended to three years and on return they were placed in their present vault, although a few are still at the Duckworth Collection in Cambridge. The cost was paid by a grant from the Royal Society.[93]

The rector drew up plans for a new crypt to house a vestry and provide 'shelters if the calamity of war were again to break upon us'. When the work began complaints poured in from local offices whose workers were shocked to see skulls and bones, so tarpaulins were hastily erected. Vandals and thieves intruded, despite police patrols, and at one point the workmen refused to handle coffins so the verger and archaeologists had to oblige. Sometimes the bones were 'mere masses of brown

St Bride. A nineteenth-century iron coffin designed to frustrate bodysnatchers.

St Bride. Charnel house - heap of bones and a line of skulls.

dust; some were a fluid slush; others were recognisable with shrunken skin. There were eight cases of adipocere where by natural process and dampness the bodies had turned to a fatty wax-like substance.[94] The lead from the coffins was sold for £3,000 (£70,933) and given to the restoration fund.

Professor Grimes, assisted by Dr Kenneth Oakley of the Natural History Museum, Dr J.C. Trevor and Dr Phillip Bury from Cambridge, removed the 240 skeletons from their wood/lead/wood coffins and placed them in metal munitions boxes purchased from the Army Surplus Stores. Regrettably there were not enough to go round so some had to share, which caused problems later. After a few years Dr F. Steel attempted to separate them all and place them in white plastic containers, which unfortunately encouraged mould growth on some of the bones. The lead nameplates also caused damage. In the 1960s Miss Rosemary Powers of the Natural History Museum compiled a catalogue of the bones and the pathologies and anomalies of each person, together with some background historical information.

During the next forty years the collection was extensively used as a research resource, but it was not until 1989 that a comprehensive conservation programme was undertaken. The Leverhulme Trust awarded a grant to Dr Louise Scheuer and Dr S.M. MacLaughlin to do this, and, together with Dr Sue Black, they have given us much important information.[95] Only ten of the medieval burials unearthed at the end of the war were still available for study, and Milne has given a careful account of these.[96]

The 244 skeletons that had been removed from their coffins were re-numbered, re-boxed and placed in the southern part of the crypt in acid-free cardboard boxes. Each was separated into cranial/postcranial remains and the coffin plates were stored separately. Smaller boxes were thus used for skulls, which often contained loose teeth, hair, hyoid bone and ossified thyroid and cricoid cartilages. Where possible a dental formula was produced for each individual – in three cases gold dentures were found. The larger postcranial boxes contained the vertebral column, ribs, hands and feet.

The skeletons had been interred between 1740 and 1852, and now the researchers listed their sex, age, condition, date of birth and death. There were: juveniles: twelve males aged 1 day–17 years; three females aged 3 years 4 months–18 years; adults: 109 males aged 20–38; 103 females aged 19–91. The dates of birth ranged from 1676–1840, but most individuals were born between 1750 and 1789. There were some familial groupings – nine members of the Devey family who had died between 1807 and 1848, and six members of the Blades family from 1788–1829. Edward Edking aged 9 days was buried on the same day as his mother Sarah, 18 February 1829. The burial registers reveal that forty were buried in the eighteenth century and 200 between 1800 and 1852, with a peak year of ten burials in 1837.

St Bride. Charnel house - a neat line of bones.

St Bride. Charnel house - skulls peer over earth still containing bones.

Some oddities were noted by the scholars. The undated coffin of Sam Lord, a hunchback cripple, contained some leather strings, which must have been the harness that supported him, and Mrs Martha Bond, who died on 1 March 1816, still had a mass of bright auburn hair. She was buried alongside her two husbands. Less surprisingly, many of the over 40s were suffering from osteoarthritis. The skull of a 24-year-old man was found to have a gunshot exit wound, but the registers record him as 'suddenly found dead'. The inquest said that his death was due to 'mental derangement' so presumably his family was being spared a suicide verdict, because that would have meant that burial was not allowed in consecrated ground.[97] Zachary Edwards, who died in the Fleet Prison in 1841, rated a mention in *The Times*. Aged 35 and formerly a lieutenant in the Lancers, he 'was accustomed to take large quantities of drink' but had died of typhus fever. During his eight months in prison he had been ministered to by fellow prisoners, including a doctor.[98]

One of the corpses is that of John Pridden, who died in 1807 aged 80. Churchwarden at St Bride's and a local bookseller, he drew a plan of the crypt bone-house, and kept careful notes of the happenings in the church and neighbourhood. In the particularly hard winter of 1788 he describes the 'two special warming machines, called buzaglas' which were installed in the building.[99] The bones of Robert Waithman, Lord Mayor 1823–24, and Samuel Holden, Governor of the Bank of England who died in 1740, are also in the collection.

In 1992, after three years' work, Dr Scheuer and her research assistant Jacqui Bowman were attempting to make more space by moving the boxes when they found an old lead coffin behind one of the stacks. It had been put to one side and forgotten in the 1950s, so as the lid was loose they prised it open to find soil and bones inside. The name plate gave them a surprise, because inside were the remains of Samuel Richardson (1689–1761), who is known as the father of the English novel. Aged 13, he had moved to London and been apprenticed to a printer. By about 1718 he had his own press in Fleet Street, and from 1723 until his death his office was next to the church in Salisbury Court.

St Bride's thus has two unique series of human remains. One is the collection described above of 244 skeletons, identified in regard to their sex and age at the time of death and thus forming a very important source of research into forensic and other forms of medicine. The other series, not open to the public, which is estimated by some to include nearly 7,000 human remains, is in a medieval charnel house. Here all the bones are put in their categories, thigh bone with thigh bone and so on, and laid in chequer-board pattern.

[*] ALL HALLOWS BERKYNGECHIRCHE-BY-THE-TOWER, BYWARD STREET

This is a site of great antiquity. At the west end of the Undercroft, under the tower, is a tessellated floor of a second-century Roman house. Above it, to the west of the nave, is a Saxon arch from the first church built on this site in about 675. The land on which this stood belonged to the Abbey of Barking, which was closely involved here until it was dissolved in the sixteenth century. Beneath the nave there are now no vaults but there are three chambers, chapels today, at the east end of the Undercroft. The seventeenth-century Oratory of St Clare is in the south-east corner. Next to it and linked by a squint is the barrel-vaulted St Francis

All Hallows by the Tower. Entrance to the crypt St Clare Chapel.

Chapel, *c*.1280, which was rediscovered in 1925. The largest chapel, under the church altar in the vicar's vault, is now a columbarium. The Revd P.T.B. 'Tubby' Clayton, founder of Toc H, told everyone when he was vicar, 1922–63, that 'a burial costs ten bob'. The price has risen since then, but owing to lack of space only the ashes of parishioners and people related to present occupants can be interred. Tubby allowed members of Toc H and of the 1st Lord Mayor's Own Scout Group to find a final resting place here.

The body of William Laud, Archbishop of Canterbury, lay in this vault for several years after his execution in the Tower on 10 January 1645. The entry in the parish burial register, which is displayed in the Undercroft museum nearby, has the word 'traitor' smeared out in ink. He was beheaded for Popish doctrines, making the communion table the centre of a church instead of the pulpit and supporting Charles I's view that he reigned by divine right. His body was taken to St John's College, Oxford in 1663. The churchyard was also used as a temporary resting place for those executed on Tower Hill, including John Fisher, the scholarly Bishop of Rochester who refused to accept King Henry VIII as supreme head of the English Church and was made a cardinal by the Pope. He was executed in 1535.

There were 2,087 parishioners in 1801, and at one time a burial ground surrounded All Hallows on its north, south and east sides. Between 1823 and 1832 there were an average of fifty-seven interments each year. This had dropped to an average of thirty-seven between 1835 and 1844.[100]

The medieval church, which had survived the Great Fire, was destroyed by German bombers in December 1940. All that remained was the brick tower of 1659, the north and south walls and part of the east end. The church was rebuilt by Seely and Paget and dedicated on 23 July 1957.

Forty years later the construction of the Queen Mother Centre to the south and east of the church meant that foundations were dug in the disused graveyard. In 2000 the AOC Archaeology Group from Twickenham, led by Melissa Melikian and Diccon Hart, reported that they had unearthed 304 burials, some in lead coffins and in varying states of preservation (286 adults and 18 juveniles), and over 107,000 disarticulated bones – loose bones within the cemetery soil. The osteologist calculated that they belonged to at least 1,736 men, women and children.[101] The burials dated from around 1770 to 1850, and the twenty-two named coffins contained fifteen men and seven women – the earliest being James Steele who died on 5 April 1776 aged 66. There were also some tenth- and eleventh-century burials, which revealed the Saxon origins of the graveyard, and pottery of that date was unearthed together with a Saxon pillow grave – a form of burial in which a stone pad was placed under the deceased's head. Beneath the graveyard the dig revealed traces of Roman floors and walls, which means that there was a substantial building here 1,000 years before the church.

All Hallows. View through the crypt museum.

All Hallows. Barrel-vaulted St Francis Chapel, c.1280. In 1452 it was a Lady Chapel, the entrance being from the chancel above.

All Hallows. Undercroft altar and columbarium, formerly the vicar's vault. The wall is fourteenth century.

On 27 November 2000, fifty-six coffins and the majority of the human remains were interred in the East London Cemetery, Grange Road, Plaistow, and the remainder on 28 July 2004. The chancellor in amending the 1999 Faculty agreed that 'half of the teeth of 18 individual skeletal remains shall be retained by the Institute of Archaeology of University College, London for analysis under the direction of one of their students in the interests of furthering forensic science'.

4

WESTMINSTER ABBEY

Queen Victoria was not amused. Lady Augusta Bruce, one of her Household and a close confidant, had at the age of 41 decided to marry a 48-year-old clergyman, Arthur Stanley, who had just been appointed Dean of Westminster in 1863. 'She has most unnecessarily decided to marry (!!!),' the queen selfishly told King Leopold. 'It has been my greatest sorrow and trial since my misfortune.' Her Ladyship persevered, but Stanley in a letter to his bride said that he had doubts about the wisdom of leaving Oxford for 'that Church of Tombs', and these fears were made worse when he met the canons. One of them, Christopher Wordsworth, had already preached against the appointment, which elicited a lunch invitation from Stanley who still remained gloomy. 'I felt no elation, nothing but depression. It seemed to me as if I were going down alive into the sepulchre.' Over the next seventeen years, however, Stanley became one of the most distinguished deans in the Abbey's 1,000-year history, and within four years he had written his scholarly, encyclopaedic *Historical Memorials of Westminster Abbey*. History had made the building a national mausoleum, but he saw each tomb not so much a dumb relic of a dead past but the eloquent mouth of one who being dead yet speaketh.[102]

The space available for burials in the Abbey was by this time very limited. Over 3,000 bodies had already been interred and it was estimated that there was room for only 100 more. There had been over 200 burials in the last twenty years of the seventeenth century but there were only fifteen during Stanley's time, and he needed to be convinced that the deceased person had great national eminence. David Livingstone was one, but his huge congregation was a contrast to the dozen mourners at Charles Dickens's funeral, on 14 June 1870, which was held in secret at 9.30 a.m. without a choir – much to their disappointment as it meant no fees. He had asked that he 'be buried in an inexpensive, unostentatious and strictly private manner',[103] but his grave in Poets' Corner was left open for two days, and at the end of the first day there were still 1,000 people waiting to pay their respects.

The Abbey has been a national monument and mausoleum for 1,000 years. King Edward the Confessor relocated England's capital from Winchester to London soon after 1042, and although the records before this time are scanty the Bayeux Tapestry has a large picture of the church on it. The Domesday survey rated Westminster seventh in order of income among fifty English monasteries. Edward wanted to build a great monastery at Westminster so work began, but he died in 1066 and was buried beneath the building which had been consecrated on 28 December 1065. His successor, William the Conqueror, was crowned there on Christmas Day, and all monarchs thereafter except for Edward V and Edward VIII have had their coronation there.

THE ROYAL VAULTS AND TOMBS. [104]

The completely preserved body of the newly canonised Edward with its white curling beard was exhumed in 1163 and placed in a shrine which has been visited by pilgrims ever since. The corpse was moved to its present place in 1269, and the coffin rests in the top part of the magnificent tomb. His wife Edith, who died in 1075, is nearby.

Forged or doctored documents make it difficult to chart the Abbey's history over the next hundred years, but by 1154 it had emerged to rival the great religious houses at Canterbury, Winchester and St Albans. Its geographical position close to the seat of power helped, and during Henry III's long reign, 1216–72, the building began to be rebuilt, and the new chapter house was used for meetings of the King's Council. Henry was buried in the space vacated by the Confessor's bones, which began the royal mausoleum, and nineteen years later he was interred in the magnificent tomb we see today, although he ordered that his heart should be taken to Fontrevrault in France. In October 1871 the tomb chest was opened after the effigy had been removed for cleaning. The marble bed on which it lay was 7ft 11in by 3ft 2in and the coffin nearly filled the space. The oak of the lid was warped but sound, and the iron chains with their rings at the foot, head and sides, which had been used to carry the coffin, were in place. [105]

Henry's son Edward I was crowned in the unfinished church, and he buried his beloved Queen Eleanor there in a splendid tomb in 1291. She had died at Hardby in Nottinghamshire, and Eleanor crosses were erected at all the halting places on the way to Westminster, the last being at Charing Cross. Her entrails were left at Lincoln and her heart deposited at Blackfriars monastery in London. Four months after his own death in 1307 Edward was buried close to the Confessor, whose shrine stood in its own chapel behind the high altar. Edward had continued the building for five bays into the nave. The king, who was 6ft 2in tall, and known as Longshanks and the Hammer of the Scots, made his son promise that after death his flesh should be boiled and his bones carried at the head of an English army until Scotland was subdued. Perhaps because of this his tomb was unfinished, being opened every two years when the wax of his winding sheet was renewed. After the fall of Richard II this gruesome practice ceased, but in 1774 the Society of Antiquaries and others opened the tomb and found Edward in his royal robes in a Purbeck marble coffin. Pitch was poured in the grave (see cover image by Rowlandson).

Queen Philippa of Hainault, who died in 1369, asked to be buried in the Abbey, and her black marble tomb-chest differs from earlier ones 'by a new veracity, both in portrait and in costume. This is specially noticeable', says Pevsner, 'in the face of the Queen and in the two happily preserved weepers at the NE end.'[106] Her husband, Edward III, lies nearby, his long flowing hair and beard agreeing with contemporary accounts. His grandson, Richard II, had a great affection for the Abbey and at enormous cost arranged the funeral there of his queen, Anne of Bohemia. Crazy with grief, he hit the Earl of Arundel so hard for being late that the earl fell to the floor covered in blood, and the funeral had to be delayed until nightfall, when a reconciliation had taken place. His own tomb, with his effigy's hand clasping Anne's,[107] was completed before his death five years later in 1399. The tomb was opened in 1871 under the supervision of Sir George Gilbert Scott, who found most of Anne's skeleton was missing as bones had been extracted by visitors through a hole in the side of the tomb. A jawbone was removed by a boy from Westminster School in 1776 but was restored in 1916. It also became apparent that the old-style box burial chamber had been made larger and was thus almost a vault. Scott discovered a chamber under the marble slab on which the effigies lay about 6½ft deep, so that the floor of the grave was 2ft 6in below the floor of the chapel: 'The lower part of the chamber is the grave, which is about 7 feet long and 5 feet wide, over it is a space transversed longitudinally by an arch formed at about mid height, so as to carry the two long slabs above, and dividing that space into two parts 8½ feet long and each about two feet wide.'[108]

The eastern end of the Confessor's chapel was cleared of an altar and sacred relics in 1422 to provide space for the great warrior king Henry V to be laid to rest, in a tomb that almost gave him saintly status. His funeral car, which came from Paris to London, had an effigy on it. Until then the body of a dead monarch had been embalmed, dressed in royal robes and regalia and exhibited to all and sundry at a lying in state. Four horses drew the coffin through the west doors into the nave as far as the choir screen, where it was placed on a bier and covered by a hearse which looked like a four-poster bed with candles stuck on its spikes. Shields, laudatory verses and the titles of the deceased might be attached to the wooden posts. Henry has his own chantry chapel at the eastern end of St Edward's chapel, in which his tomb-chest was completed in 1431.

Henry V's widow, Katherine de Valois, probably because she had remarried, was placed 'in a badly apparelled state' in a plain coffin. She had successfully been embalmed because she 'continued to be seen, the bones being firmly united, and thinly clothed with flesh, like scrapings of fine leather' for the next 274 years. She travelled around the abbey because, having been buried in front of the lady chapel altar in 1437, she was taken up when Henry VII demolished the chapel in 1502 and put above ground in a new wooden chest near her husband's tomb, 'to be seen and handled of any who will much desire it'. Samuel Pepys paid her a visit and noted in his diary that 'I did kiss her mouth, reflecting upon it that I did kiss a queen, and that this was my birthday, 36 years old, that I did first kiss a queen.'[109] She was moved to the Villiers vault in 1776 and finally deposited beneath the altar slab in her husband's chantry chapel in 1878.

For the rest of the fifteenth century St George's Chapel, Windsor, became the favoured burial place for the royals, until the arrival of the Tudors in 1485. Henry VII wanted to transfer the remains of the saintly Henry VI to Westminster, but this was never done.

The Tudors

Henry VII, not known for his liberality, decided to build at the east end of the Abbey a chapel dedicated to Our Lady, so the old chapel and the White Rose tavern were demolished, and building began in January 1502/3. Ten years later it was completed, and is, with all its glorious elaborations and fan tracery of the fashionable Perpendicular style, one of the finest buildings in Europe. Henry meant it to be the mausoleum for himself and his family, so when his queen, Elizabeth of York, died in 1503 she was eventually laid to rest there. Henry followed six years later in a black velvet coffin marked by a white satin cross from end to end. It was placed not in a raised tomb but in the cavernous vault beneath by the side of his queen. The archbishops and bishops struck their croziers on the coffin with the word 'Absolvimus'. The monument above the vault was completed within twenty years by Pietro Torrigiani, who is best known as the rowdy youth who punched his fellow pupil Michelangelo on the nose. An observant antiquary considered that the king's features on his effigy cast by Nicholas Ewen indicated 'a strong reluctance to quit the possessions of this world'.[110]

The Dissolution of the Monasteries by Henry's son, Henry VIII, was a serious threat to the Abbey, for on 16 January 1540 in the chapter house Abbot Boston and twenty-four of his monks signed the Deed of Surrender. The king received much of the monies and lands but fortunately St Edward's body was removed and hidden. Two years later a cathedral foundation with a dean and chapter was endowed and established but when Henry died and was buried at Windsor near his Yorkist grandfather, Protector Somerset pondered the building's destruction. It was probably saved by the royal tombs – and by the seventeen manors and good farms that were given to him. Many of the treasures were removed and the tombs despoiled, but the royal bodies remained. The Roman Catholic Queen Mary ordered the monks to return and restored the abbey's privileges and wealth – almost alone among the monastic bodies. The bones of St Edward were returned to his shrine, which was repaired and encrusted with new jewels. The queen also ensured that her predecessor and young half-brother, Edward VI, was buried close to Henry VII instead of beside their father at Windsor. Stanley comments that it is a great paradox 'that the first Protestant Prince should have thus received his burial from the bitterest enemy of the Protestant cause, and that the tomb under which he reposed should have been the altar built for the chanting of masses which he himself had been the chief means of abolishing'.[111]

Mary was interred in Westminster Abbey when her brief reign ended in 1558, and the black draperies were torn down by the jubilant congregation before the ceremony ended. Elizabeth, her sister, who was crowned two months later, sent the monks packing and established the Collegiate Church that we know today. On 21 May 1560 possession was given to a new dean, William Bill, and twelve prebendaries. She took a close interest in their affairs and almost always entered the Abbey to pray before opening Parliament. On her death in 1603 she was brought by the Thames from Richmond to lie in Henry VII's vault. There is some confusion as to whether Elizabeth's body was embalmed, because John Manningham, the contemporary historian, says that this was not her wish and that it was 'wrapped up in cerecloth, and that very ill too'. However, Dr Litten notes that Elizabeth Southwell, a courtier, reports that Lord Cecil ignored her wishes. In a recent biography John Clapham states that her body was left alone for a day or two, 'and meane persons (embalmers) had access to it' before it was laid in the anthropoid lead shell-coffin.[112] Elizabeth I is the last monarch buried in the Abbey to have a monument erected above her, and the corpse was moved in 1606 to rest above her sister Mary I in the north aisle.

The Stuarts

King James I arrived from Scotland and decided that his illustrious predecessor should be commemorated with a magnificent monument made of white marble and touchstone costing £765, which is still one of the most visited tombs in the Abbey. It was the last time a sovereign paid tribute in this way to a predecessor. James ordered that the body of his 'dearest mother', the ill-fated Mary Queen of Scots, should travel south from Peterborough and be placed in a vault below the south aisle of Henry VII's chapel. He wanted to honour her with an even grander monument, and this soon became a place of pilgrimage for devout Scots who regarded it as the shrine of a canonised saint. 'I hear,' said Thomas Demster, 'that her bones, lately translated to the burial place of the Kings of England at Westminster, are resplendent with miracles.'[113]

Dean Stanley called part of the north aisle 'Innocents' Corner', because here lay two of King James's infant children. They are Princess Mary, who at her death aged 2½ in 1607 said, 'I go, I go, away I go' three times, and Princess Sophia, who lived only three days and was placed in an alabaster cradle which is her tomb. In the south aisle are the bones of James's eldest son, Henry, who died in 1612, thus catapulting his brother, the unfortunate Charles, towards the crown and martyrdom. Henry's funeral was attended by 2,000 mourners. King James died in 1625 and was interred not beside his wife or children but in the vault beside Henry VII, which presumably meant disturbing the boy king, Edward VI. Nothing came of a scheme for a monument in classical style, possibly by Inigo Jones who designed the king's hearse – by now these wooden or plaster frames decorated with hangings were only used in grand funerals.

After his execution at Whitehall in 1649 the body of Charles I was not taken to the Abbey, where he had interred his infant children Charles and Anne, but to Windsor. At the Restoration his remains were to have been returned to London and taken to Henry VII's chapel, but there was difficulty in finding them – which is odd as they were discovered in 1813 where they had originally been placed. The grant of £70,000 to pay for transport costs and a memorial by Christopher Wren was presumably pocketed by his son Charles II. Stanley loftily comments: 'The Abbey, no doubt, was fortunate to escape the intrusion of what would have been, architecturally, the only thoroughly incongruous of all the regal monuments.'

The Commonwealth

The Abbey's constitution changed under Oliver Cromwell, but its fabric was surprisingly untouched and the royal monuments were unharmed. However, Torrigiani's altar in Henry VII's chapel was desecrated: Sir Robert Harley, chairman of the Parliamentary Committee, 'brake it into shivers' and then took the chapel's stained glass to his home.[114] Two companies of soldiers were quartered in the church and they caused much havoc, smashing the organ to bits, but despite episodes like these the Abbey's finances and fabric were preserved. Perhaps this was because Oliver Cromwell soon made it clear that he and his family expected to be buried in the royal vaults. Henry Ireton, his son-in-law, had a sumptuous funeral; Cromwell's mother, Elizabeth, was laid to rest in 1654 aged 96; his sister Jane two years later; and his favourite daughter, Elizabeth Claypole, in 1658. Finally the Protector himself expired on 3 September 1658, the anniversary of his victories at Dunbar and Worcester. It is uncertain when his body was placed in what became known as Oliver's vault at the east end of Henry VII's chapel, but it was probably within a fortnight as the embalming process went wrong, and despite being laid in two coffins of wood and lead 'The filth broke through them all', according to Dr George Bate, his physician.[115]

Cromwell only rested in his vault for just over two years, because on 26 January 1661, soon after the Restoration of Charles II, the Speaker of the House of Commons arrived in the Abbey to witness the corpse being dug up, together with those of Henry Ireton and Bradshaw, the judge who had condemned Charles I. They had cheated the executioner in life so in death they were to hang at Tyburn. The bodies of the regicides were then buried beneath the gallows, but their heads were hoisted on poles outside Westminster Hall and were still there twenty years later. The grand hearse in Henry VII's chapel was speedily destroyed, and the effigy was hung by its neck outside a window in Whitehall. It survived until

1689, when it was seen in the Banqueting House, and it may be the effigy on show today at the Bargello Museum in Florence.[116] Cromwell was not commemorated in the Abbey until Stanley inserted a tablet in what is now the RAF chapel, and the Cromwell Association later placed a stone at the east end of Henry VII's chapel: 'The burial place of Oliver Cromwell 1658–1661'.

The Restoration

Members of the House of Stuart, including Elizabeth of Bohemia, 'The Queen of Hearts', were now once again laid to rest in Henry VII's chapel, usually in the vault of their ancestress, Mary Queen of Scots. These were joined by a considerable number of the illegitimate progeny of the Merry Monarch, who had apologised for taking an 'unconscionable time a-dying' on 6 February 1685. A new vault, known as the Royal Vault, was made for him, and John Evelyn reports that the obsequies were done 'very obscurely' at night, and that 'all the great officers broke their staves over the grave according to form'. In the same narrow space William III was interred in 1703. He was followed by Queen Mary, then Queen Anne, accompanied by her eighteen short-lived children and her ten brothers and sisters who had died in infancy. No inscription marked their graves until the time of Dean Stanley.

Queen Anne was buried in 1714. Her unwieldy frame filled a coffin even larger than that of her gigantic spouse, Prince George of Denmark, who had been interred there six years earlier. The vault had no more room so was bricked up.

The Hanoverians

George I, having arrived in this country from Hanover in 1714, returned there to be buried in 1727, but his son, having lived longer in England, decided that he and his queen, Caroline of Anspach, should be interred in the Abbey. Powerful and much loved, she died on 20 November 1737 and was buried on 17 December in a new vault constructed in three weeks beneath the three westernmost bays of the nave of King Henry VII's chapel. The funeral was chaotic, for the psalms were not sung and the lesson was omitted, but the day was saved by Handel's magnificent music: 'How are the mighty fallen! She that was great among the nations and Princess among the provinces.' The Chapter complained to the earl marshal that three of their number had been insulted during the preparations and demanded he dismiss the offender, which he did. However, the penitent Secretary Hutcheson attended a chapter meeting to apologise. He was reinstated.

George II had no love for his eldest son, Frederick, who predeceased him and was laid in the Hanoverian vault on 13 April 1751. No members of his family attended. 'This has been a fatal year to my family,' the king remarked that December. 'I have lost my eldest son, but I was glad of it.' This is probably the first time an undertaker was used at a royal funeral, as there is a bill from a Mr Harcourt for £43 9s 6d (£8,331) for the work involved.

Historians have not been kind to George II. Although a vain, irascible, ridiculous and sometimes contemptible figure, his fundamental good sense guided England through an armed rebellion, two threats of invasion and at least three parliamentary crises.[117] He died aged 77 in 1760, and as he had left instructions that his remains should be mingled with Caroline's, the two coffins were placed in a large black marble sarcophagus with their names inscribed and their sceptres crossed. As the queen had been dead for twenty-three years, mingling their bones must have been an unpleasant task.

Horace Walpole witnessed George's interment on 11 November 1760, the king's heart having been taken to the vault two days before:

> Do you know, I had the curiosity to go to the burying t'other night; I had never seen a royal funeral; nay, I walked as a rag of quality, which I found would be, and so it was, the easiest way of seeing it … When we came to the Chapel of Henry VII, all solemnity and decorum ceased; no order was observed, people sat or stood where they could or would; the yeomen of the guard were crying out for help, oppressed by the immense weight of the coffin … the Bishop read sadly and blundered in the prayers … the anthem besides being immeasurably tedious, would have served as well for a nuptial.

Walpole is obviously biased, but even he had to admit that it was a reminder of centuries of royal, religious ceremonies – 'absolutely a noble sight'. As Thomas Cocke has pointed out, 'The Stuarts had allowed their funerary vaults to be created in an informal and even chaotic manner', but King George had commissioned a new vault twenty-three years earlier. Care had to be taken in the rush not to undermine the foundations, because the vault designed by Henry Flitcroft was large: it has three square bays with equal aisles to north and south and a larger bay at the east end. It is entered by a staircase and vestibule at the west end.[118] The huge sarcophagus in black and yellow marble containing the royal pair is 7ft long and 4ft 4in wide.

George II was the last sovereign to be interred in the Abbey, and his younger son William, the 'Butcher' Duke of Cumberland, followed five years later. Augusta of Wales, the mother of George III, was interred in 1772. Farmer George decided to break with tradition so constructed a vault beneath the Wolsey chapel – now the Albert memorial chapel – in St George's Chapel, Windsor, where he, his queen and most of their large family now rest. His two youngest sons, Alfred and Octavius, who had died aged 2 and 4 respectively and had been placed on each side of George II and Queen Caroline in the Abbey, were removed to Windsor. The new vault was an almost exact copy of his grandfather's at Westminster, and in it there was room for eighty-one coffins. After Queen Victoria's remodelling this was reduced to sixty, and there are still thirty vacancies.

Ten other coffins rest in the Abbey's Hanoverian vault, each with a scarlet Genoese silk velvet outer covering and accompanied by a viscera chest similarly upholstered. As well as Frederick Prince of Wales and his wife Augusta, their children Elizabeth, Frederick, Edward[119], Henry and Louisa lay together with George II's children, William,[120] Caroline and Amelia.

THE NINETEENTH-CENTURY EXCAVATIONS

The Stuart vault was opened again in 1867 when workmen attempting to install heating in Henry VII's chapel removed some rubbish from under the floor of the eastern bay of the south stalls and found a brick arch. The stalls dated from 1725 so the arch was obviously earlier. A hole was made, and someone crawled in to find that the floor sloped southwards and ended in a flight of five steps leading into a vault containing the coffins of Charles II, Mary II, William III, Prince George of Denmark and Anne with urns at the feet. The wooden cases were decayed and the metal fittings were loose or fallen. The lead of some of the coffins, especially of Charles II, was much corroded, and his silver breastplate had fallen into the coffin. Until this moment it had not been certain where exactly these sovereigns lay.

The south-east corner of the chapel now received attention. A plain brick vault was found beneath, and there in the centre of the wide, well-swept space lay a lead coffin shaped to the form of the body, but the brass plate revealed that it was not King James I but his consort, Anne of Denmark. Its length of 6ft 7in attested to the lady's remarkable stature. The lead had corroded and collapsed on to the body, and the workmen reported that this was the only room with foul air. Contemporary accounts record that James was buried with his wife, so where was he? Two leg bones and a skull were found embedded in the western wall: had Cromwell's soldiers dispersed the remains of the founder of the Stuart dynasty? Could James be resting beside his mother? Having found several members of the Sheffield family in a vault near her, it was decided to enter the vault of Mary Queen of Scots herself by removing stones on the south side of the chapel's southern aisle, one of which was marked 'WAY'. In his *Memorials* Stanley describes what happened:

> This led to an ample flight of stone steps, trending obliquely under the Queen of Scots' tomb. Immediately at the foot of these steps appeared a large vault of brick 12½ ft. long, 7ft. wide, and 6ft. high. A startling, it may almost be said an awful, scene presented itself. A vast pile of leaden coffins rose from the floor; some of full stature, the larger number varying in form from that of the full-grown child to the merest infant, confusedly heaped upon the others, whilst several urns of various shapes were tossed about in irregular positions throughout the vault ...

The first distinct object that arrested the attention was a coffin in the north-west corner, roughly moulded according to the human form and face. It could not be doubted to be that of Henry Frederick Prince of Wales … On the breast was soldered a leaden case evidently containing the heart.[121]

Having discovered this young man, whose death in 1612 meant that England would have to endure a brutal Civil War under his brother, Charles I, Dean Stanley went on to find the coffin of Mary Queen of Scots, which was saturated in pitch. Pressing down on it but not damaging it was the frail coffin of a cousin of James I, Arabella Stuart, whose bones and skull were visible. The many other Stuart coffins stacked around included the children of James II and Anne. Stanley was horrified:

It was impossible to view this wreck and ruin of the Stuart dynasty without a wish, if possible, to restore something like order and decency amongst the relics of so much departed greatness. The confusion, which, at first sight, gave the impression of wanton havoc and neglect, had been doubtless produced chiefly by the pressure of superincumbent weight, which could not have been anticipated … In the absence of directions from any superior authority, a scruple was felt against any endeavour to remove these little waifs and strays of royalty from the solemn resting-place where they had been gathered round their famous and unfortunate ancestors. But as far as could be they were cleared from the larger coffins and placed in the small open space at the foot of the steps.

A small space opening to the west contained three coffins one above the other, members of the Lennox family. Stanley and his researchers were baffled, and agreed they should now look beneath the tomb of Elizabeth I. By now the chapel must have resembled a building site. Two coffins were seen: Queen Mary's beneath and the Virgin Queen's above with its wooden sides crumbled. Part of the lid had been drawn down, but on the floor they found a fragment of it with the Tudor badge, a full double rose, and on each side ER, and below it 1603. The quiet calm of this secluded spot, the dean reflected, contrasted with the confusion and multitudinous decay of the Stuarts' last resting place.

The northern side of the chapel, where records said that James was buried, had now all been explored, so the vault of the young King Edward VI who had died in 1553 was opened. In the centre of the chapel, it was found to be only 7½ft by 2½ft, and was only a few feet below the pavement. When the stone covering was removed at the back of the coffin the skull of the king became visible. The winding sheet had fallen away, and it became obvious that he had no hair – which is corroborated by Froude, who reported that the 15-year-old's last illness caused his hair to fall out.

The indefatigable dean then examined a 6ft skeleton dug up in the south-east corner of the chapel, but James I was a much smaller man and this turned out to be Charles Worsley, Cromwell's 'great and rising favourite', who died aged 35 in 1656. Every conceivable place had now been explored except one, the tomb of Henry VII, but was it likely that the first Stuart king would lie next to the first Tudor king? The only possible way in was from the west so the pavement was removed, the earth cleared and a large stone like a wall was discovered. It was an entrance, and soon an arch was revealed. On 11 February 1869 Stanley was much excited:

> It was with a feeling of breathless anxiety amounting to solemn awe, which caused the humblest of the workmen employed to whisper with bated breath, as the small opening at the apex of the arch admitted the first glimpse into the mysterious secret which had hitherto eluded this long research. Deep within the arched vault were dimly seen three coffins lying side by side – two of them dark and grey with age, the third somewhat brighter and newer.

James I had been found. Three anthropoid coffins lay within the tomb, containing Henry VII, Elizabeth his queen and James I, all in good condition and shaped at the head and shoulders. The vault is narrow (8ft 10in long, 5ft wide and 4½ft high) so the wooden outer coverings of the first two occupants had been removed to make room for James, who still had his wooden case. The lead of Elizabeth's casket is unadorned except for a large appliqué Maltese cross on the breast, and Henry's also has a smaller Maltese cross preceding the inscription which is on a lead plate, 24in by 4in. After 'H' is written '*Hic est Henricus, Rex Angliae et Franciae ac Dominus Hiberniae, hujus nominis septimus, qui obit XXI. die Aprilis, anno regni sui XXIIII et incarnationis dominicae MVIX*' which translates as 'Here lies Henry VII, King of England and France, and Lord of Ireland, who died 21 April 1509 in the 24th year of his reign'. Presumably the silk pall marked with a white cross that had been wrapped around it was removed when the vault was

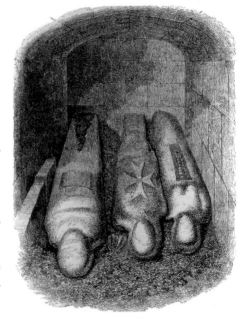

Westminster Abbey. Henry VII's vault showing from left to right, the anthropoid coffins of James I (d. 1625), Elizabeth of York (d. 1503) and Henry VII (d. 1509).

opened to admit the Stuart king. Two workmen who had pushed James's coffin in had scratched their names with the date on the other coffins – E.C. and John Ware 1625. Another workman had been smoking – his pipe was found near the entrance. James, who had published *Counterblast to Tobacco*, would not have been amused.

The Scottish James had thus chosen not to be laid next to his wife, mother, children or even his great predecessor but with the first Tudors. Stanley was overjoyed at the discovery and asked the Archbishop of Canterbury, Archibald Campbell Tait, to come immediately. 'Stand back! Stand back!' the dean shouted theatrically. 'Let the first Scottish archbishop look upon the first Scottish king of England.'[122]

OTHER BURIALS IN THE ABBEY

Dean Stanley's beloved wife Augusta died on 1 March 1876 and eight days later, with the permission of Queen Victoria, her mistress and friend, she was given the great honour of burial in Henry VII's chapel close to a royal exile, Antoine, Duke de Montpensier, younger brother of the French King Louis Philippe. The queen and three of her daughters came to the funeral. Arthur Stanley was broken hearted. 'With her departure,' he wrote, 'the glory of the Westminster life, if not its usefulness, is brought to an end – the mine worked out, and no energy to continue the old routine.'[123] He joined his wife in 1881.

The monks of the Benedictine monastery were presumably buried in the Abbey grounds, and a few saintly prelates were interred in the church, including Richard, Bishop of Rochester, in 1250 and Roger Ford, Abbot of Glastonbury, eleven years later. It was not until the fourteenth century that it became the custom to put commoners alongside the royal family. Richard II's courtiers and favourites were honoured, and John of Waltham made it into the Confessor's chapel 'not without a murmur of general indignation'. The fashion slowly grew, and Henry VII gave permission for an Abbey burial for Sir Humphrey Stanley, who had been with him at Bosworth Field, and also to his cousin Sir Giles Daubeny. Bishop Thomas Ruthall of Durham, his favourite secretary, was also accorded the honour, but he made the fatal mistake of sending a list of his private wealth to Henry VIII instead of a state paper. Queen Elizabeth I had restricted Abbey burial to 'those especially … who have well and gravely served about our person, or otherwise about the public business of our kingdom', but this was disregarded after her death.[124] The burial in Henry VII's chapel of the handsome young George Villiers, Duke of Buckingham, adored by James I and Charles I, set 'a disastrous precedent, so that increasingly these chapels became filled with monuments and the stonework hacked about to get them in'.[125] His murder in 1628 may explain this 'first intrusion of any person not of royal lineage into the mausoleum of princes', and in the vault rest his three sons, and six members of his family.

It is difficult today to know who lies beneath the floor and who is only commemorated, but among those in Abbey soil are the poets Chaucer, Spenser, Dryden and Tennyson; politicians Charles James Fox, the two Pitts, Gladstone and Attlee; composers Handel, Purcell, Stanford and Vaughan Williams; actors Garrick, Irvine and Olivier; writers Johnson, Sheridan, Dickens, Hardy and Kipling; scientists Newton, Hunter, Darwin and Rutherford. Voltaire, watching Newton's burial at night, remarked, 'His countrymen interred him as though he had been a king who had made his people happy', and J.W. von Archenholz, astonished at the grandeur of Garrick's obsequies, told a friend, 'When shall we see our German actors honoured in this manner?'

The dean decides who is to be buried or memorialised in the Abbey. In former centuries, according to Dean Edward Carpenter, high social rank was one of the criteria used to make a decision, as was great distinction in the arts of peace and war, 'But there was no *policy* to restrict burial to any particular category although a large monument to an obscure person with no pretensions to distinction of any kind would not have been contemplated'. He thought that a wide tolerance was exercised.[126] The privilege did not, of course, come free of charge. This important source of income caused concern in 1745, when it seemed that accommodation was becoming limited. There was a proposal to use St Margaret's churchyard, then an open space inhabited by 'dogs and swine and other nuisances', but fees would then have had to go to that church, so the proposal was dropped. Instead the cloisters and the newly available north green, where houses had been demolished, were used.

Fees have always varied. Dr Samuel Johnson was laid to rest in Poets' Corner near Garrick with no choir or anthem, 'merely', said Charles Burney, 'what is read over every old woman that is buried by the parish'. The cost of £54 (£6,804) was thought to be excessive for such a slovenly affair. The choir funeral, brick grave and gravestone for William Wilberforce in 1833 cost the family £129 17s 6d in fees (£13,104).

The funeral of Queen Elizabeth the Queen Mother in 2002, which was followed by interment at Windsor, was the first funeral in the Abbey of a king or queen for almost 250 years. Rehearsals for it took place regularly over the last twenty years of her life, and although they were held in secret before dawn, her treasurer, Sir Ralph Anstruther, told me she would occasionally ask at breakfast, 'Did it all go well?' It is said that Queen Elizabeth II's funeral service will also be in the Abbey.

The Abbey is not simply a heroes' acre. Defoe writes: 'It is become such a piece of honour to be buried in Westminster Abbey that the body of the church begins to be crowded with the bodies of citizens, poets, seamen and parsons, nay, even with very mean persons if they have but any way made themselves known in the World; so that in time, the royal ashes will be thus mingled with common dust.'[127]

5

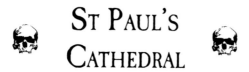

St Paul's
Cathedral

The present building, one of the most famous in the world, is the fifth to be built on the site. According to Bede the first cathedral was founded in 604, and over the years many histories have been written, the most recent, a scholarly account that I have heavily relied on, being published in 2004.[128] The Norman cathedral, with its spire which was struck by lightning in 1561 and not replaced, was begun soon after 1087, and had a crypt at the east end where the relics of St Erkenwald rested, until on 14 November 1148 they were taken upstairs to the apse, behind the high altar. A screen divided the crypt into two equal areas. At the east end was a chapel of the Holy Name of Jesus, and the western part was used by the parishioners of St Faith, whose church was demolished to create the new choir.

St Paul's. The thirteenth-century Gothic crypt of the old St Paul's Cathedral looking east. Etching by Hollar from Dugdale, 1658.

There are several references to pre-fire interments within the cathedral, but of the thousands of medieval burials inside and outside the building only about 100 are recorded. 'Carpenters and trunkmakers' occupied part of the pre-fire crypt, and sections of it were rented out as stock rooms for the publishers located in St Paul's Churchyard.[129] The chapel beneath the south aisle was leased to a glazier, whose cart wheels had damaged the steps at the south door. In 1663 Wren, then aged 31, had been asked to renovate this Romanesque building, and had unsuccessfully recommended demolition. Three years later it was destroyed by the Great Fire.

Samuel Pepys visited the ruined cathedral five days after the fire, and on 7 September 1666 saw 'a miserable sight of Paul's Church, with all the roofs fallen, and the body of the choir fallen into St Fayths' below. Two months later he saw 'The body of Robert Braybrooke, Bishop of London that died in 1404. He fell down in the tomb out of the great church into St Fayth's this late fire, and is here seen his skeleton with the flesh on; but all tough and dry like a spongy dry leather, or touchwood all upon his bones ... Many flocking to see it.'[130]

After the conflagration it was discovered that the monument of Dean John Colet, who died in 1519, had been broken. John Aubrey has left this account, written in about 1680:

Somebody made a little hole towards the upper edge of his Coffin which ... was full of a Liquour which conserved the body. Mr Wyld and Ralph Greatorex tasted it and 'twas of a kind of insipid tast, something of an Ironish tast. The Coffin was of Lead, and layd in the Wall about 2 foot ½ above the surface of the Floor. This was a strange rare way of conserving a Corps: perhaps it was a Pickle, as for Beefe, whose Saltness in so many years the Lead might sweeten and render insipid. The body felt, to the probe of a stick which they thrust into a chinke, like boyld Brawne.

Dr Litten asks how much of the liquor in this anthropoid coffin was body fluid, because the construction of such coffins meant that it would be practically impossible to have introduced much liquid preservatives.[131]

After the Great Fire Wren had to clear the cathedral site, and it is thought that the human remains were taken to Finsbury Fields where 1,000 cartloads of bones had been taken in the late sixteenth century.[132] John Donne's memorial by Nicholas Stone survived the fire; originally it was in the crypt but it is now in the south choir aisle. It shows his shrouded body released from its urn and awaiting the resurrection.

The new crypt was constructed beneath the whole area of the cathedral. Sir Christopher Wren had strong views against intramural burial, but the *memento mori* (remembrance of death) cartouches over the entrances reveal that the dean and chapter wished the undercroft to be used for interments.

Indeed, Wren overcame his distaste, and in 1723 was buried there in a pink shroud and a double coffin of elm and lead. His remains were laid close to the south-east corner of his building. His first wife, his daughter and his sister followed him. The grave was covered with a heavy ledger slab in 1723, and the dark, gloomy vault was hardly suitable for his famous epitaph, *'si monumentam requiris circumspice'* ('if you seek a memorial look around').[133]

In the seventeenth and eighteenth centuries most parish churches relied on fees from burials and monuments, but the dean and chapter resisted erecting monuments on the cathedral's ground floor until the 1790s, when the sculptor John Bacon provided memorials to John Howard, Samuel Johnson and William Jones. Sir Joshua Reynolds, buried in the crypt in 1792, has a memorial under the dome by John Flaxman. In the crypt, however, burials began soon after the cathedral was consecrated, but all were beneath the floor. The tomb of John Martin, a City printer who died in 1680, possesses a relief of swaddled babies.

St Paul's. A full-flowing shroud clings to the body of Dr John Donne on his effigy by Nicholas Stone, 1631, in St Paul's.

The crypt soon became a place for the burial or commemoration of national heroes, and distinguished architects, painters, sculptors and writers.

Nelson's body was interred in the crypt using a sarcophagus prepared for but not used by Cardinal Wolsey. The year 1806 ushered in a new era in the crypt's history and it became a place of pilgrimage. However, by 1852 it had 'a forlorn, dismal and dirty aspect'. Nonetheless, help was at hand with the interment, after a state funeral, of the Duke of Wellington that year.[134] Unfortunately his coffin was left literally in mid-air in the crypt, dangling in chains until a suitable sarcophagus, designed by Francis Penrose, could be prepared. This took several years, and is the one we see today. Arthur Wellesley was laid in it on 15 April 1858 – the new gas lighting banishing the gloom surrounding it. The public were now admitted to inspect the new tombs, for some time free of charge on Mondays, Thursdays and Saturdays.

St Paul's. Wellington's coffin suspended on chains above Nelson's sarcophagus. After the state funeral in 1852 Wellington's remains were held here until his tomb was ready six years later.

The remains of Lieutenant General Sir Thomas Picton were buried in St Paul's crypt in 1859; Picton fought with Wellington in the Peninsular War, then at Waterloo where he was the most senior officer to die. His body was interred in the Bayswater Cemetery of St George, Hanover Square, but when this was closed his remains were reburied in the crypt of St Paul's near Wellington's tomb. He was 'respected for his courage and feared for his irascible temper'.

St Paul's. The remains of Lieutenant General Sir Thomas Picton being buried in St Paul's crypt, 1859.

In 1861 Wellington's funeral car, weighing 12 tons and complete with model horses, was placed in the eastern part of the crypt. By 1871 the horses were so decrepit that they were removed. Seven years later the central crypt was cleared of all lumber and rubbish and the car was moved to the west end. Visitors were charged a 2*d* admission fee, which brought in extra income for the virgers. Estimates of the amount in the 1860s varied: the virgers said that it was less than £300 pa each (£31,920), whereas the jealous vicars-choral put the figure at £750 (£79,800). The chapter soon stepped in, and reserved the right to dispose of the income from 'The new attractions' as they wished.[135]

By the end of the nineteenth century crypt interments were getting out of hand, and Dean Gregory told the 1891 Royal Commission: 'For a long time it has

St Paul's. Wellington's funeral car, designed by Richard Redgrave in 1852. Weighing 12 tons and 20ft in length much of it was cast from guns captured at Waterloo. It took twelve dray horses over four hours to pull it from Apsley House, Piccadilly to St Paul's.

been exceedingly difficult to get consent for any funeral at all. There are certain people who have claimed the right of burial there, such as the minor canons and the virgers, and that right has not been contested; but for the future we should object to it.'[136]

St Paul's. Today's restaurant in the cathedral crypt.

In 1968 Dean Sullivan, determined to open the cathedral's doors especially
to young people, used the crypt for a 'festival of youth' with speakers discussing
moral and religious issues, and the following year a new monthly 'worship in
the round' service was held there. However, until the 1980s the crypt resembled
a museum, with Wellington's funeral carriage, the Great Model,[137] constructed by
two London joiners William and Richard Cleere in 1673, and Penrose's discarded
pulpit alongside all the monuments. In the 1990s the carriage was dispatched to
the duke's house at Stratfield Saye in Hampshire, and the model and pulpit are
now on the floor above. Today the western part of the crypt houses staff rooms,
lavatories and the offices of the works department. There is also a restaurant
and a cafe. To the south is a new song school and music library. The mausoleum
character of the central area remains, with Nelson's sarcophagus and Wellington's
sarcophagus. There are monuments that mark a burial place, and memorials that
commemorate the life of a famous man or woman. The last person to be buried here
was Admiral Earl Beatty in 1936, but since then there have been many interments
of ashes. The crypt and nave above is now a pantheon – a place of worship, but also
one of remembrance and pilgrimage.

St Paul's has always been surrounded by a large churchyard, and, although now
paved, it still is. Until the opening of the New Churchyard,[138] consecrated but not
owned by the Church, near Broad Street in 1569, this was heavily used, particularly
by City parishes with inadequate burial space. Many of the shops in St Paul's
Churchyard were owned by printers and publishers. The churchyard and precinct

of the medieval St Paul's Cathedral was 'used for a variety of trading and secular activities … and disorderly assault both verbal and physical might be expected'. An Act of Edward VI had addressed 'Outrageous and barbarous behaviour … committed by divers and ungodly and irreligious persons, by quarrelling, brawling, fraying and fighting openly in Churches and Churchyards'.[139]

ST AUGUSTINE-WITH-ST FAITH

When the old St Paul's had been extended eastwards in 1256 the tiny church of St Faith was demolished, and its congregation worshipped in the cathedral's crypt, or Shrouds as it was known. At the Reformation they were moved to the Jesus chapel in the cathedral. In 1670 the parish was united with St Augustine by St Paul's, whose building was rebuilt in 1680–07 by Wren after the Great Fire.[140] Parishioners were given the option of being interred in the cathedral crypt or in a new graveyard of 25,810sq.ft to the north of the cathedral. Houses, buildings and alleys had been purchased to create this. The number of burials was not great; in the thirty years 1722–52 only seventy parishioners and fifty-four strangers were interred in the vaults (some ledger stones can still be seen), and 371 parishioners and forty-three strangers in the churchyard. Between 1753 and 1757 an acrimonious dispute arose about this,[141] and on 13 April 1757 it was agreed that the parish could use 2,600sq.ft in the vaults providing they paid 6s 8d to Dean Secker and the chapter, and the same amount to the clerk of works. They might also use the north-east churchyard for 3s 4d per burial. By 1841 the parish had a population of only 289, and burials averaged thirty each year.

In *Parentalia* Wren writes 'Under the Quire was a noble Vault, wherein were three Ranks of large and massy Pillars, which being made a Parish-church, was dedicated to St Faith.'[142] The area of the old crypt church of St Faith (on the north side of the building) is defined today by a brass strip in the cathedral crypt floor.

ST GREGORY-BY-PAUL'S

This church, first mentioned in 1010, nestled next to the medieval St Paul's. For four months in 1631, while the old cathedral was being restored following a fire, services had been held there, and ten years later Inigo Jones had been summoned to the House of Lords by the enraged parishioners who accused him of partly demolishing their church to construct the cathedral portico. He was compelled to put the stones back.[143] The Great Fire destroyed the church and it was not rebuilt.

The churchyard lay to the west of the present cathedral,[144] and to the north of it was the cathedral's Pardon churchyard. St Gregory's also possessed vaults under the cathedral's western steps. As the new cathedral was built 70ft to the east this meant that the vaults were now under the road. On 28 September 1714 it was proposed that the vault and burial ground be given to the cathedral in return for land in the south-east churchyard close to the south portico, on which a 60ft by 20ft vault would be constructed with a flight of steps.[145] The vestry agreed, and on 31 October the Clerk of Works of the cathedral surrendered the land and its vault, which measured approximately 33ft by 34ft and 10ft high, to the parish.[146] The vestry decided that corpses should not be interred on the vault floor but beneath it to a depth of 8ft, and to assist the sexton 'a rod of eight foot shall be kept there' for measurement. Coffins could be placed one on the other and if the ground sank another corpse could be interred there. The fee would be £1 (approximately £175) for an adult and 10s for those under 12. The gravedigger's fee would be extra. There had been no burials in the churchyard above, so care had to be taken not to damage the cathedral's drains. Burial there would cost 2s. With an eye to the future the vestry, noting that 'solemn cavalcades' passed by, agreed that the land could be let. They accepted 'The natural curiosity of Mankind inducing all sorts to desire to see such sights'.

In 1909 the Dean of St Paul's asked the rector, Lewis Gilbertson, and his wardens if he might have part of the vault. He explained that he would like the northern half in connection with 'a scheme for more efficiently warming the Cathedral'. The cathedral is not known for its warmth, and in the 1830s Sydney Smith, a residentiary canon, had written: 'To go to St Paul's is certain death, the thermometer is several degrees below zero. My sentences are frozen as they come out of my mouth, and are thawed in the course of the summer, making strange noises and unexpected assertions in various parts of the church.' There were no coffins in the vault because all the burials were below the floor, and the last interment, on 8 February 1853, had been that of Mrs Mary Procter, aged 78, who lived at No. 78 St Paul's Churchyard. The parish vestry meeting discussed the matter on 8 October 1909 and agreed to the project, providing their rights to erect stands over the vault, to view processions on great occasions, would be respected. The recent royal jubilees and the annual lord mayor's days had obviously been very lucrative.

Advertisements were placed in *The Times*, the *Telegraph* and other newspapers, which elicited a letter from Mr William Ridley Richardson of Bromley, Kent, asking if the body of the Revd William Reyner, sub-dean in 1737, had been found. He was an ancestor of his wife and his portrait had been painted by Sir Joshua Reynolds; his coffin had been placed in the vault on 22 March 1764. Mr Richardson was assured that no remains were to be disturbed and that the memorials would be transferred to the southern part of the vault; a brick wall would divide it from the new boiler room, the floor of which would be hermetically sealed with concrete.

The fourteen tablets set into the floor commemorated a total of thirty-seven people, the earliest being that of Joseph Grimstead, who died on 10 October 1719 aged 63. The twelve wall tablets listing twenty-one men and women were dated 1719–1814, and included four generations of the Verinder family. The date of the vault's construction was surprisingly left blank on the faculty by which the boiler was installed, issued on 3 February 1910.[147]

6

CITY OF LONDON CENTRAL

The over 100 City churches, past and present, have been divided into four chapters by their geographical areas; then two chapters, with shorter descriptions, list other parishes with cleared and uncleared crypts.

[*] ST LAWRENCE JEWRY, GRESHAM STREET

The workmen who re-paved Guildhall Yard after the new art gallery had been built in 1999 were surprised when their pneumatic drills broke through into a vault outside the north-east corner of St Lawrence. Work stopped immediately, and eventually the eighty coffins stacked inside were removed to the East London Cemetery. The vault was then filled with concrete, and bollards were placed around the site.

Until their expulsion by Edward I the Jews inhabited this area, hence its name. After the church had been destroyed in the Great Fire, Wren strengthened the foundations in 1671–77, and built a new one based on one of the designs he had prepared for St Paul's Cathedral.[148] In 1801 the inhabitants, 'highly respectable' according to Malcolm, numbered 1,007. From that year until the vaults and churchyard closed in 1853 there were 529 burials there. The vaults beneath the church included Little, Great, Chancel, Porch, South and several others. In 1864 the Commissioners of Sewers removed all the coffins and bones from the churchyard to the north of the building and paved the area. Their plan to place a urinal close to the north-east side of the church elicited a protest on 29 June 1863 from Mr G. Holmes, who wrote: 'I have several females residing in my house and consider that such a place immediately opposite to my windows would be disgusting … you cannot prevent indecent conduct … to say nothing of the effluvium which is sure to arise.'[149]

The church was gutted by bombs in 1940, and the present building was restored by Cecil Brown between 1954 and 1957. Steps on the south side of the building were found blocked up: these may have been an entrance to the crypt.[150] On 9 April 1954 the priest in charge and churchwardens successfully petitioned for a faculty to remove to the City of London Cemetery the remains stacked in the north-west vault and any other bodies found during the underpinning of the foundations.[151] During her wanderings around the City at this time the writer Mrs Robert Henrey met William George, general foreman of Dove Bros, which was restoring St Lawrence. A Norfolk man, aged 52, he told her that he and his twenty-four workmen had unearthed about 200 coffins. He explained to her that Wren, having to rebuild fifty-one churches, did not always use solid blocks of Portland stone but put a stone skin on the outside and another on the inside of a wall, then filled it with rubble and gravestones from the earlier church. At St Lawrence he had found part of a human jaw in rubble 60ft above the ground. 'Everything was grist to the builder of Wren's walls.'

Today the north-west vault and another leading from it are empty, but contain a number of coffin plates, clay pipes and other items found during the restoration. Since 1782 St Lawrence has been the church of the City of London Corporation, which owns the freehold of the site and the patronage of the living. The Revd Basil Watson, vicar from 1970 to 1986, always boasted that he wore a dinner jacket more than a cassock.

ST MATTHEW, FRIDAY STREET

The church, first mentioned in 1261, stood a few yards to the south-east of St Paul's Cathedral. Henry Burton, the rector in 1637, preached a fiery sermon that landed him in the pillory at Westminster minus his ears. He was then thrown into prison for life but released after three years. St Matthew was burnt down in the Great Fire and Wren rebuilt it 1681–87; 'a small plain church with the east end backing on to the street'.

The burial registers, which begin in 1538, show that it was not a populous area, because from the sixteenth century there were only six to nine interments each year until the registers end in 1812. From 1739 until 1812 there were 450 interments, half of which were in the vaults. These were not very secure, as in the nineteenth century they were cleared every ten to twelve years.

On 11 September 1846 evidence was given before Mr Broughton, the magistrate at Worship Street, that several loads of bones and human remains had been dumped in a field belonging to a Mr King in Haggerston by a dust contractor named John Gould. Fortified by gin, Samuel Wright, the driver of the cart, had gone with his mate John Roffey to St Matthew at 3 a.m. on 5 September and, assisted by the gravedigger, removed the remains, being promised 4d per load. One of King's employees, John Roe, said that the rubbish was 'entirely composed of broken coffins, plates, handles and human bones'. John Gardiner, a hawker, of No. 6 Southwark Street, Haggerston, testified that the human bones had flesh on them, and Samuel Shearman admitted that he had purchased 44lb of metal coffin plates and handles that had been brought to his shop. The churchwardens denied that the bones were from St Matthew, but agreed that rubbish had been removed from the church. The vicar's vault had sunk during the construction of a new sewer eighteen months earlier, and the 'intolerable effluvia' had made them clear the vault. For nearly a week they had personally inspected the rubbish and reinterred any bones. The magistrate clearly did not believe them and, after reprimanding the wardens and giving bail to Wright and Roffey, referred the matter to the parish authorities in Shoreditch.[152] There is no mention of the incident in the vestry minutes.

The church was demolished in 1881, and exhumation took place during July 1883 when fifty-six coffins were removed from the crypt; nearly all had plates to identify their contents. They had been placed there between 1741 and 1846. Among the coffins were those of a former rector, George Hatch (1837), his wife and three family members; forty-two name plates unattached to coffins were found.[153] Human remains from the vaults and the churchyard, to the west of the building, now rest in the City of London Cemetery.

ST MARY ALDERMANBURY

In the Middle Ages the church had a large display of the bones of exhumed bodies in the cloisters. Wren replaced this medieval church destroyed in the Great Fire with a simple church with no spire. It stood to the north of the Guildhall, where Love Lane meets Aldermanbury. Burials in the 1670s were in the Great Vault or Chancel Vault and the notorious Judge Jeffreys, who died on 19 April 1689, was interred in a vault under the communion table on 2 November 1693.[154] In 1810 the coffin was found 'still fresh with the name of the Lord Chancellor Jeffreys inscribed upon it'. There was no trace of it in 1863, but the breastplate of his eldest daughter Mary's coffin was found.[155]

On 1 January 1778 William Ashton interred his brother in a lead coffin and placed it in the vaults of St Mary, but it was stolen on 7 March. The previous day James Gould, George Roach and Robert Elliot, three carpenters repairing the church, unscrewed all but two of the coffin's screws and returned the following morning at 5 a.m., unscrewed the last two, turned the coffin upside down and removed the outer coffin. They cut the lead into two pieces and screwed down the wooden case containing the body and put it on a shelf. They then took the 42lb of lead to Jonas Parker of Grub Street, who gave them 3s 6d (£24) for it. However, their employer's apprentice reported them to the authorities, and although the men ran away they were taken into custody. At the Old Bailey the following month Roach and Elliot were sentenced 'to labour three years on the Thames' and Parker was sent to prison for the same period.[156] Presumably Gould, having given evidence, was not charged.

Interments in church in the 1830s had to be in lead and were under the aisles, or in Mr Hog's vault, Mr Smith's vault or in 'The new vault at the Christening pew'.[157]

St Mary was gutted by bombs in the Second World War and not rebuilt. The Portland stone walls were shipped to Fulton, Missouri, USA, and re-erected as a memorial to Sir Winston Churchill, who had delivered his 'Iron Curtain' speech there in 1946. The remains from below the church were taken to the City of London Cemetery in 1965. A garden of approximately 1,190sq.yds, owned by the City Corporation, now covers the foundations and the churchyard, where Hemming and Condell, two of Shakespeare's actors, are buried.

[*] ST MARY WOOLNOTH, LOMBARD STREET

This church of St Mary is first mentioned in 1273, but legend says that it was founded earlier by Wulfnoth, a Saxon prince, hence its full name. Rebuilt in 1442, it was repaired by Sir Christopher Wren after the Great Fire, then rebuilt by Nicholas Hawksmoor in 1716. At this time the population of the parish was approximately 600, a third of whom were prosperous goldsmiths, merchants, scriveners and factors. Burials took place on any day of the week, Sunday being popular, and could be held on Christmas or Easter Day.[158] The wealthiest parish family was probably the Viners, whose grand funerals meant that there was a long delay between death and funeral. Sir Thomas, a former lord mayor, died on 11 May 1665 and was buried on 1 June, and Sir George, his son, died on 5 July 1673; he and his wife's funeral was held on 18 August.

In 1891 the rector, the Revd James Brooke, complained about the smell in the church and asked the architect Mark Judge to investigate. He visited the building, now acknowledged as one of Nicholas Hawksmoor's masterpieces, and on 15 December reported that openings had been made in the floor: he was confident that 'The source of the mischief' was not drains or disused wells but the closed vaults. 'The basement of the church', he wrote, 'has an open well-ventilated vault[159] extending from north to south on either side of which are large closed vaults in which human remains are deposited. The Eastern vault is more than twice the size of that to the West.'

The eastern vault had a lower ceiling because in 1886 a concrete floor carried by iron girders had been inserted above it in the church. The vault was nearly filled with lead coffins: some were intact but many had collapsed, 'and the bones and debris of the coffins form one mass'. The western vault had wooden coffins closely packed together, 'Though in process of decay they are mostly intact, the bodies remaining with the flesh upon their bones'. In both vaults the ventilation flues had been bricked up, the arches and ironwork were dripping with moisture and the smell was offensive. The Medical Officer of Health, Dr Sedgwick Saunders, was called in, but it was not until 7 November 1892 that he closed the church. A faculty[160] was issued the following month and 358 cases containing wood and lead coffins and 301 cases of bones were taken to the City of London Cemetery. It was reckoned that around 1,500 skeletons left the vaults between 18 November 1892 and 3 March 1893. Among them were the bones of Edward Lloyd, buried at Woolnoth in 1712: he was owner of Lloyd's Coffee House and gave his name to the insurance market. After the removal of the remains, some of which had probably been transferred from St Michael Crooked Lane, Bank tube station was built below the church.

A partly hewn granite block marks the cemetery site, and the chancellor was told that the 40sq.yds that were needed would cost around £1,000, which he thought excessive, so he ordered that the Corporation should be asked for a reduction because City residents were being interred. On 22 December the principal clerk at the Sewers Office in Guildhall wrote to say that coffins would be buried for 15s each instead of 20s, but he regretted that the charges for excavating and building vaults 'do not admit of reduction'. The final cost of the project was £2,000 (£215,191). Several families were allowed to remove the coffins of their ancestors, and two former rectors travelled to new destinations – Dr Samuel Birch, who died in 1843, went to Kensal Green, and the Revd John Newton and his wife went to Olney in Buckinghamshire. This was at the request of the serving incumbent as no family could be traced, and the cost was born 'by their admirers'. Newton, incumbent from 1780 until his death in 1807, was an early Evangelical who had inspired Wilberforce in his campaign against slavery, because he had served in slave ships in his youth. He wrote the hymns 'Amazing Grace' and 'Glorious Things of Thee are Spoken'.[161]

Today the church receives visitors perhaps with more grace than Mr Brooke, who wrote in 1890 that 'dozens and dozens of times men and women have actually made a public convenience of the sacred building; others have come in and stripped themselves nearly naked in the darker corners, for what reason no one can say; others come for the sole purpose of altercation with the attendant ... between one and two o'clock it is regularly used as a luncheon room'.[162]

ST MICHAEL BASSISHAW, BASINGHALL STREET

The Medical Officer of Health for the City called at St Michael's in 1892, and on 5 June wrote to the vestry clerk telling him that he had 'seen a considerable quantity of human remains which have been exposed by the removal of the floor of the church in the course of the repairs now going on'. They had to be removed. A faculty was issued the following May and work began in the three vaults below the church. However, three weeks later Mr Low, the superintending architect, reported that although the workmen had only dug 7ft below the floor any further work would seriously interfere with the stability of the structure: 'The columns of the nave arcade are of a most unsatisfactory character', and he had been able to pass a stick through one of their foundations. He said that the vaults should be filled with clean dry earth, and the nave floor should be laid on concrete (9in was Dr Sedgwick Saunders's suggestion).[163] Dr Tristam, the chancellor of the Diocese of London,

ordered the work to stop on 6 June 1893 because repairs were estimated at over
£5,000 (£544,090). There were only seventy ratepayers in the parish, and they could
not raise such a sum.

This small brick church, which stood on the west side of Basinghall Street
behind Guildhall, had been designed by Wren in 1676 and named after the Basings,
a wealthy City family who had a house here in the thirteenth century. It was a
small parish, with only 747 inhabitants in 1801, and one burial a year in the mid-
nineteenth century, until an Order in Council of 25 November 1853 closed the vaults
and churchyard on 6 December. In 1893, realising that repairs were too expensive,
the vestry agreed to demolish the church and merge the parish with St Lawrence,
Jewry and St Mary Magdalen, Milk Street, so this was done by an Order in
Council of 3 May 1897. The earlier faculty was renewed in December 1898, and the
remains in the vaults – 129 coffins and 197 boxes of human remains according to
the memorial – were removed to the Great Northern Cemetery in New Southgate.

The chancellor told two families that they could remove the remains of ancestors
to other places. Mr Edmund Woodthorpe was given permission to take the bones
of his grandfather Henry, who had been town clerk of the City and was buried
on 9 March 1842, to Highgate Cemetery along with those of his wife, Mary Ann,
and their three children, all of whom had predeceased him. Mr George Braikenridge
took the body of his great-uncle, Dr William Braikenridge, a former rector of
St Michael, to a separate grave at the Great Northern. He had been interred under
the chancel on 8 August 1762 and his wife, Helen, and their six children were also
discovered there and removed. The church was demolished in 1899, and the site sold
to the City Corporation for £36,000 (£3,917,454). An agreement made thirty-four
years earlier had already vested the churchyard in the Corporation, providing that
they used it as an open space and did not build on it. When the present steps were
placed there in 1968 another faculty had to be issued.[164]

ST MILDRED, BREAD STREET

In January 1897 Bishop Frederick Temple of London received a letter of complaint:
'I am an aged clergyman laid aside by severe illness but I have with much effort risen
from my sick bed with trembling hand to appeal to your Lordship. I am greatly
distressed that the remains in the underground vaults of St Mildred Church in
Bread St are being disinterred.' It came from the Revd Samuel Charlesworth, the son
of a former rector. He had recently worshipped in St Mildred's, where his uncle was
buried, and, noticing no smell, was surprised at the clearance of the vaults. On that
January morning the bishop also received another letter – from a parishioner, who
was certain that the rector, living in Croydon, 'has for many years been very desirous
of having the church pulled down'. The bishop ordered an inquiry into the church's
affairs, and to his horror discovered that the churchwardens, acting on the authority of

an Order in Council of 27 November 1896, were already removing the pews, furniture and fittings in order to dig the floor up. Soon the coffins in the vaults were to be taken away. When quizzed by Mr Lee, the registrar, the wardens sent him a copy of the City's Medical Officer of Health's report dated 25 September of the previous year:

> In the course of some repairs in the interior of the church the floor has subsided to some extent owing to the shrinkage of the sub-soil from the human remains buried there. Having made openings a vault was found extending the whole width of the building containing 150 coffins in various states of decay. In parts some rats' nests were discovered lined with human hair which has been taken from a female whose head had been dragged half out of the coffin by the rats. Another vault exists at the eastern end and under the altar containing 12 coffins. A third vault, in the middle of the church, is saturated with water and smelt abominably, so foul indeed that the workmen refused to enter it. Another vault was broken into and coffins were within two feet of the floor level. In this spot the ground was over-run with rats that had eaten into the coffins.

Dr Sedgwick Saunders ordered that the crypt be cleared. As with all City vaults there had been no interments since 1853, and so the churchwardens, having obtained an Order in Council, declined to apply for a faculty, and Dove Bros removed twenty-eight cases of remains on 26 June. Work then stopped, as Saunders would not sanction removal in hot weather, and also demanded a fee of 100gns (£12,392) because supervision of the project was not part of his job. He eventually received 35gns.[165] The chancellor, Dr Tristram, was angry, and on 16 August summoned the four churchwardens to appear before him, listing their misdemeanours. They were 'to answer to certain articles heads positions or interrogatories to be administered to them … concerning their soul's health and the lawful corrections of their manners'.[166] Presumably they saw the error of their ways, because a faculty was issued on 15 December 1897. Although nineteen families asked about removing one of their forebears, when the work continued into the following year only the coffin of Sir Nicholas Crispe, 'a Farmer of the Customs to Charles I', was moved to St Paul's Hammersmith where his heart already lay in a stone urn. He had died on 27 February 1665, aged 67. The rest of the 450 coffins arrived in Brookwood Cemetery in 1898 and were placed in plot 87, close to St George the Martyr Avenue.[167] The cross erected that year at Brookwood is now (2012) in a parlous state, leaning at an angle. The legal fees of Mr G. Steinberg totalled £220 11s 11d (£24,784), and his twenty-seven-page bill gives us a very good account of an exhumation.[168]

St Mildred's on the east side of Bread Street was a Wren church which had replaced a medieval building after the Great Fire. Having been bombed in 1941, it was not rebuilt. The church site and the churchyard were sold by Act of Parliament in 1969.

[*] ST STEPHEN WALBROOK

The first church, mentioned before 1100, was on the west bank of the Wall Brook, but in 1429 it was replaced by a new building on the east bank. This was destroyed in the Great Fire, and the vestry entertained Wren several times 'to incuridg and hast in ye rebuilding'. With the same motive Lady Wren was presented with 20gns in a silk purse. The ruse worked, and in 1679 a dinner at the Bull's Head Tavern, at which the architect received a hogshead of claret, marked the project's completion.[169] Sir Christopher gave his clients one of the most stunning buildings in London. The first interment in the building was in 1677, a year after consecration.

The earliest of four burial registers covers the period 8 November 1557 until 19 November 1716. It is 18in high, 7½in wide, made of parchment, strongly bound and fitted with two brass clasps. Until 1666 interments took place in the graveyard, part of which survives as a garden to the east of the church, or in the church itself, usually 'under a great stone'. The clerk locates these as 'upper end of middle aisle, in ye south ile, in the mens little ile or at the middill door'. Clergy and important people were placed 'in chancel or in ye quier in the parson's ground by vestry door'. Between March 1615 and March 1616 nine bodies including two clergy were interred in the church and five in the churchyard, and soon afterwards vaults are mentioned for the first time. On 27 October 1642 and during the months following, the family vault of Mr William Van Brugg was used to bury five of his stillborn children. It is in this vault that the famous architect Sir John Vanbrugh was placed when he died in 1726. This is ironic, because he and Wren always condemned burials in church as unwholesome.

An Order in Council closed the crypt and churchyard on 3 August 1853, but the remains of the Revd Dr George Croly, rector, were placed illegally in St Stephen's vaults on 1 December 1860, joining those of several previous incumbents.

The rich seventeenth-century fittings and furniture survived the Blitz, but the building was more badly damaged than at first thought. The dome had suffered from the 1941 incendiary bombs, and flying 'doodle-bugs' split the tower, which, according to the architect, Robert Potter, was 9in out of plumb. In 1972 the church had to be closed for nine years, but it reopened to display a magnificent Henry Moore central stone altar donated by Lord Palumbo, a churchwarden.

The crypt survived intact because, although the church had been settling unevenly, concrete piles were installed below the columns to support them. Behind brick walls, coffins covered with earth still take up approximately three-quarters of the space, while one quarter – at the west end – was used by the rector, Chad Varah, to house the Samaritans, which he founded in 1953 to befriend the suicidal. They have now vacated the crypt, which at the time of writing is being renovated as a meeting room, offices, kitchen and lavatories.

After his ordination Varah went to a curacy in Lincoln, where he had to conduct the funeral of a 14-year-old girl who had committed suicide when she started bleeding between her legs. Unable to talk to anyone about it, she thought she had a shameful disease. After the mourners had gone Varah looked into the grave and said, 'Little girl, I never knew you, but you have changed my life. I promise you that I will teach children what they need to know about sex even if I get called a dirty old man.' When he arrived in the City eighteen years later, the war-damaged St Stephen's had been hastily repaired, but there was no congregation. He started services in the church, and in the crypt fifty volunteers began taking distress calls for Samaritans on Mansion House 2000.[170]

7

City of London East

[*] ST BOTOLPH-WITHOUT-ALDGATE, ALDGATE HIGH STREET

The present church, designed by George Dance, replaced a medieval church that stood east-west and was demolished in 1741. Surprisingly an Act of Parliament went through in a matter of months, enabling the new church to be erected on condition that the graves and vaults were not disturbed. This must have proved impossible, because the new building was sited north-south with four tunnel vaults under it. The large graveyard to the north was untouched.

An anonymous pamphlet dated *c.*1747 in the possession of St Andrew Holborn describes:

> Two young knaves who, by some Means or other, got into the vaults of St Botolph, Aldgate where they stripp'd all the Coffins of their Nails and Hinges, which they afterwards sold. The Upshot of their Villainy was, that they were both discover'd, seiz'd and committed to Newgate, an Indictment was laid to be the Property of P'sons unknown; and on this Charge they were found Guilty, ordered for Transportation, and transported accordingly to the Plantations in America for seven Years.

The church vaults and the churchyard were not the only burial place in Aldgate. Sir John Cass, a wealthy businessman and alderman of the ward, had built a three-storey building close to the church's west wall to house his new school for fifty boys and forty girls on the first floor. The ground floor contained shops, and the basement had burial vaults. These were a mixed blessing, because workmen were often sent to remedy 'The intolerable stench arising therefrom'. The school transferred to new premises in 1762, and today the infant/junior

Sir John Cass's school is situated to the west of St Botolph's, with the senior school in Stepney.

The parish was always populous – in 1719 there were 26,400 parishioners – but by 1801 there were 8,689. A small strip of the western churchyard was sold to the City Corporation for £3,500 (£380,863) in 1889, so that they could widen Houndsditch, and when work began forty-one lead coffins were discovered there in three vaults. As the site was at the corner of Houndsditch and Aldgate High Street, it was possible that these came from the Cass vaults. A faculty was granted by the chancellor to remove these to the crypt, and this was done. They joined other coffins that were already there, and a wall had to be built 'to prevent effluvia from coming into the church'. However, the City's Medical Officer of Health was horrified, and in a report to his committee on 24 March 1891 pointed out that the boiler in the east crypt tunnel made the air hot and thus foul. Not only that, 'The floor of the vault is fine, dry earth intermixed with human bones in great quantities on and beneath the surface … the vaults contain sunken brick graves in all probability containing human bodies in every stage of decay'. Tombstones that were horizontal and upright suggested that the bodies were indeed under the floor. He recommended that all the coffins and remains should be taken to the City of London Cemetery. The chancellor visited St Botolph's and agreed to vary his faculty so that the forty-one coffins and 116 wooden cases

St Botolph Aldgate. Crypt homeless centre, 1978. Azella lived in a cardboard box in a car park until a truck backed over her. She was a very lively, friendly woman who was always game for a drink and a laugh.

(each 4ft by 1½ft by 1½ft) should be removed from Aldgate to Ilford. As each box contained the remains of twelve persons, it was reckoned that about 1,432 skeletons were removed to their new home. The Commissioners of Sewers paid the £1,200 bill (£129,114) – much to vicar Hadden's delight. They also concreted the crypt floor and limewashed the walls and roof.

In 1957, soon after his arrival as rector of Aldgate, George Appleton realised that homeless men and women, many of whom were drunk and in a bad way, were gathering in the churchyard. Their leader, Jimmy, suggested an evening canteen in the crypt, so it was decided to clear the junk out of the two eastern crypt tunnels to create a daytime canteen. Washbasins, baths and lavatories were installed, the walls were painted and a kitchen built.

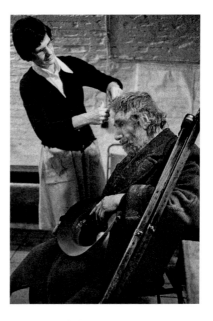

St Botolph Aldgate. Crypt homeless centre, 1978. Mr Sheridan has his hair cut by volunteer Bobbie Beecroft. Two years later Daly Maxwell, senior worker, took him to a Yorkshire farm to live.

St Botolph Aldgate. Crypt homeless centre, 1978. A general view.

Appleton also established a youth club in the two western tunnels of the crypt and around fifty East End teenagers arrived each day. Ten years later membership had trebled, and the Cass School gymnasium was used for boxing and badminton. The then rector, Derek Harbord, told a visitor that 'members dislike being organised and run as would members of the Athenaeum, so we make a point of respecting their independence'.

When I arrived as rector in 1974 numbers had dropped dramatically and the membership was solely Bangladeshi. Other clubs were opening in Spitalfields, so our club was closed, and the space was used by the homeless centre, which usually had seventy people each evening in the canteen. I realised that a full-time staff was needed, because volunteers, as good as they were, could not provide continuity of care and form friendships that would enable a change of lifestyle. Accordingly the staff grew over the next few years, hostels were opened, and the premises modernised and enlarged to welcome the 200 to 300 people who visited daily.

The crypt floor consisted of gravestones laid across brick walls, between which were stacked coffins. In 1985, when the floor in the western tunnel was being dug up and replaced, I shone a torch downwards, thus revealing the Vink family vault. Much to my surprise the next morning I received a letter from Major Kenneth Vink of Carshalton asking me if I knew where his family vault was located. I immediately telephoned him and, much shocked by the coincidence, he, his wife and son came to see the vault. I asked him what had made him write to me, and he said that he was reading the family history, so thought he would try and find out where his ancestors were buried in the church. We agreed to place a memorial on the floor above the coffins, the last of which was dated 28 July 1843, and when Major Vink died in 1986 I interred his ashes in the vault.

In 1988 it was decided to clear the vault under the church front steps to create further space. This proved a difficult task, as we found thirty-five lead coffins dating from the early nineteenth century and huge piles of bones that had been dug out of the churchyard many years before and thrown into the vault, which was as wide as the church and stretched approximately 30ft towards the road. A large wooden wall surrounded the area and a workman lived on site in a caravan for several months. Malcolm Kimber and the Necropolis Ltd operatives did a skull count, which totalled 6,000. All were reverently removed in heavy gauge black bags, which were hermetically sealed then transported to the East London Cemetery, where a marble headstone marks their burial place. During this project another vault was discovered under the small piece of garden between the church and the next door office block, but we were reluctant to do more work.

A door and passage now had to be made under the church main entrance to join the new space to the main crypt, which was a few feet higher. A local builder was contracted to do the work, and on 29 August 1990 one of his workmen arrived in my study and breathlessly reported that he had dug up a skeleton. It turned out to be the remains of Mrs Mary Hague, who according to the breastplate had died on 24 August 1812. The coffin wood had disintegrated and the lady's skull, still with wig-like hair on it, was separated from the bones of the body. I asked him to rebury her reverently, and said a prayer. An hour later he came into the church and told me that he had found a male skeleton. Although this was not her husband the builder was all smiles and said, 'I have put them together so they should be happy now.'[171]

In 2003 the homeless project went bankrupt owing to mismanagement, although the four hostels in Hackney were taken over by another charity. In 2011 the crypt space is not being used, but a new rector is preparing plans.

ST JAMES DUKE'S PLACE

This church, founded in 1621 and rebuilt in 1722, had no crypt but a map of 1853[172] shows a churchyard to the north of the building, 50ft by 36ft towards Duke St. The building was demolished in 1874 when *The Times* of 15 August reported 180 chests of human remains from the churchyard were removed to the City of London Cemetery, to the south of Central Avenue, where a huge stone block records the details. Sir John Cass's Foundation School was later built on the site. It was here in the early hours of 30 September 1888 that Catherine Eddowes was killed by Jack the Ripper. She had been released from Bishopsgate Police station earlier, but her throat was cut and she had been brutally mutilated.

ST MICHAEL ALDGATE

Although this church was demolished in the sixteenth century, its empty crypt survived beneath houses near Leadenhall/Fenchurch streets. It had groined arches, which are seen in two prints in the Guildhall Library.[173] It was destroyed in 1876.

St James, Duke's Place. The block of stone records the removal of 180 chests of human remains in 1874.

HOLY TRINITY CLARE STREET, MINORIES

In 1978, when I was rector of St Botolph Aldgate, I had a surprise visitor. Gerald Legge, the 9th Earl of Dartmouth, walked into my study bearing a large cardboard box labelled 'Fairy Lights'. Inside were nine breastplates of silver, copper, brass and lead ripped from the coffins of the Dartmouth family, removed from the vaults of Holy Trinity when it was deconsecrated in 1950. His ancestor, Colonel William Legge, who owned the land on which the church was built, had been buried beneath the chancel in 1672. His son became the first Earl of Dartmouth and many family members were placed in the vault.

Minories, on the eastern edge of the City in Aldgate, takes its name from the Minoresses, an order of Franciscan nuns who had a convent here until Henry VIII dissolved them. The chapel eventually became a parish church, and was replaced by a new building with vaults beneath it in 1706. Presumably the Dartmouth coffins were transferred to the new vaults. The churchyard was small, and in 1689 and 1763 it had to be emptied to make room for new burials.[174]

Scandal stalked the parish. Not only did the incumbents do a brisk trade in marrying thousands of couples without banns, but in 1786 Mr Smalcole, the beadle, was dismissed after being caught in the crypt sawing up coffins for firewood or to make floorboards for his house.[175]

Holy Trinity Minories. Depositum plates taken from the Dartmouth family coffins in the crypt when the church was demolished in the 1950s. Hon. Elizabeth Keen. Rectangular, brass, 1801.

Anne, Countess of Dartmouth. Rectangular, brass, 1751. Coat of arms in a lozenge denotes she died when still married.

George, Viscount Lewisham. Silvered shield, 1823. What one would expect for a boy of 16 months.

Hon. Frances Legge. Lozenge, lead. Die-stamped and engraved lead, 1789. Lozenge denotes spinster.

Hon. Anne Legge. Lozenge, copper, 1752. Lozenge denotes spinster.

Hon. Charles Legge. Lozenge, copper, 1785. Unusual; should be rectangular – the undertaker might probably have selected this shape if the gentleman was unmarried.

In 1852 a gruesome head embedded in sawdust, which had preserved it, was found in the vaults beneath Holy Trinity. The hair and beard fell off, and word went round that it was the unfortunate Duke of Suffolk, father of Lady Jane Grey, who had been beheaded with her on Tower Hill. The Revd E.M. Tomlinson, vicar of

Holy Trinity, placed it in a glass case for public perusal, and it eventually found its way to the sacristy of St Botolph Aldgate where George Appleton, the rector, referred to it as 'one of the amenities of Aldgate'. His successor buried it in the vault beneath the church's front steps. I found it there in its biscuit tin when we cleared that vault, and I reburied it under the floor of the west crypt.

Burials continued at Holy Trinity until 1853, and between 1849 and 1852 there were seven interments in the vaults and eleven in the churchyard. The church was destroyed by enemy action on 9 September 1940 and sold for a paltry sum nineteen years later, half being given to St Botolph. Today the church still owns a tiny part of the former burial ground, which is now a car park for the office building built on the site of Holy Trinity; one space is reserved for the rector.

The coffin of Anne Mowbray (1472–81) was unearthed here in 1963 during building work. Daughter of the Duke of Norfolk, when she was 7 she married King Edward IV's second son Richard Duke of York, then aged 4, one of the princes later murdered in the Tower. When she died her lead coffin was placed in Westminster Abbey's chapel of St Erasmus, but it had to be moved to Minories when the chapel was demolished in 1502 to make way for Henry VII's chapel.[176] About 450 years later she returned to the Abbey to be placed near her husband. The workmen reported that her red hair was still on the skull and a shroud was still wrapped around her.

[*] ST BOTOLPH-WITHOUT-BISHOPSGATE

A church has stood on this site since the early thirteenth century. The building escaped the Great Fire but was demolished in 1724, and a new church designed by James Gould was opened in 1728 at a cost of £10,400. The builder's specifications mention using material from the old church, and ashlar limestone blocks which are possibly medieval are to be found in the vaults today. In the early nineteenth century the building was surrounded by squalid houses, and a cleric refused the living in 1820 because the rectory was at the mercy of an 'irremediable nuisance of rats'. Charles James Blomfield, later the reforming Bishop of London, accepted it, but kept his parish of Great Chesterford, Essex. The census of 1801 reports that 10,314 people lived in the parish, not many more than 100 years earlier.

Under the church Gould provided three tunnels running (liturgical not geographical) east-west, and mourners would have descended the stone staircase at the west end. The steps are still there, but in the 1990s the entrance was covered over to provide an office, so the entrance to the crypt is now outside on the south side. The vaults are barrel-vaulted and constructed in brick, and the earth floor which is not paved has thirteen huge ledger stones on it. There are only four small family vaults, two at the east end and two at the west end, and they are bricked in. In 1991 the then incumbent, Prebendary Alan Tanner, needed to know if it was possible or desirable to develop the crypt space, so a research paper was prepared by Dr Roberta Gilchrist and Jez Reeve. Necropolis Ltd was asked to make small openings in the crypt floor and to do a trial dig on the south side. Four deteriorated lead coffins were recovered at a depth of 1½ft in the south aisle, and a further seven coffins in a brick-lined grave at 3½ft. Eleven individuals were exhumed, of which five could be identified by their coffin plates. They had died between 1834 and 1847.[177]

Many disarticulated remains were recovered and reinterred in the brick-lined grave. The researchers concluded 'that considerable portions of the foundations of the crypt will be medieval in date, used to support eighteenth-century vaulting'. We know what happened to the bodies resting below the old church, because at a vestry meeting of 9 November 1724 the members 'Resolved that a vault from the south doore of the Church, towards the sexton's house, be built for the reception of the bodies taken out of the Church', and 'that a piece of ground or graves be found but for the laying the bones in'. A year later the bearers 'Brought in their bill for Removing the Corps from the Church into the New Vault', and it was resolved 'that the man that stood at the Door be paid 2 pence per day for 17 days, and the four Bearers three shillings per day for twenty-three days'. The operation took ninety-two working days, so the numbers reinterred must have been considerable, and the bodies must still lie close to the south door as this land has not been disturbed since.[178]

Nearly all the burials in the crypt must have taken place beneath the floor in the soil and, unlike Christ Church Spitalfields, very few coffins were placed on the floor itself. The vestry minutes of 10 March 1729 confirm this: 'no grave shall be dugg in the vaults under the Church less than 6ft and an halfe deep. Nor more than seven foot deep. And that all of Earth and Rubbish after any such grave shall be filled up shall be immediately carry'd away out of the said vaults.' Graves were to be marked by flat stones, and several have survived – including one commemorating Benjamin and Margaret Wood and their five children, who died between 1771 and 1822, and another huge ledger of Isaac Taylor, buried beneath the middle aisle after his death on 23 June 1816.

Dr Gilchrist considers that, given the space in the crypt and the 120 years it was in use until its closure in 1849, approximately 600 individuals are interred here. The Necropolis excavation suggests that the depth of the deposits extend no more than about 8ft below the crypt floor, so possibly the coffins are in piles of up to five. In the 1850s they would have been covered with soil and charcoal. Of exceptional value, she says, are the burial registers, which unlike those of other parishes give the age of death from as early as 1600 and the clerk, using the Searchers' Reports, noted the cause of death from 1792 until 1800. Comparisons can be made between those in the churchyard and those in the vaults. Only those in the more prosperous crypt population were diagnosed as dying of 'decline', gout, diabetes or apoplexy. The Searchers also tell us where families liked to be buried: Shannons, Judds and Fossicks in the north aisle, Davises in the middle aisle; Taylors and Thompsons in the south aisle, and Schooleys and Goodenoughs in their reserved vaults.[179]

During the Second World War the crypt was used as an air-raid shelter. Today an ancient organ blower and a central heating boiler stand on concrete but the rest of the crypt floor is soil and charcoal, which have been well trampled. Beneath are the coffins. Having taken advice and received the 1991 Report, the rector and churchwardens decided not to proceed with modernising the crypt.

ST DIONIS BACKCHURCH, LIME STREET/FENCHURCH STREET

First mentioned in 1198, the church was hidden behind houses, and Cobb suggests that the name derives from a Mr Bac who was a clerk there. It was rebuilt in 1450 but destroyed in the Great Fire and replaced by a small, lofty building costing £5,737 10s 8d, built by Wren in 1670–84. In March 1845 a committee appointed by the vestry to report on the condition of the churchyard was shocked to discover that the selection of the place and depth of burial was 'entirely left to the option or caprice of the labourer employed', and the 'most revolting and disgusting scenes' had taken place 'especially at the interment of Mr Thompson'. The grave dug for him had revealed another coffin containing a body 'in an entire state'.

The church possessed a fifteenth-century rector's vault under the chancel, which the architect G.E. Street described in 1858 as a parallelogram 9ft 6in north-south and 13ft east-west internally. 'Covered with a quadripartite vault: the vault has diagonal ribs but neither wall nor ridge ribs. The ribs are', said Street, 'of the simplest kind, but spring from good corbels in the angles of the crypt and at their intersections there is carved a bold and effective rose. The height from the floor to the spring of the vault is only 4ft and the vault rises a similar height, its arches being everywhere four-centred ... The filling-in of the vault is chalk whilst the ribs are, I think, executed in Calverley stone.' It was filled with bodies.[180] Obviously Wren kept this vault intact when he built his new church, which incorporated the Kentish ragstone of the medieval building. When interments ceased the vicar, the Revd W.H. Lyall, asked for the Medical Officer of Health's advice, and on 15 July 1858 Dr Letherby ordered that as there was no offensive smell the coffins should not be moved but rearranged and covered with 12in of earth and 3in of charcoal. Street was asked to install ventilation and, having laid concrete over the coffins in the nave, to put down a new pavement.

The church was demolished in 1878 to widen Lime Street, and exhumation of the bodies from the vaults began on 16 May and ended on 31 July. Advertisements were placed in national newspapers and several families, including the Hargreaves, Hankeys and Rawlinsons, removed their family coffins, although twelve bodies asked for by relatives could not be traced. The Anderson relatives removed four but left three behind. The Ironmongers Company claimed two coffins containing Sir Robert Jeffery and a family member. A total of 436 coffins and cases were removed, but only 158 of these dating from 1679 to 1844 were named. There were eighty-three unnamed

St Dionis Backchurch. City of London Cemetery, House tomb with Gothic tracery, 1879. (The plot contains 436 coffins and cases of bones.) In the background is the All Hallows Lombard St Memorial, 1939, by Jabez Drewitt.

lead coffins and the rest were cases of bones.[181] These were all taken to the City of London Cemetery, where there is a house tomb monument with Gothic tracery on St Dionis Road. During the upheaval a medieval lead coffin was discovered, and the Guildhall Library possesses a sketch of it by Henry Hodge.

[T] ST DUNSTAN-IN-THE-EAST, GREAT TOWER STREET

First mentioned in 1271, the medieval church on the west side of St Dunstan's Hill presided over a prosperous parish. The building was extensively repaired in 1633 when Portland stone was used to reinforce the outer walls, which may explain why the main body of the church withstood the 'dismal fire', and Wren only had to repair it. Later he built a new and graceful tower and steeple supported on flying buttresses, which survive today. When a hurricane swept London in 1703 Wren was told that every City steeple had been damaged. 'Not St Dunstan's, I am sure,' he commented correctly.[182]

There were vaults beneath the church. Stow mentions that 'in the quire John Kennington, Parson, was buried there, 1374'. Many notable people were also interred there, including on 31 August 1556 Mistress Sawde, wife of Queen Katharine's keeper of the exchequer. Mr Machyn, a local tradesman who was 'a supplier of funeral trappings on a considerable scale', noted in his diary that afterwards the company retired to Master Greenways 'to drink and spicebread; and the morrow a mass and sermon and after a great dinner; and the morrow after there was given for her both wood and coals to the poor people'.[183]

In 1941 the building was gutted by enemy action, but the tower was restored at the end of the war, although its bells crossed the Atlantic and now hang in the tower of a Californian winery. In 1957 it was still hoped that the church would rise again, so on 17 April the Revd Richard Tatlock and his churchwardens petitioned for a faculty to remove 'no less than 76 bodies in lead coffins in the vaults below the church and re-inter them in the City of London Cemetery at an estimated cost of £500'(£10,208). The skeletons were to be removed from their coffins and the lead sold 'for the benefit of general church funds'. Permission was given by the chancellor, but the plan came to nothing, and today the land is an open space.

[*] ST HELEN, BISHOPSGATE

The IRA bombs of 1992 and 1993 badly damaged this church, which had been repaired in the 1630s and survived the Great Fire and the Blitz. A Benedictine convent was founded here in about 1204 and the nuns shared the church with local parishioners until the Dissolution in 1538. They must have been a feisty group of ladies, because in 1385 they were scolded for kissing 'secular persons' and wearing ostentatious veils. There was also too much conviviality in cloister and kitchen, with 'waving over the screen' that separated the two sides.[184] Traces of the nunnery remain, including a squint at the east end. The crypt of the convent survived until 1799, because the building above it had been used as the Dining Hall of the Leathersellers' Company, who purchased it from St Helen's in 1538 when the priory was dissolved. The building was demolished and rebuilt to the east.

There have never been large vaults beneath the church because the bodies of wealthier parishioners were placed below the stone floor in intramural graves, although there was an impropriator's vault.[185] The parish has never been populous. The first entry in the St Helen burial registers is that of John Byngle, 17 April 1575, but vestry records began in 1558 and five years later it was decreed that corpses buried in church must be 'coffened in wood'. There was an annual average of only thirty-four burials in the ten years following January 1666. The sexton gives very precise locations in 1667: 'close to the Railles of the Communion'; 'near Mr Robinson's vault'; 'Under the great Stone which is Crackt in the middle'.[186] Only rarely are there instructions about interments, but for 19 January 1698–99 a bricklayer was told he would be paid 5s for every grave in church and told to keep the pavement level. The incumbent was censured on 9 August 1699 for appropriating ground in the chancel to make a vault without asking the vestry's permission, and on 17 April 1718 regulations were laid down about the times of burials in church and yard. From Lady Day to Michaelmas they could be until 10 p.m. and at other times until 9 p.m.; after that double fees would be charged.

In 1891 J.L. Pearson was asked to repair and reorder the building, and he began work on 1 September. Immediately it became apparent that the ground below the floor of the church was in a bad state, containing coffins and bones in abundance. The Home Office ordered that these must be reinterred, but the faculty granted on 18 February ordered that certain members of the gentry who had monuments in the church should stay. They were to be 'covered over with a bed of concrete 18 inches thick with liquid cement grouted in, and so hermetically sealed as to guard against any possible injury of health arising therefrom'.[187] An Order in Council of 9 May authorised this and the exhumation began on 27 May: 129 lead coffins with inscriptions and 131 without, together with seventy cases of bones, were moved to Central Avenue in the City of London Cemetery. Among them were the bones of Robert Hooke, the 'Leonardo of London' and City surveyor, who cooperated with his friend Sir Christopher Wren in restoring St Paul's and designing some of the City churches. He died on 3 March 1703.[188] All the wooden coffins had perished and disappeared but most of the lead coffins still had an outer wooden case. The earliest of these dated from 1609 – Sir John Spencer and the last to be buried was in 1851. Under the chancel and choir lay sixty coffins, including those of Dame Mary Langham (d. 1660) and the Revd James Bleukarne, incumbent of St Helen from 1799 until his death in 1836. The parish vault, only 8in below the floor of the nave, had coffins 'placed close together like bales of merchandise'.

The report by the rector, the Revd J.A.L. Airey, and his wardens, signed in December, three months after the work finished on 13 September, suggests that the remains of about 700 to 1,000 people had been found. As the St Helen burial register records 4,355 interments in church and yard between 1651 and 1853, it seems that an unusually large percentage of parishioners were given intramural burial. Very few coffins were found entire, as the lead had decayed and in some cases shrivelled or flattened down, the remains inside being reduced to dust and a few bones. One coffin below the chancel contained only stones and bricks. Many bodies were wrapped in brown or yellow cere cloth, and some 'particularly in the Gresham vault had coarse and bushy hair'.[189]

St Helen Bishopsgate. City of London Cemetery. Memorial, 1892. The plot contains 700–1,000 skeletons including Robert Hooke, City Surveyor, who died 1703.

The gentry whom the chancellor directed should not be moved from below their monuments are listed below:

Sir John and Lady Crosby (1476) buried on the south side of the chancel. No remains were found.

Sir John Spencer, Lord Mayor, who died in 1609, and was buried with his wife in the Pickering chantry, Chapel of the Holy Ghost. In 1696 his vault was forfeited to the parish because the Earl of Northampton refused to repair it.[190] His lead anthropoid coffin was found on 28 June 1808 12ft below the chancel, but there was no sign of his wife buried here on 7 April 1610.[191]

Sir William Pickering died in 1574 and was buried on the north side of the chancel. His remains were discovered in a narrow brick vault 4ft below his monument.

Sir Thomas Gresham, Elizabethan financier and founder of the Royal Exchange,

LEADEN...SHROUD

containing the remains of Sir John Spencer, with inscription upon it in raised characters. Date, 1609.

[from a Photograph]

St Helen Bishopsgate. Leaden shroud containing the remains of Sir John Spencer buried in a new vault, 22 March 1609.

who died in 1579, was buried in the north-east corner of the church. A large lead coffin, together with 'a confused mass of loose remains', lay in a large vault 8ft below his monument.

Sir John Lawrence (lord mayor during the Great Plague) was buried in the south-west corner of the church. No remains were found, but Mr R.H. Hills wrote to the rector while the clearance was underway suggesting that the body had been stolen for its leaden wrapper earlier in the century, during repairs to the building.

Alderman Thorn Robinson was buried in the north-west corner of the church. Some remains were found in a large brick vault only a few feet below his monument.

Sir Julius Caesar died in 1636 and was buried in the chantry. Only the coffin of Jemima Perry who died on 1 February 1834 lay here 'with a confused mass of loose bones'; these were removed.

Alexander Macdougall, died 21 November 1835. His coffin 'in a state of perfect preservation' lay 6ft below the surface of the chantry next to that of Thomas Alston, who died on 5 August 1844. The family of the latter removed him to Highgate Cemetery.

The Boddington family was buried below the east end of the nuns' choir. A 'vault of considerable size and depth' was discovered containing several lead coffins, the uppermost of which, standing upright, belonged to Eleanor Boddington, 27 March 1795. She was placed horizontal and left undisturbed.

Sir Francis Bancroft, buried in 1728 beneath the north aisle, having paid the parish £95 (£17,837) for the ground, required that his coffin should open and shut like an ordinary trunk – in case he was buried alive or was late for the final Judgement.[192] There was a piece of square glass in the lid of the oak coffin over his face. His remains were found together with a small chest possibly containing his heart and entrails. His coffin and 9sq.ft tomb, 'like a house' with a door so that the sexton might enter and clean it, were now put in a new vault and the Drapers' Company ensured that they retained the ownership of this portion of land. An empty stone coffin split in half, possibly thirteenth century, was found here.

These vaults were 'arched over, covered with concrete and hermetically closed'.

[*] ST OLAVE, HART STREET

Samuel Pepys and his wife Elizabeth lived in Seething Lane, and on 24 August 1660 he notes in his diary that, aged 27, he went to St Olave's 'to find out a place where to build a seat or a gallery to sit in'. Two days later on the Lord's Day he endured 'a dry and tedious long sermon' but was pleased to be 'placed in the highest pew of all' where the congregation bowed to him as he arrived, probably because he held office in the nearby Navy Office. On 5 June 1703 at 9 p.m. Pepys was 'buried in a vault by ye communion table' in the same grave as his wife Elizabeth. At her death in 1669 he had placed a beautifully sculpted marble bust of her by John Bushnell 'in our church' on the north wall of the sanctuary, and this survived the Blitz because it was stored in the crypt of St Paul's Cathedral. His coffin was seen when the floor was lifted during the alterations of 1954. The Pepys coffins joined a large number of others interred under the church floor, and they are still there.

In 1800 the parish had 1,216 inhabitants. Charles Dickens was fascinated by this churchyard and in his *Uncommercial Traveller* calls it St Ghastly Grim. Acknowledging 'The attraction of repulsion', he would make special visits at night during thunderstorms to peer through the gateway and soak up the atmosphere, watching as lightning illuminated the tombstones. 'As I stand peeping in through the iron gates and rails, I can peel the rusty metal off, like bark from an old tree. The illegible tombstones are all lopsided, the grave-mounds lost their shape in the rains of a hundred years ago.'[193]

Prebendary Wellard, the rector, reported in 1933 that while removing the font to give it to St Olave Toronto the floor of the baptistery had collapsed to reveal a small crypt beneath the tower. He crawled into it over an accumulation of rubbish and found it led to a somewhat larger room, which was obviously late thirteenth century and under the western part of the nave. Constructed of Caen stone, it consists of two bays with groined vaulting in four divisions to each bay. With the permission of the chancellor[194] the rector paved the floor and inserted a narrow staircase from the base of the tower. The chapel, which was dedicated on 19 November 1934, is now regularly used for midweek services. An unglazed window in the west wall barely shows above the ground outside, but the most surprising feature of this crypt is the well standing next to the altar in the south-east corner of the chapel, 20ft deep and lined with brick; its stonework is in a fine state of preservation. Thought to date from *c.*1250, it is covered with a wrought-iron grid. Was it once a holy well visited by pilgrims?

8

CITY OF LONDON
NORTH

[*] ST ANDREW HOLBORN, HOLBORN CIRCUS

A four-bay crypt designed by Sir Christopher Wren can now be seen for the first time here because 1,300 coffins and around 1,600 skeletons that filled it almost to the ceiling were cleared in 2001–02 and reinterred in the City of London Cemetery.

There they joined the 11,000 to 12,000 bodies removed in 1863–69 from the churchyard to the north of the church so that Holborn Viaduct could be constructed. Soon after the coffins arrived to the south of Central Avenue in the City of London Cemetery a St Andrew's cross was erected. This now has an inscription to mark the new arrivals. Their exhumation and removal, carried out by Pat Toop and his operatives, took seven months and cost £1.2 million.

A church has stood on this site for 1,000 years – a charter of Westminster Abbey mentions it in 951. The medieval building, which was restored in 1632, escaped the Great Fire of 1665, but was rebuilt in 1684–90 by Wren, who used the medieval stone foundations which can still be seen.

St Andrew, City of London Cemetery, St Andrew Cross, 1863-69, (11,000 corpses removed from churchyard).

St Andrew. City of London Cemetery, 2002. Inscription on Cross (burial of 1,300 coffins and *c.* 1,600 skeletons from crypt).

The church vaults soon began to fill up, but in 1747 a scandal brought publicity to St Andrew's because John Lamb, the sexton, and William Bilby, the gravedigger, appeared at the Old Bailey accused of stealing lead from the coffins committed to their charge. When Bilby was apprehended by the 'vigilant and worthy constable, Mr Chance', the old, 'grey headed and infirm' Lamb went into hiding, but a reward was offered and he soon joined his partner in Newgate Prison.[195] At their trial on 14 October evidence was given by several men who had assisted in the operation under the impression that the Revd Geoffrey Barton, the rector, had ordered the removal. Bilby persuaded the rector that because the crypt was waterlogged a hole should be made in the outer wall for drainage. It was through this hole that bodies were dragged at night to be thrown into a pit in the churchyard, while the lead from the coffins was cut up and taken to the men's houses; when the constable visited them he found a hundredweight of lead worth 13*s* (£150). The two men were sentenced to seven years' transportation, but their helpers were acquitted.[196]

It appears, according to an anonymous pamphlet, that Bilby already had a notorious reputation, and it was not the first time this had happened. There were also 'Pranks the villains had played with the Dead'. Two months before this offence he and Lamb's son had:

decoyed a poor Fellow into the Vaults, and having stuck up a dead Corps against the Wall, covered with a Sack in which they used to carry away the Lead (a pipe being stuck in the Corps's Mouth with a lighted Candle in it), they desir'd the Man to rake away some Dirt just where the Corpse was placed, and young Lamb getting behind, unty'd a Rope which held up the Corpse, when the same fell down violently upon the poor Man, which frightened him so much that he was near losing his Senses.[197]

In the nineteenth century the church remained important and busy. The sexton's accounts 1812–15 reveal that on some days there were two or three interments in the various yards with a usual fee of 4s 6d for children and around 9s for adults. A vault might cost 13s 6d, and a burial below the church porch £1 6s 2d (£80).[198] There was no charge for the poor. The present building, 105ft by 63ft, is the largest of Wren's churches, and his four crypt tunnels which have a clay floor take up all the space underneath except for the area under the western tower with its vestibules on each side, and a narrow area under the sanctuary and vestries at the east end. S.S. Teulon drastically restored the church in 1871, but the vaults remained untouched.

St Andrew. Lamb and Bilby stealing lead, 1747.

St Andrew. Jumbled coffins before clearance in 2001/2.

On the night of 16 April 1941 incendiary bombs rained down, destroying everything but the tower, walls and floor of the building. The crypt was untouched, but the rubble soaked up moisture and transmitted it via the walls to the foundations at the north-west and eastern ends. Dampness has always been a problem, and Wren had to put conduits below the crypt floor in all the tunnels, running east-west. The water presumably ran into an underground stream, perhaps the Fleet. In 2001 during the clearance a well was discovered in the south-west chamber. It had been dry for some years, but when the water table recently rose it caused dampness to that part of the building and explains why the walls were wet in the vestibule above. Wren's conduits had been blocked by earth. Seely and Paget restored the church, and it was reconsecrated on 25 October 1961.

Until 2001 coffins and skeletons filled the four vaults, and it was difficult to enter through the doors which are in the middle of the north and south exterior walls. Mounds of earth were found at several places in the four tunnels, which suggest that when the 1961 rebuild was taking place holes were made in the nave floor, through which rubbish was shovelled. The earliest coffin found was that of Alexander Napier, who died aged 45 on 5 December 1691, and the last interment was of an unknown person in 1853.

When the project began Mr Toop, a South London builder, opened the south crypt door on 14 November 2001 to find twenty skeletons piled against the steps. The bodies were listed on the 29th and a conveyor belt was installed to carry earth

Left: St Andrew.
Lead coffin.

Below: St Andrew.
Two skeletons share
a coffin.

into a large tent on the south side of the building, where it was examined for bones, coffin furniture, etc. An archaeologist from the Museum of London kept a careful eye on the operation. Oyster shells in abundance were found, which presumably contained the eighteenth- and nineteenth-century workmen's lunch – 'Poverty and oysters always seem to go together,' remarked Sam Weller in *The Pickwick Papers.*[199]

Most of the coffins, usually stacked four to five high, dated from the first thirty years of the nineteenth century, although three vaults contained several from the eighteenth century. There were few family groupings, although four members of the Powell family (1808–41) were in vault 4 and three Taylors in vault 3. Sad stories must lie behind the coffins of John Fortesse aged 18 months and his brother Anthony aged 13 weeks, who both died on 7 May 1790, and the tiny caskets containing William Luttly aged 8 months and Bertha Luttley aged 6 months.

Steps had at one time led from the chancel to the vault beneath, but these had been bricked up. The coffins in this area had been disturbed and were upturned, with some opened and some leaning against the walls, suggesting that thieves had entered by breaking through the north wall. A distinguished occupant was Professor G. Tralles from Berlin, who died aged 60 on 19 November 1822. When aged 22, he was appointed professor at the Academy in Berne then moved in 1810 to be a professor at the University in Berlin. Despite the holding chains on the walls, the coffins, all of which were simple in design, had obviously been moved around, and breastplates that had become detached were lying separately. The last coffin – that of Charles Perry, 46, who died in 1813 – left St Andrew's on 21 May 2002.

The oldest resident of the church was discovered at the end of the project. A square area under the north-east vestry remained untouched and there seemed no way through. The wooden floor of the vestry was lifted, and after the 1960s concrete underneath was broken up a chamber was revealed, filled with earth, bones and bits of wood. As the hole was too small to remove this earth, a decision was made to break

through the medieval stone wall of the crypt; the stones were numbered so that they could be replaced. At the base of the chamber, below the crypt floor level, a lead anthropoid coffin containing a male skeleton was discovered. Dan Gallagher, a member of St Andrew's staff since 1996 who was present throughout the exhumation, considers that the burial had been unceremonious and hurried. Carbon dating showed that the body is $c.1650–70$, so it predates the 1684 church. Presumably Wren had cleared away all the other bodies to erect his building, so why did this man remain? Was he a famous personage? Had he been removed from the western end? He and his coffin remain

St Andrew. Anthropoid coffin containing an unknown man. Is this Mr Thavie?

today at St Andrew's, and as there is no name-plate to identify him he is now known as 'The Thavie Man'. 'He is our oldest resident,' says Dan. 'We need to give him a special place so that he can welcome visitors.' There is, however, no evidence that he is connected to John Thavie, whose benefaction of 1348 still maintains much of the church fabric and work.

In 2011 the four-tunnel crypt is a magnificent venue for parties, receptions and launches. Each individual bay can be controlled separately to produce an event. Ideally suited for fringe theatre, the red Wren brick produces a great backdrop for filming.

[*] ST BARTHOLOMEW THE GREAT, SMITHFIELD

St Bartholomew's crypt, which today is accessed by a staircase to the north of the lady chapel, dates from the fourteenth century and extends under the two eastern-most bays of the lady chapel, with which it is coeval (*c.*1335). It was used as a charnel house and is described as such in the will of Walter Whytefeld dated 1451, where he willed to be buried 'in the cemetery of the priory of St Bartholomew before the entrance of the charnel house outside the processional path in West Smythfeld'. The internal dimensions of the crypt – which is rectangular – are 25ft 6in long, 23ft 9in wide, and 9ft high: the thickness of the walls is 3ft. It consists of six bays. The vaulting was originally built with chalk blocks, of which small portions remain in the north-east and north-west corners. There were five vaulting arches and a vaulting wall rib at each end. The rib on the eastern wall is original, excepting where the doorway breaks it.

The walls and pilasters are original, excepting the upper portions of the west wall which had been destroyed. In the western bay of the south wall there was originally an opening measuring 2ft 8in wide by 2ft 6in high. It could hardly have been intended for an entrance, but may have been for a bone shute. As no other entrance could be found, either from the chapel above or from outside, the sill was lowered in 1895 to form a doorway 7ft 6in high, with five steps down to give access to the vault. The house or cottage that blocked the window of the third bay of the lady chapel on the north side, and which fell in the year 1904, also blocked the crypt window. The present opening is as it was found in 1905, when the cottage was removed.

At the restoration in 1895 the crypt was made into a mortuary chapel for the use of the inhabitants of the crowded courts and alleys round the church. An altar was erected at the east end, where Holy Communion was celebrated for the first time on 29 June 1895. Later on the same day the crypt was opened as a mortuary chapel by the Duke of Newcastle, after a short service of dedication by the Bishop of Stepney. In the centre of the floor was a low dais for the bier, around which stood six tall wooden candlesticks for light in the death chamber. This space is used today as a choir vestry, but if funds are available a treasury will be installed.

A tiny portion of churchyard survives around the walls of the lady chapel, and a columbarium is planned for the south-east corner, accessed from the lady chapel. The architects Welters have designed an L-shaped stone construction with decorative coloured pillars. There will be 196 niche chambers each able to take two caskets.

[*] ST BOTOLPH, ALDERSGATE

The Revd S. Flood Jones, vicar, reported that there was an odd smell in the church. He told the members of his vestry that it obviously came from under the floorboards where bodies lay just below the surface. It was 1892, and the Charity Commissioners had recently taken control of the city church funds so there was no cash to pay for an investigation. However, the commissioners had already instituted an enquiry into the fabric of St Botolph's, which had been rebuilt by Nathaniel Wright in 1788–91. Apart from the east front being stuccoed in 1831, it remains untouched today.

The closure of the vaults and churchyard came in August 1853, by which time there had been fifty-five burials that year.[200] In 1892 members of the Home Office visited and pronounced that the situation was 'injurious to health', and issued a licence to remove the coffins. On 21 April 1893 the chancellor declared the building unfit for public worship, and the vestry asked him to grant a faculty to remove all human remains beneath the floor of the church to a depth of at least 6ft. Special care would be

St Botolph, Aldersgate. Marble monument 1893, and large enclosure, Brookwood, containing 237 coffins and 296 boxes of bones. The small memorial at the rear is of Holy Trinity, Kingsway, 1909.

taken not to endanger the stability of the structure by interfering with its foundations. The work was to be supervised by Dr W. Sedgwick Saunders, the Medical Officer of Health for the City of London. Notices were inserted in the press asking for relatives of the deceased to come forward, but no one did. On 6 June 1893 *The Times* reported: 'The last interment here was in 1852. There are two large vaults with at least 100 coffins exposed to view, and there are coffins lower down which are not exposed. There is a large quantity of human remains outside the vaults buried without coffins under the floor of the church. The wood of the coffins has perished.'

The chancellor granted the faculty on 20 October 1893 and work began on 15 December, continuing until the following June. It took thirty-nine days – usually starting at 7 a.m. – to remove the 173 lead coffins with nameplates dating from 1710 to 1849, sixty-four lead coffins without any identification and 296 boxes of bones with eight detached breastplates. There were 'small loads owing to Bad Weather' on two days in January,[201] and after these had been removed the vaults were filled with clean, dry earth, and the church floor complete with brown and yellow tiles was relaid upon a bed of concrete. The remains are at Brookwood in plot 85 on St George the Martyr Avenue, where the unkempt enclosure around a marble monument has sunk several feet.

[*] ST GILES CRIPPLEGATE, FORE STREET

The church, founded in the eleventh century on the swampy ground outside the Gate, was rebuilt in 1537 and again eight years later after a disastrous fire. It escaped the Great Fire, but apart from the tower and walls it was reduced to rubble on 29 December 1940. Godfrey Allen rebuilt it as the parish church of the Barbican development, so it still has a large resident population. Reopened in 1960 after years of neglect, it stands 'like a respected but not well understood older person at a party'.[202]

The parishioners of St Giles suffered greatly from the plague: the burial register has seventy-one pages for July 1665, and in August, when the heat intensified and the stench was appalling, the deaths take up 101 pages. On 18 August alone there were 151 funerals, taken presumably by the curate as the rector had fled. It is estimated that in the Ward of Cripplegate Without there were 8,000 deaths including the parish clerk, five churchwardens and the sexton.

A burial took place in the churchyard in about 1706 of William Maw. No one knew that the coffin was empty except his wife, 'a cunning baggage'. Maw who lived in Golden Lane had been a cabinet maker, but gave that up for a life of crime. He had been fined, then 'burned in the hand', and after a robbery he asked his wife to help him disappear by arranging a mock funeral. In 1711 he met a man called Watkins, who knew him and had watched the coffin go past the Red Cross ale house where he was drinking. Watkins told the authorities, and Maw was arrested, convicted of five indictments and executed on 29 October 1711.[203]

As well as the churchyard, the parish possessed the Green Churchyard[204] which still exists hidden away to the south-west of the church between Bastions 12 and 13. In 1662 land in Bath Street was purchased as a pest-house ground for plague victims, and a shelter was erected for £6 10s 0d to protect priest and mourners in rainy weather; 14s was paid for 'biskitts' at the consecration ceremony.

John Milton's grave under the chancel of St Giles was opened on 3 August 1790. He had been buried there on 12 November 1674, and although a lead coffin was unearthed it had no breastplate. However, everyone was convinced it contained Milton's corpse and Philip Neve has left a contemporary account:

> Between 8 and 9 o'clock on Wednesday morning, the 4th, the two overseers (Laming and Fountain) … went with Holmes, a journeyman, into the church and pulled the coffin … into daylight … Holmes immediately fetched a mallet and chisel and cut open the top of the coffin … Upon first view of the body, it appeared perfect, and completely enveloped in the shroud, which was of many folds; the ribs standing up regularly. When they disturbed the shroud the ribs fell. Mr Fountain told me, that he pulled hard at the teeth, which resisted, until someone hit them a knock with a stone, when they easily came out. There were but five in the upper-jaw, which were all perfectly sound and white … Mr Laming lifted up the head and saw a great quantity of hair. Mr Taylor, a surgeon, took up the hair, as it laid over the forehead, and carried it home.[205]

After this the caretaker Elizabeth Grant took the coffin under her care, charging 6d to anyone who wished to view it, later reducing her fee to 3d and finally to 2d ('The price of a pot of beer'). Milton still rests in the vaults under St Giles as, apart from a boiler house being constructed at the west end, they have not been disturbed since.

Interments continued in the church often under a favourite pew, but after 1828 all corpses had to be in lead or other metal coffins.[206] By 1841 the parish had a population of 13,255 and there were approximately 400 burials each year.[207]

Today the church serves the Barbican Estate, and has close links with the Guildhall School of Music and Drama and the nearby City of London School for Girls. A columbarium and small garden has been created below the pavement at the east end of the church.

ST LUKE, OLD STREET

One of the last churches built under the Act of 1711, which provided for fifty new churches in London, St Luke was built in 1727–33 to minister to the large parish of St Giles Cripplegate, and it became a separate parish in 1733 just beyond the City border. It was designed by John James, though the obelisk spire, a most unusual feature for an Anglican church, west tower and flanking staircase wings were by

Nicholas Hawksmoor. It was built on marshy land and had to be underpinned four times, but there was no substantial war damage. A calamitous subsidence occurred in 1959 and the building was declared unsafe. It then became a dramatic ruin for forty years, overgrown with trees despite being a Grade I listed building. The site was closed in 1964 and the roof was removed two years later for safety reasons.

In July 1964 it was found that coffins in the crypt had been disturbed, and in one case the lead interior had been taken apart from the case and the top forced off, revealing the remains in an advanced state of decay of Mrs Esther Tomkies, aged 53, who had died on 2 December 1853. Holes in the nave floor had been made by the intruders to gain access to the crypt, which contained three layers of coffins. Mrs Tomkies was placed in a new zinc coffin with an outer wooden case and reinterred in the crypt.[208]

Although the 1711 Act forbade crypt burials, by 1740 the vestry minutes list fees for them. In his *Gatherings from Graveyards* (1839) Dr George Walker reported that 'The vaults underneath the church are less used than formerly, but the smell from these vaults is particularly offensive – so much so, that I was informed by the Rev Dr Rice, the present Curate, that he never ventured to descend, but invariably performed the funeral rites whilst standing in the passage, at the top of the entrance to the vaults'. The vaults closed in 1853.

On 19 August 1964 a meeting was held of the diocesan authorities, Dr Brook, Chief Medical Officer of Health for Finsbury, and the London Necropolis Ltd. By the end of the month Dove Bros were asked to brick up all the openings to the crypt, which they did in November. The parish was reunited with St Giles in 1959.

On 14 November 1994 the architects Biscoe and Stanton reported that vandalism had increased: 'The internal area of the church has also re-grown quite luxuriantly as there seems to be a favourable micro-climate within the sheltering wall.' £150,000 was being spent on the tower.[209]

After several controversial proposals to redevelop offices inside the retained walls, it was converted by the St Luke Centre Management Company Ltd for the London Symphony Orchestra as a concert hall, rehearsal, recording space and educational resource. The conversion was designed by Axel Burrough at London architects Levitt Bernstein, who installed a heavy concrete slab roof to keep out traffic noise from the nearby road. Though this is similar in profile to the former eighteenth-century roof, its great weight is supported on tall steel columns inside the hall, described by the designer as 'tree-like'. The interior acoustic can be varied for different events, from full orchestra to soloists, by the use of absorbent surfaces that unroll like blinds across the ceiling and down the walls, while the seating and staging is also highly flexible. The project had a budget of £18 million and was partly funded by the Heritage Lottery Fund. The external walls were underpinned and additional space was provided at basement level after the human remains were removed. The crypt had four parallel brick bays with barrel-vaulted roofs

St Luke. A coffin in a crypt vault before clearance, 2001.

about 13ft wide by 82ft long. No burials were found beneath the crypt floor. All sealed or substantially sealed lead coffins remained so, and were then sleeved on site and removed for reburial. The use of wooden coffins ended in 1810.[210]

A Home Office Order was granted on 21 January 1999 subject to agreement with the chief environmental scientist for the London Borough of Islington. A database records details of coffin furniture and osteological information, and a photographic record was maintained. The exhumation was carried out by Necropolis Ltd. A documentary entitled *Changing Tombs* covering the removal of the burials was produced at the time.

Between July and December 2000 the Oxford Archaeological Unit worked with Necropolis Ltd on behalf of St Luke Centre Management Company in advance of the construction work to be undertaken by the LSO; 1,053 burials from crypt and the north and south churchyards were recorded and removed, of which 336 were named. Basic demographic information was recovered, stature was calculated where possible, a detailed dental record was compiled and pathology recorded where seen[211]: 354 bodies were in the crypt, 398 in the north churchyard, and 300 in the south churchyard. In addition there were ten chest tombs and fifty-five vaults and brick shaft graves. In all fifty-eight corpses were dated as eighteenth century and 429 to the first half of the nineteenth century. The earliest vault interment was 1756 and the last was of Cordelia Scotter, who died on 12 August 1853. The vestry minutes record a letter to Lord Palmerston asking that burials could continue, but this was rejected, and interments ceased at the end of 1853.

Of the 732 coffins recorded, 430 were lead alloy/wood triple shell and 257 were wood single shell. Among the artefacts found were four wedding bands and dentures, which consisted of a copper alloy plate into which human teeth had been fixed. The majority of bodies were adult (86.4 per cent), and 62.8 per cent of these were over 40 years of age; 121 bodies were under 17. The coffins and remains from St Luke were buried in Randall's Park Cemetery, Leatherhead.

[*] ST CLEMENT, KING'S SQUARE

There are sixty-two lead coffins in the crypt of this church, which was conse-crated on 12 June 1826 after four years of wrangling and disputes. Originally dedicated to St Barnabas, it was a chapel of ease of St Luke Old Street, which is a short distance to the south. The vestry of St Luke's resisted the proposal, believing that a new church would 'impose on the inhabitants a needless and oppressive expense' and that 'no additional chapels are necessary'. It is more likely that they were worried about the considerable loss in fees, because this part of their parish was becoming more populous: orchards were giving way to houses on the northern edge of the City. King Square, named after King George IV, seemed to be an ideal spot to place one of the new 'Waterloo' churches, financed by a £1 million (£84 million) grant from Parliament, so the vestry grudgingly gave way. Designed by Philip Hardwick, the architect

St Clement. The well-preserved security cage of the Bedggood family vault.

of Euston station, it was built in the Greek Ionic style with a spire attached. The tall main doors led directly into the church, and the doors on either side of the porch led up into the galleries or down to the crypt, which is the same size as the church.

St Clements. The passage showing the entrance to the Gall family vault.

St Clements. Stacked coffins at eastern end of crypt looking north.

St Clements. Coffins in the Bedggood vault, off the south aisle.

St Clements. The entrance to the family vault of Mr Thomas Gall of King Square.

St Clements. The cobwebbed east-west passage on the northern side, looking west.

In 1842 St Barnabas became a separate parish, and other churches were built nearby – presumably on the principle that if you open more pubs you sell more beer. The Second World War destroyed three of them, including St Clement, Lever Street, and they were not rebuilt. St Barnabas had not been severely damaged and was being used as a store of ecclesiastical furniture, so it was decided to make it the parish church and change its name to St Clement. The Bishop of London rededicated the new church on 11 June 1954, and during the next twenty years the old damaged tenements gave way to high rise developments, mainly owned by the local authority.

The crypt, about 100ft by 45ft, is now strewn with piles of soil, stone, rubble and clinker. It is in a sad state and visited by cats and foxes, so there are animal and human bones among the cobwebs. It has a centre aisle, and there are nine arched tunnels running north-south across it. The side aisles have recessed, arched bays, and on each side there are coffins in three of them behind locked iron grilles: the family would have kept the keys. At the east end under the altar lies a priest in charge, the Revd William Thompson, and two members of his family. All those interred here are local people, including five Sowters of Wharf Road, five Bedggoods of Regent's Terrace, City Road, and William Jacob and three relatives, who lived in King's Square. The Gall vault has three coffins and the Clement vault, dated 1826, contains three coffins. On the floor of the open tunnels there are thirty-one coffins, all lead encased in wood. They are in good order, although the outer fabric has perished, as would be expected.

St Clements. North-south tunnel, the outer wooden coffin cases are beginning to crack.

St Clements. Coffins beginning to disintegrate after over 170 years.

In 2011 the parish priest, Fr David Allen, has been told that to clear and modernise the crypt would cost around £2 million, so he is consulting the local community to find out how the space might fill their needs. Only one vault is at the west end, so its three coffins could be moved to the east end and bricked up with the others. The floor where it can be seen is brick. It may be that coffins are below, which would increase costs. A wall tablet commemorating a Mr Behm, who died in 1852, says that he is 'buried beneath'.

9

City of London
West and South

[T] CHRIST CHURCH, NEWGATE STREET

The Greyfriars monastery founded here in 1224 had the second largest church in the City because of the patronage of Queen Margaret in the fourteenth century. She and several queen consorts were buried here. When the monastery was dissolved by King Henry VIII its church was renamed Christchurch and a parish was formed from two demolished churches (St Nicholas Shambles and St Ewin) and part of St Sepulchre. Parishioners could only use the choir because after 1553 Christ's Hospital, a school for poor children where they wore blue coats, used the nave. Although the building was destroyed in the Great Fire, funerals were still held, and in 1681 the wife of Richard Baxter was 'buried in the ruins in her mother's grave'. The new church by Wren costing the large sum of £11,778 opened in 1691.[212] It was 114ft by 81ft – one of the widest in the City – and was built on the eastern part of the site, leaving the western part as a burial ground.

On 30 July 1790 a vault was discovered under the old vestry door with a flight of seventeen steps, 18ft wide, leading to the north aisle. Only one body was there, and it was placed erect in a deal case with a longitudinal door. In 1803 Malcolm viewed it: 'The body is entire throughout … the flesh is firm … the head fallen back and extremely bald … the colour of parchment. The worms have begun their operations and it is perforated in many places as they pierce a decayed book.' Malcolm decided not to enter the vault again 'at least while alive'.[213] Fees in the 'New Vaults' were expensive in 1830 – £8 2s 4d (£773), and £14 6s 8d (£1,354) for a non-parishioner. The vaults and churchyard were closed on 6 December 1853. The school moved to Horsham in 1897 and the church was gutted in 1940, leaving Wren's tower, which was restored in 1960 by Lord Mottistone. Presumably coffins and remains are still below the churchyard to the west of the tower.

[*] ST DUNSTAN-IN-THE-WEST, FLEET STREET

The only early nineteenth-century church in the Square Mile, the present octagonal building, was consecrated on 31 January 1833. Two years earlier the medieval church had been demolished and its vaults cleared, although eighteen coffins dating from 1783 to 1831 were transferred to the vaults under the new church. Mr George Carden visited the crypt before the rebuilding, and in 1825 reported that the dead there were in wooden coffins, which meant that the coffins below were crushed by those placed on top of them, and that he saw 'The remains of the recently-interred corpses forced in part out of the coffin, and in a state of decomposition too disgusting to be described'.[214]

The earliest known reference to this church is in a document of 1185 held in Westminster Abbey, which originally held the advowson. The dean saved St Dunstan's from the Great Fire of 1666 by sending forty boys in the middle of the night, armed with buckets of water to douse the flames. A change of wind helped. Because the parish was well populated the church vaults and graveyard were extensively used – in 1665 there were 1,623 burials, 958 of which were plague victims. When John Graunt, a parishioner living in Bolt Court whose house was destroyed in the Great Fire, died on 18 April 1674, the only place that could be found for him in St Dunstan's according to his contemporary John Aubrey was 'in the body of the same church under the

St Dunstan-in-the-West crypt, central vault. Gate to catacombs on right.

St Dunstan. Gate to north catacombs.

piewes (alias hoggsties) of the north side of the middle aisle. What pity 'tis so great an Ornament of the Citty should be buried so obscurely.'[215] As Dr Litten notes, it was better for him to be under a pew in church rather than outside in the churchyard, where security of grave tenure could not be guaranteed.[216]

In 1813 there were 107 interments – ten in the vaults, thirty-eight in the churchyard and fifty-nine in Fetter Lane burial ground. By 1852 when interments ceased the number had dropped considerably.

The crypt space is approximately 72ft by 95ft. The central area is surrounded on all sides by ten smaller vaults, including an oblong vault, 30ft long, with stone shelving to the north, which contained forty-four slots on its western side and forty-eight to the east. The Hoare family vault lay to the east – their bank, founded in 1672, has been in its present location opposite the church since 1690, and many members of the family have been churchwardens and benefactors. William Sands, the builder who estimated £50 (£5,261) for the building work needed to close the vaults, listed the position of the coffins: fifty were in the west vault, thirty-two in the northern catacombs, twenty were in the south vault and the rest in the smaller rooms.[217] An Order in Council dated 31 July 1858 directed that all coffins be placed in one vault and be covered with earth and powdered charcoal. Those in the catacombs

St Dunstan. Inside catacombs.

St Dunstan. Arch to the Hoare family vault.

to the north should be bricked up, and 'McDougall's powder, chloride of lime and other disinfectants be employed'. The Hoare vault containing six coffins was sealed and a wooden door inserted.

The vaults were used by the St Dunstan's Troop, the 6 City of London Boy Scouts in the 1920s and 1930s, who constructed their dens and held meetings in the midst of the coffins, which were behind iron grilles and wooden doors. The fifty-eight members used the main area as a playroom/gymnasium and other rooms as offices, workshops and canteen. The space was used as an air-raid shelter in the Second World War, and local solicitors stored their drawings and other records in the smaller rooms until 1970.

In 1980 Gale, Heath and Co. drew up a feasibility study to convert the crypt into a community centre for use by the Rumanian community, but there were many disadvantages. Ventilation would have to be installed, doorway heights increased and kitchens and lavatories built. The dangerously small entrance stairs made access difficult, and the vaults containing coffins would have to be sealed. Eventually it was agreed that the timber props installed during the air raids could be removed without the ceiling falling in. Some restoration was undertaken, and in 1986 it was decided to remove the coffins. A faculty was issued on 22 December on the condition that there should be no publicity, and a tablet be erected to commemorate the removal.[218]

St Dunstan. Author in the Hoare vault. The boxes contain ashes.

Mr Boakes of Necropolis Ltd, assisted by six operatives, took nearly four months to clear the vaults, and on 18 February 1987 the last consignment arrived at the East London Cemetery. The remains of 101 adults and thirty-two children, each named and labelled, together with 108 unidentified skeletons, were reinterred; 107 lead coffins were removed, among them being the eighteen from the pre-1833 church vaults. All had breastplates, which revealed that the earliest was Mary Garrett, who died on 19 April 1788, and the last was Paul Harrovman, who was buried on 22 August 1831, only days before the old church was demolished.[219] As yet no memorial marks their new grave in Plaistow.

St Dunstan. Hoare vault.

St Dunstan. Staircase to crypt.

A wine bar was proposed to fill the vacant space in 1996, but despite two years of discussion the plan collapsed. The crypt remains empty.

For over 200 years people have been thrilled and horrified by the story of Sweeney Todd, who in 1795 is said to have had his barber-surgeon's shop at No. 186 Fleet Street next to St Dunstan's Church, in the square formed by the projecting façade of the old building. When the unfortunate client sat in the chair to be shaved; Sweeney cut his throat and pressed a lever with his foot, which made the chair disappear into the cellar with its hapless occupant. Another chair swung up for the next customer. Meanwhile an assistant stripped the body and pushed it through a hole into the church vault, where it was dissected. Tasty morsels were made into pies by Mrs Margery Lovett, who had a shop in Bell Yard. After a while worshippers in the church complained of the stench and the churchwardens investigated. Todd was arrested, but there is no record of him being a resident in the nearby Newgate Jail. The story is pure, or rather impure, fiction, but it may have been based on a gory local murder in the eighteenth century. As Anna Pavord observed in the *Observer*, 'We all need bogeymen and he was bogier than most.' *Victorian Penny Dreadfuls*, the 1936 film starring the appropriately named Tod Slaughter, Stephen Sondheim's 1979 musical thriller and Tim Burton's 2007 film have ensured the story has reached a huge audience.

[*] ST JAMES GARLICKHYTHE, GARLICK HILL

A church has stood here since the twelfth century; in 1598 Stow says that garlic was sold nearby, hence the name. The building was rebuilt in 1326 but destroyed in the Great Fire. Wren completed the rebuilding in 1683. The burial registers contain the clerk's notes about cause of death including gripe of the guts, lethargy, worms, stoppage of the stomach and tooth. A high percentage of eighteenth-century interments were in church – 30 per cent of the 267 burials between 1709 and 1718, and 40 per cent of the eighty-six between 1779 and 1782. In 1801 the parish population was 595, but by 1841 this had fallen to 520 and burials averaged twenty each year. The burial registers mention vaults at the west end and beneath the pulpit and the middle aisle.

Interments ended in 1853, and four years later on 6 January 1857 the vestry agreed that the coffins should be moved to the 'north end of the vault and that a wall should be built across the vault from side to side and go to the top enclosing them all'. Presumably the coffins are still there.[220] Today the only part of the crypt which is accessible is under the east end of the building, reached by a door in the east wall. There are two rooms, together 25ft by 25ft, one of which is a boiler room.

In January 1993 a report from the Museum of London gave details of a north-east burial vault, 11ft 6in by 8ft 2½in, entered two months earlier.[221] It is outside the building and contained five lead coffins in two stacks. The arched barrel chamber was 5ft 8½in high and a passage led westwards into the vaults blocked by two stone slabs. Coffins may have entered the vaults through this space or through a bricked-up entrance in the south-west wall of the building. Only one coffin had a breastplate – of Robert Henry Slaney, who died on 5 June 1833, and was interred in the east vault five days later. His was a triple shell coffin, but the others were in a poor state and one had exploded.

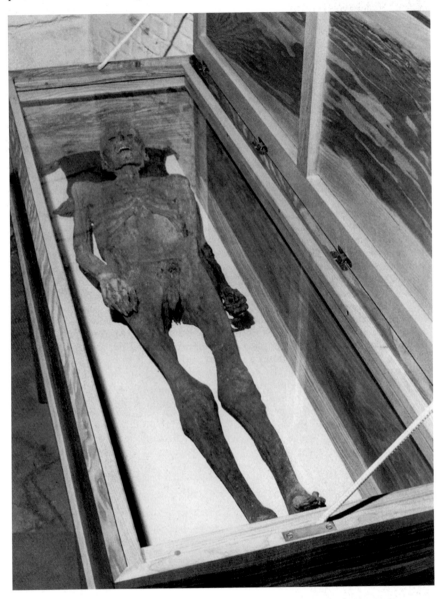

Above and right: St James Garlickhythe. The desiccated seventeenth-century corpse 'Jimmy'. Jimmy is still resident in the church.

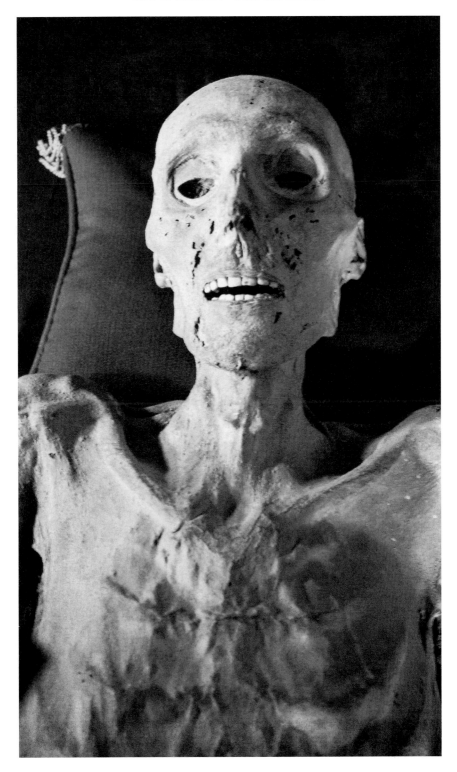

The church possesses a desiccated mummy of a man whose identity is unknown but who is known as Jimmy Garlick. He has been moved around the building over the years, sometimes on view, sometimes not. By the 1850s he was an established attraction for people who came from other parts of London; for a modest fee they were taken to his cupboard and could even touch Jimmy if they wanted. He spent several years in this cupboard in the narthex, and Canon Roy McKay, the incumbent, tried unsuccessfully to send him to Brookwood Cemetery in 1968, with the corpses removed that year from Huggin Hill Cemetery. On 4 August 2004 a faculty was issued[222] so that Atlantic Productions, who make scientific programmes for television, could ask three scholars[223] to examine Jimmy. They reported that he was around 140lb, had pierced ears, was going bald and lived between 1641 and 1804. He had been embalmed, which was unusual in the eighteenth century, although his internal organs are intact. All the water in the body has disappeared, and although desiccated the front of the body is well preserved, but the rectal area is badly decomposed, suggesting that he was lying in his own decomposition fluid. The teeth are well worn so he is an older man of high status – his finger nails are excellent and there are no signs of the labourer's complaint, osteoarthritis.[224] Jimmy, shrouded in an alb and placed in a wood casket, now resides in the tower, but in 2011 plans are being made for him to be buried beneath the floor of a small parish room to be built on the churchyard to the north-east of the building.[225] Mr Ellis Pike, the present honorary verger who has made a careful study of Jimmy, suggests that he was discovered in the mid-nineteenth century, because Emma Garrod, who lived nearby, has left memories of seeing him in the 1860s.[226] Also in the tower room is a wooden coffin with a circular hole at the head end. It fits Jimmy exactly, but could be the parish coffin used before Jimmy's arrival.

[*] ST MAGNUS THE MARTYR, LOWER THAMES STREET

London Bridge has dominated this church since 1067, and Stow says that 'many men of good worship' have been buried here. Its most famous vicar so far is Miles Coverdale, who while in exile produced the first complete English Bible, and in 1538 made a translation of the New Testament based solely on the Latin Vulgate. In 1551 he was made Bishop of Exeter by the young Protestant king, Edward VI, but had to flee into exile on Mary's accession. However, Elizabeth welcomed him home in 1559, and when he died nine years later his body was interred in St Bartholomew-by-the-Exchange. When this church was demolished to make way for a new Royal Exchange in 1840, his remains were taken to St Magnus, where they now lie in a vault below the south-east corner of the building. The monument in the church extols his virtues but has a gold mitre above it, which seems strange because the Puritan Coverdale disapproved of clergy dressing differently, and would certainly never have worn a mitre.

St Magnus was destroyed in the Great Fire, which started only a few yards to the north, but was rebuilt by Wren in 1671–76, and the 185ft steeple was added in 1705. A survey of the building undertaken in 1806 by a Mr S. Robinson[227] notes that there are four parish vaults containing fourteen coffins, one parish vault 9ft high and 50ft by 15ft across the width of the church, which was half full.[228] Three private vaults belonging to the Green, Preston and Scott families contained three, five and six coffins respectively[229] and all were full. A vault 20ft by 20ft outside in the churchyard to the north of the portico was 9ft high and contained thirteen coffins. It was entered from the church and had no ventilation. A reordering of coffins took place in 1845, and the last interment was on 21 February 1853.

In January 1893 the City's Medical Officer of Health, Dr Sedgwick Saunders, closed the church and directed that 'in the interests of public Health' all human remains found beneath the floor, which was subsiding in many places to a depth of at least 6ft, should be removed. On 22 March he told the vestry that bore holes had been made and bodies were 'a short distance' below the floor. On either side of the altar about 8ft below the floor were vaults containing lead coffins, and the 'stench was very bad'. It was decided to empty the crypt of all coffins, but the faculty of 2 November exempted the remains of Bishop Coverdale. His vault was 'overlaid and surrounded by concrete so as to prevent effluvia'. As he had died 325 years earlier this seems an unnecessary precaution.

The Necropolis Company of Brookwood Cemetery quoted 15s for each case received, and pointed out that it would only need one horse to take a cart to Waterloo station, whereas two horses would be needed to travel to Ilford, where the City of London Cemetery had quoted 19s per case. Brookwood Cemetery[230] got the job, and eventually charged £366 15s 0d (£39,827). John Shepherd, builders and undertakers of No. 26 Leadenhall Street, moved 534 cases of coffins and bones at a cost of £1,586 4s 0d (£172,585).[231] I have found no record of names of those reinterred. Work was completed by March 1894: Dr Saunders wrote on the 16th saying that the vaults must be concreted as the 'subsoil is saturated with the debris of human remains'. An obelisk, now badly damaged, marks plot 87 on St George the Martyr Avenue where the remains lie (see image on page 26). Mr John McAndrews was allowed to remove the coffins of six of his family interred from 1783 to 1828 to his family vault at Nunhead, and Mr George Aston was given permission to take five of his family's coffins to his father's grave at Nunhead 'free of cost'. Also to go to Brookwood, but in separate plots, were four members of Mr John Closs's family, and fourteen of the Child family, whose coffins had been placed in the crypt in 1756 to 1846.

In August 1893 a letter arrived for the rector from Charles Gooding of Gooding's Patent Sanitary Coffin Company, Princes Street, Cavendish Square, asking to view the human remains in the crypt as he needed information on their condition. His plan was to 'practically dispose of a body in 12 months'. A coffin was lined 'with a powdered chemical preparation which absorbs the moisture and decomposing matter emanating from the body contained therein, and ultimately causing the gradual destruction of the remains … It acts as a perfect sanitary system and prevents the possibility of germs and infectious matter escaping from the coffin … Many doctors and scientists have given their unqualified approval.'[232] His offer was not accepted.

The vault running north-south towards the western end of the crypt was made a parish room by Henry Fynes-Clinton, rector 1921–59, and it still is. He assumed that the next vault to the east would also run across the width of the church, and asked permission to break through the wall and renovate it.[233] However, a number of small vaults behind brick walls were found, so only a small central vault beneath the nave was renovated to extend the existing room. Fr Fynes-Clinton offered to sell the church's sixteen Chippendale chairs valued at around £210–£270 to pay for this, but was persuaded to change his mind. Today the area is used after services as a meeting room and kitchen, and on the tiny staircase leading to it is a plaque: 'This vault was built Anno 1705.' Today the Irish Genealogical Research Society use part of the crypt to store their records.

[*] ST MARTIN WITHIN LUDGATE, LUDGATE HILL

The medieval church first mentioned in 1174 was destroyed in the Great Fire, and Wren's rebuilding, 1677–84, has given the church a graceful, slender steeple. Beneath the church are two large vaults and three smaller ones, which were reached by a staircase near the reading desk. A committee of the vestry was appointed to inspect these on 1 April 1709 to decide if more space was needed. Two years later it was decided to buy land from the Stationers' Company and build a vault 43ft by 16ft below their garden to the north of the church.[234] Burials have never been numerous; in 1768 there were only fourteen and twelve in 1803 when parishioners numbered 1,529.

In 1842 the beadle, William Ford, told the Select Committee that the church's five vaults contained 400–500 bodies which smelt in damp or hot weather. Twice he had cleared a vault to make more room, and the previous year ten cartloads of wood had been removed. He reported that wood coffins were still allowed, but strangers had to be laid in lead coffins.[235] The last interment was on January 1849.[236]

In June 1893, when the nave floor was being levelled, some human remains were found beneath, and Dr Sedgwick Saunders, the City medical officer, entered the vaults and immediately ruled that the building was unfit for worship. An Order in Council and a London diocesan faculty gave permission for the church vaults to be cleared.[237] On hearing the plans the Stationers' Company asked if the vault under their garden could also be emptied. These were in unconsecrated ground and access was only from the church vaults. The ninety-nine-year lease granted by the Company in 1711 had long expired. Work began on 14 October in the vaults below the Stationers' Company garden, and Dove Bros removed 219 boxes. Only forty-seven coffins could be identified, and these had been interred between 1773 and 1845; all except eight were nineteenth-century. Twelve lead coffins had no nameplates. Beneath the church eighty-one named coffins were found dated 1742–1848, thirty-two being eighteenth century. In all 176 boxes of bones were removed, and two coffins, one of George Hilditch, an ancestor of the only objector to the faculty, were taken by their family to Richmond Cemetery for reburial.[238] Nameplates that had become detached in all the vaults filled two boxes. All the remains were moved to plot 85, St George the Martyr Avenue in Brookwood Cemetery, Woking. A memorial cross marks the area. In 2011 the land, covered in fox holes, had sunk, and the cross was leaning over at an alarming angle, probably about to collapse.

The crypt is still empty, and can be accessed through a hatch in the church floor and by dropping down a ladder.

St Martin Ludgate. Memorial Cross, 1893, Brookwood (219 boxes from churchyard; 81 coffins and 176 cases from crypt). At the rear is the Cross of All-Hallows-the-Great and -Less, 1893. (This plot contains 146 lead coffins and 190 boxes of bones.)

[*] ST MARY-AT-HILL, LOVAT LANE

Sir Christopher Wren's church, which replaced a medieval building destroyed in the Great Fire, survived the Blitz – but the disastrous fire that broke out on 10 May 1988 did severe damage. It took eight hours to extinguish, the dome collapsed, and the volume of water used caused subsidence to the floor and much harm to the furniture and organ. The architects The Conservation Practice did a splendid restoration, and the building reopened at Christmas 1991.

A scene 'not very creditable to the parochial authorities' took place at the funeral of a murdered man, James Burdon, on 26 September 1841. It was attended by a very large crowd:

> The rush to get into the ground was tremendous … an attempt was made to lower the coffin containing the body when it was found that the grave had not been dug sufficiently capacious, or that from the extremely crowded state of the ground, some of the coffins which were to be seen piled one on the other on either side had shifted from their situation.

The coffin was placed as far in as it would go, and after the service it was drawn up and placed on the side of the grave, 'The lower part of which appeared filled with pieces of broken coffins, and human limbs partly decomposed were seen projecting across the aperture'.[239] On 21 May 1846 the crypt and churchyard were closed.

In 1850 Mr W. Lewis visited the vaults, which he found were in a 'disgraceful condition' of which the churchwardens were unaware. 'In one spot 13 coffins are piled one upon the other, many of them broken and crushed; the bones from the upper coffins dropping down among those of the lower, and mixing with them in all stages of decay, are most revolting to the senses of smell and vision.'[240] The vaults were officially closed by an Order in Council in 1859, and coffins were laid on the floor and covered with 18in of earth and 6in of powdered charcoal.

When the church closed for repairs in 1892 the City Medical Officer of Health found human remains only 6in below the church floor. He considered that the situation was 'injurious to public health', so the vaults were emptied and 3,000 bodies were taken to the South Metropolitan Cemetery in Norwood, where a small burial ground, 72ft by 63ft, was purchased for £567 (£61,006). In granting a faculty on 12 September, the chancellor gave permission to Lord de Ramsey to remove the coffins from his two family vaults.[241] All the vaults except that under the nave were then back-filled with soil.

Dr Paul Jeffrey in his *St Mary at Hill* has described how the Museum of London studied the archaeology of the site in the months following the 1988 fire. Four incomplete truncated supine Christian burials, which cannot be dated precisely, were discovered under the foundations of the south arcade, but their depth suggests that they were connected with a pre-thirteenth-century church and cemetery on this site. During the excavations a number of seventeenth- and eighteenth-century brick-built burial vaults were found under the east end of the building. The earliest of the larger chambers intended for multiple burials is that of Joshua Marshall, 1670–72, which is below the south aisle of the church. It is 7ft deep and measures 18ft by 9ft. The Great Vault of *c.*1715 was built under the centre aisle, with an entrance below the tower.[242]

The building is now shared with the Lutheran Church of St Anne.

10

OTHER CITY OF LONDON CRYPTS (CLEARED)

[T] ALL HALLOWS-THE-GREAT, UPPER THAMES STREET

Wren erected the new building in 1683, but the tower and north aisle were demolished in 1876 to widen Upper Thames Street. The tower, rebuilt that year on the south side, is all that remains of this church because it was pulled down in 1893/4.

The last burial took place on 29 January 1853. The contents of the vaults were removed in 1893–94 to Brookwood, where they rest in plot 85 on St George the Martyr Avenue: the memorial is in good order today. There were 146 lead coffins, ninety-three of which could be identified, and 190 boxes of bones. The earliest coffin was that of Theodore Jacobsen who died in 1706, and the latest was John Drew, 1848. Half were eighteenth-century interments and half nineteenth-century.[243]

ALL HALLOWS, LOMBARD STREET

The building stood on the north side of Lombard Street to the west of Gracechurch Street. First mentioned in 1053, the church was rebuilt in 1494–1516 but destroyed in the Great Fire, and was the last of Wren's churches to be built. Burial here in the 1830s was expensive – around £15 (£1,450) in church under the aisles or churchwardens' pew.

The church was demolished and the site sold in 1937–38. The human remains from the vaults – which included one for the rector – and churchyards to the north and south[244] were reinterred in the City of London Cemetery in a plot 35ft by 19ft, where a memorial by Jabez Druitt was erected (see page 113). Lead coffins were found under the aisles but a large number were found in a large brick vault at the west end of the building. Some were in a bad state, but all were placed in wooden boxes painted black, pitched inside, with charcoal at the bottom and sides; forty-eight

All Hallows. Father Time and the Grim Reaper. A wooden archway leading to the churchyard, 1693, was topped by statues of these two gentlemen.

coffins were identified, the earliest being two dated 1735 and the latest 1848. One was made of very light sheet copper. 'A vast number of bones and skulls' were also found, which suggested that the men and women were tall and well built. Sets of teeth were in very good condition. Two flights of steps, one leading to the north door and one to the body of the church, had been sealed.[245] Another 153 cases containing bones and coffins were removed from the churchyards at a total cost of £7,983 (£455,031).[246]

The white stone, 104ft tower was rebuilt at All Hallows Twickenham, which also received the seventeenth-century reredos, the eighteenth-century

All Hallows. Father Time. The arch is now in All Hallows Twickenham.

furnishings and the wooden gate to the churchyard, which is approximately 12ft high with columns each side decorated with carvings of bones, skulls and hourglasses. Dated 1693, it is topped by statues of the Grim Reaper with his scythe and Old Father Time.

[T] ALL HALLOWS, STAINING, MARK LANE.

First mentioned in 1177, its name may have been derived from the land on which it was built being owned by the manor of Staines. The church survived the Great Fire, but in 1671 it collapsed because of excessive burials[247] – the sexton who was digging close to the wall narrowly escaped with his life. It was rebuilt three years later, but was demolished in 1870 except for the fifteenth-century tower. The Clothworkers' Company purchased the church site in 1871 on the understanding that they were responsible for the upkeep of the tower and churchyard of 773sq.yds.

The bodies in the rector's vault were reinterred in a vault in the graveyard, and the others were taken to the City of London Cemetery. Below the 70ft-high tower, which stood at the south-west of the building, is a Transitional Norman crypt of c.1300 brought here by the Clothworkers' Company in 1873 from the former Lambe's Chapel in Monkwell Street.

[T] ST ALBAN, WOOD STREET

Wren's fine sturdy tower is now on a traffic island close to the City police station near Guildhall. First mentioned in 793, the church, standing on the east side of the street at the corner of Little Love Lane, was rebuilt in 1682–85 by Wren after the Great Fire. The building was destroyed in 1940 and demolished in 1955. All human remains from the church and churchyard, which was to the north and east of the tower, were taken to the City of London Cemetery in 1962. There were 130 cases of unidentified bones, and twelve cases containing lead coffins and named remains dating from 1783 to 1844.[248]

[T] ST ALPHEGE, LONDON WALL

On the north of today's road London Wall are the sad-looking remains of the tower, north transept and crossing of the first St Alphege church. This was demolished in 1923. The Ecclesiastical Commissioners agreed to the scheme, but the congregation insisted that the steeple, porch and vestry remain, because the rector would lose £1,200 p.a. in tithes from local warehouses if the building disappeared completely.[249]

As there were bodies beneath and around the building, a public notice was issued asking for relatives to come forward. Only one reply was received – from Charles Hayward, who lived near Honiton in Devon. He claimed the remains of an ancestor whose monument was in the church, Sir Rowland Hayward, and these were transported to St Michael's, Owliscombe, Devon. The rest were packed in twelve cases and in 1920 taken to the City of London Cemetery which charged 35*s* per case. The new vault there cost £84 13*s* 1*d* (£4,301).

ST ANTHOLIN, WATLING STREET

The medieval church, first mentioned *c.*1119, was destroyed in the Great Fire and replaced by Wren in 1678/82 with one of his finest buildings. The vaults were used for interments but there were only seven between 1849 and 1852.

The building was destroyed in 1875 to make way for Queen Victoria Street, although the majority of the site was not used. Some bodies were taken from the churchyard in 1875 to the City of London Cemetery where an obelisk marks the place of burial to the north of Central Avenue, and some were moved to the rector's vault, which had to be enlarged.[250] Other remains were interred in plot 70, south of St Agnes Avenue in Brookwood Cemetery. The marker here is incomplete as one section suggests it was erected on 29 December 1880. The memorial in 2012 was a heap of stones.

Henry Wright visited the churchyard which remained in 1882 to find it 'a public rubbish dump', and fourteen years later Mrs Holmes writes 'very little left except one great vault'.[251] This was only 12sq.ft on Sise Lane and was sold in 1955 to property developers and the proceeds given to St Stephen Walbrook.[252]

ST BENET, GRACECHURCH STREET

First mentioned in 1181, St Benet was repaired in 1630–33 and destroyed in the Great Fire. Wren rebuilt it in 1681–87. The building stood on the east side of the street at its junction with Fenchurch Street. It was a small parish with only fifty houses and 429 inhabitants in 1800. The church was deconsecrated on 8 February 1867 and demolished to widen Fenchurch Street. The human remains below the church could not be reinterred in the churchyard because it was full, so they were taken to the City of London Cemetery and £2,104 6*s* 8*d* (£199,484) was paid to the undertakers and the cemetery. A list was prepared of the 235 coffins dating from 1730 to 1842 in the vaults, which included those of a rector, the Revd Dr George Gaskin, who died in 1826, and his wife Elizabeth, who died in 1813. Seven bodies were interred in the rector's vault, nineteen under the chancel and one in Mingey's vault. The churchwardens ordered that 'distinct coffins' in a good state should be moved 'in decent mourning carriages' and be placed in the catacombs. Other remains were deposited in black elm shell coffins and laid in the earth at the cemetery.[253]

ST GEORGE, BOTOLPH LANE.

First mentioned in 1180, St George was repaired in 1627 but destroyed in the Great Fire. Wren used rubble from the old St Paul's to rebuild it in 1674. The building, which stood on the west side of the lane, was declared unsafe in 1903 and demolished the following year. The coffins and remains in the vaults were taken to Brookwood Cemetery by the London Necropolis Company and a handsome obelisk of blue Aberdeen granite marks the site – plot 85 (see page 184).[254]

ST KATHARINE COLEMAN, FENCHURCH STREET

Probably built by a Mr Coleman sometime before 1346, this church escaped the Great Fire and was rebuilt by James Horne in 1739 – 'most ugly and inelegant' according to George Godwin.[255] The large vaults beneath it were originally not used, because burials only took place in the churchyard which was then extensive. The building was closed during the First World War; then a poll of parishioners revealed that seventy-eight wanted the building demolished and twenty-seven were against. It was decided to sell the site and the wardens wrote to the Ecclesiastical Commissioners regretting the delay because 'City values are declining'.[256] The building was demolished in 1925.

Messrs Dove Bros removed the human remains for £1,173 2s 6d (£56,445); there were 218 cases interred in thirty graves at the City of London Cemetery. In the crypt the workmen dug down 11ft 6in, and the work was completed on 6 November 1922. There was no chancel vault, but eighty-one coffins with their names were found in the rest of the crypt, with another six in Arthur Tite's vault. In total forty-nine coffin plates were found, and nearly all the coffins and bones were from the nineteenth century.[257]

St Katharine Coleman. City of London Cemetery, Celtic cross, 1921 (the site contains 218 cases of bones from the vaults).

[T] ST MARTIN ORGAR, MARTIN LANE

A few yards to the south of St Clement Eastcheap is the tower of St Martin Orgar, all that survives of the church that replaced the medieval building in 1666. The congregation moved to St Clement's, and Huguenots worshipped here for 150 years until the building came down in 1820.[258] They had their own burial vault beneath the church and ten interments are recorded in it between 1813 and 1820. Other vaults were used by St Clement, Eastcheap – the rector's, the Great and Corner vaults and one under the vestry. A faculty of 26 January 1825 giving permission for the building to be demolished ordered that the vaults beneath be preserved as a burial place. In 1986 a Faculty was issued so that Necropolis Ltd could remove the human remains in 'fresh wooden shells' or other suitable containers to the East London Cemetery.

ST MARTIN OUTWICH, THREADNEEDLE STREET

Situated on the west side of Bishopsgate at the south-east corner of Threadneedle Street, this was first mentioned in 1216. Cobb thinks that the name comes from the Oteswich family. Rebuilt in 1403, it survived the Great Fire but burnt down in 1765, and was rebuilt with an oval interior by S.P. Cockerell. Burial was in the north or south vaults of the church or in the churchyard, which closed on 6 December 1853, and the church was demolished in 1874. The human remains were taken to the City of London Cemetery. One vault contained a family all over 7ft tall.[259] There were 110 coffins dating from 1722 to 1848, of which forty-one had no identification. The rector's vault yielded sixteen, the north vault forty-five and the south vault twenty. The rest were in 'The ground of the church'. There were sixty-five cases of bones and fifteen coffins were removed by the families.[260]

[T] ST MARY SOMERSET, UPPER THAMES STREET/LAMBETH HILL

First mentioned in 1335, the church stood on the north side of Upper Thames Street. Its name comes from a local wharf, Somershithe. Repaired in 1624, it was destroyed in the Great Fire and rebuilt by Wren in 1686–95. Malcolm was unimpressed by the parish and found 'nothing remarkable for the gratification of the senses, either in domestic, public or ecclesiastical architecture, nor are the streets and courts pleasant or comfortable'.[261] The last service was held on 1 February 1867 and the building was demolished, except for the tall Portland stone tower.

St Mary Somerset and St Mary Mounthaw. City of London Cemetery, Gothic house tomb, 1868, with a list of interments on the side.

In 1867 Wadham College asked if they might have the bones of a former warden, Gilbert Ironside, Bishop of Hereford, who was interred here in 1701, but eventually they were taken to the lady chapel of Hereford Cathedral.[262] While removing bodies from the interior of the church, the foundations of the earlier church were discovered.[263] The human remains from here now lie to the north of Central Avenue in the City of London Cemetery. The monument there is a Gothic house tomb with a list of interments on it.

ST MARY MAGDALENE, OLD FISH STREET/KNIGHTRIDER STREET

A twelfth-century church, it was destroyed in the Great Fire and rebuilt by Wren. In the seven years 1798–1804, when there were 521 parishioners, there were 147 burials, only four of which were in the vaults. The last interment was on 10 July 1853. In 1845 R.H. Barham, author of *The Ingoldsby Legends*, was buried in the rector's vault. Damaged by fire on 2 December 1886, the church was demolished and the site was compulsorily purchased to construct Queen Victoria Street. The human remains are in the Great Northern London Cemetery.[264]

ST MICHAEL, CROOKED LANE, FISH STREET HILL

First mentioned in 1271, the church was burnt in the Great Fire and rebuilt by Wren in 1684–89. In 1817 the vestry ordered that coffins interred in church or in the New Vault had to be lead or copper properly soldered – lead 5lb to the foot and copper 1lb. The building had to be demolished in 1831 to make way for King William Street, the new approach road to London Bridge. When the church was demolished coffins from the vaults were taken to St Martin Orgar, St Peter Cornhill or St Clement Eastcheap.[265]

ST MICHAEL QUEENHYTHE, UPPER THAMES STREET

The building stood on the north side of the street between Huggin Hill and Little Trinity Lane. First mentioned in the twelfth century, its name may come from a hythe, a haven for unloading ships. Burnt in the Great Fire and rebuilt by Wren in 1676–77, it was demolished in 1876. There were 330 coffins, 1712-1850, of which 205 had no breastplates, removed from the crypt to a vault in the churchyard. Eleven lead coffins, 1791–1850, of the Randell family were found in their vault below the eastern end of the building. Six coffins of the Wilcox family, five lead ones of the Toppitt family and seven lead coffins of the Jarvis family were removed from their vaults. Five coffins went to Petersham and five Smith coffins went to Brompton Cemetery.[266] The site was compulsorily purchased by the City Corporation in 1969 and the human remains were reinterred at Ilford.

ST MICHAEL, WOOD STREET

First mentioned in 1170, this church stood on the west side of the street. Stow says that the head of James IV of Scotland was buried here. After being slain at Flodden Field in September 1513, his body encased in lead was taken to Sheen monastery in Surrey. When this was dissolved at the Reformation, Stow saw the body 'thrown into a waste room amongst the old timber and other rubble … workmen for their foolish pleasure hewed off his head'. Launcelot Young brought it to St Michael's where the sexton buried it in the charnel house.[267]

St Michael. Brookwood Cemetery, memorial, 1894, and enclosure.

The church was burnt in the Great Fire and rebuilt by Wren 1670–75. It was one of his cheapest and plainest buildings, but the delighted parishioners gave him a dinner in 1672 and a gift of £15 15s 0d, which was repeated on completion. Vaults were built under the church including a rector's under the chancel. Bodies were placed beneath the three aisles, north, south and middle, and a new vault 7ft by 5ft was dug in 1820 for William Hayter, a Goldsmith, between the south and middle aisles 'for the sole use of him and his family'.[268] The church was demolished in 1894 and the human remains taken to plot 85 in Brookwood Cemetery. The memorial, which is in good order, records that those buried 1559–1853 in St Michael's are reinterred in the enclosure.

ST MILDRED, POULTRY

First mentioned in 1175, it stood on the north side of Poultry. The church was burnt in the Great Fire and rebuilt by Wren in 1670–76, the tower being added in the early eighteenth century. The parishioners of St Mary Colechurch, whose building was not rebuilt, unsuccessfully objected to joining St Mildred's parish because it was noisy and disturbed by carts and coaches, and 'wants sufficient place for burials'. There were three main vaults beneath St Mildred's which received the majority of interments in the eighteenth century – vestry, great and chancel. Several bodies from here in the late seventeenth century were taken to the Bethlem Ground known as the New Churchyard.

In 1691–92 there were thirty-two burials (thirty in the vaults) and in 1725–26 there were twenty-five (thirteen in the vaults). This is a very high number of intramural interments. In 1872 the building was demolished and human remains were taken to the City of London Cemetery, where there is a Celtic cross monument to the north of Central Avenue marking the site.

[T] ST OLAVE, OLD JEWRY

Today one approaches Wren's tower (topped by the sailing ship weather vane from St Mildred, Poultry) through a well-kept narrow strip of churchyard in Ironmonger Lane, and at its door one realises that it is the entrance to a modern

St Mildred, Poultry, Celtic cross, 1872.

office block. This church on the west side of Old Jewry was first mentioned in 1181 and the churchyard, which was 306sq.yds in the 1840s, lay to the south. Restored in the seventeenth century, the building was destroyed in the Great Fire and rebuilt by Wren in 1670–76. Fees in c.1820 varied from around £11 (£900) for the chancel, vestry and parish vaults, and £1 3s 6d for burial in the churchyard.[269] Non-parishioners were charged double.

St Olave's nave was demolished in 1888,[270] and the tower was incorporated into a new building which was changed to offices in 1986. The human remains, consisting of 216 coffins and 279 cases of bones, were taken in 1888 from the vaults and the churchyard to the City of London Cemetery by Mr John Shepherd, an undertaker of No. 55 Bishopsgate Street. In the rector's (chancel) vault there were sixty-one coffins, including that of the Revd Dr Samuel Shepherd and his family; there were also twenty from the vestry vault and thirty-five from 'The right hand vault'. The Frederick family's vault with twenty-seven coffins, 1610–1799, contained baronets, an admiral, a judge and Sir Humphrey Weld, Lord Mayor, 1608.

ST PETER-LE-POER, OLD BROAD STREET

On the west side of the street, it was known until the sixteenth century as St Peter de Bradstrete. First mentioned in 1181, it was rebuilt in 1540 and escaped serious damage in the Great Fire. It was rebuilt as a circular church with vaults beneath by

Jesse Gibson, 1788–92. In 1801 there were 867 parishioners, and Malcolm observed that there were 'few districts within the City of London so rich, or where more excellent houses may be found as I believe the parish to be almost destitute of poor persons'.[271] There was no churchyard in 1850 when interments in the vaults were only one each year. The building was demolished in 1907 and the human remains were reinterred in the City of London Cemetery by the London Necropolis Company who charged £217 10s 0d (£22,106). They identified 132 coffins dating from 1711 to 1853, including seven members of churchwarden Edward Vaux's family and nine of the Tessier family.[272]

ST STEPHEN, COLEMAN STREET

First mentioned in 1214, the parish suffered greatly during the Great Plague. Defoe in his *Memoirs of the Plague* tells of John Hayward, the under sexton, who 'went with Dead-Cart and Bell to fetch the dead-bodies from the houses where they lay'. The parish had a great number of tiny alleys so he had to use a hand barrow to take them to the carts. He 'never had the distemper at all but lived about 20 years after it and was sexton of the parish at the time of his death'. The church was rebuilt by Wren in 1674–76 after the Great Fire. The funeral of Lady Hodge in May 1717 was particularly splendid. Malcolm states that the 'chief mourners had seven train bearers, the hearse had 32 branches with wax candles and 500 torches lighted the lady to the grave'. As she was Spanish the Spanish ambassador attended with his suite, and there were 300 coaches of friends.

The parish was populous and had 3,225 inhabitants in 1801. The Select Committee of 1842 was told by the parish clerk that forty to fifty burials took place each year, either in the churchyard, where there was a common vault for the lower classes, or below the building in the vaults, where the best vault was under the belfry. The chancel vault belonged to the vicar,[273] where in 1827 an interment cost £7 14s 6d (£626) with £5 extra for a lead coffin.[274] In 1835–41 the churchwardens received an average of £35 (£3,019) per year in burial fees. In a debate in the Common Council, 23 September 1846, on intramural burial, St Stephen's graveyard was described as paved, 'but effluvia escapes through holes in the tombstones'. Having been bombed in 1940, the building was demolished and the site sold.

ST SWITHIN LONDON STONE, CANNON STREET

First mentioned in 1420, a Roman milestone was set in the wall of the church, which stood at the south-west corner of St Swithin's Lane. Wren in 1677–81 used the stones of the burnt-out building to erect a new church with an octagonal dome and a walled churchyard. Burial was in the chancel, the long or the north vault, and the cloisters, or in the churchyard which stood on the opposite side of Salters

Hall Court. The building was bombed in 1940, and the site sold in about 1960. In February 1958 the human remains from the church and churchyard were taken to Brookwood Cemetery and reburied in plot 70, south of St Agnes Avenue. The memorial is in good condition.

ST THOMAS CHAPEL, LONDON BRIDGE

Dedicated to St Thomas of Canterbury, this was erected over the central pier (ninth from the north) of the first stone bridge – jutting out on its east side – in 1176–1209. It had an entrance from the river as well as from the street and was reached by a newel staircase at the south-west corner. It was 60ft long, 29ft wide and 110ft high with a vaulted crypt beneath it, in which Peter de Colechurch, the bridge builder, was buried.[275] It was closed in 1548, then used as a house and a store until it was demolished in 1757, when George Dance and Sir Robert Taylor removed the houses on the bridge and replaced the two central arches with a single navigation span. The bones in the undercroft were tipped into the river.

[*] ST VEDAST-ALIAS-FOSTER, FOSTER LANE

Known in the sixteenth century as St Foster's, it is possible that Vedast and Foster are the same word.[276] First mentioned in 1170, it was rebuilt in 1519 but destroyed in the Great Fire, and Wren's building of 1700 was bombed in 1941. It was restored by Stephen Dykes-Bower, who added a rectory and colonnaded cloister on the site of the burial ground to the north.

In 1724 the chancellor defined the 'Minister's Ground', which 'should contain 340 sq ft on each side of the communion table to extend Westward as far as the first pew but not to be in the middle aisle'.[277]

In 1850 Dr Waller Lewis visited St Vedast and reported that the vault under the church containing 200 lead coffins was in 'a tolerable condition', but that the three vaults under the churchyard were not. Damp had caused the 200–300 coffins there to disintegrate, so that only the bottom and one side of each remained, and 'The contents, black and rotting, lie around'. Usually the sexton regularly removed the remains to the cellar of a nearby house but this had not been done.[278] This was just as well because the room above was used by the school of a nearby parish.

In 1881 all the pews and furniture had to be removed so that the coffins in the crypt could be taken to the City of London Cemetery. All empty vaults and walled graves were then filled with fresh dry earth and charcoal, and the floor of the church was covered with a layer of concrete, 9in thick.[279]

11

Other City of London Crypts
💀 (Uncleared) 💀

[*] ALL HALLOWS, LONDON WALL, NO. 83 LONDON WALL

George Dance the Younger called this building his 'first child' when he designed it in 1765–67 to replace a medieval church that had escaped the Great Fire. In the mid-1840s the rector of Bishopsgate considered that the rectory house, situated on the north side of London Wall and built on the old churchyard, was uninhabitable because of 'The noisome vapours with which the air is loaded'. The small churchyard to the east and west of the building closed on 6 December 1853.

[*] ST ANDREW-BY-THE-WARDROBE, QUEEN VICTORIA STREET

First mentioned in about 1244, the building received its name from the nearby King's Wardrobe at Blackfriars.[280] The church was destroyed in the Great Fire and rebuilt by Wren in 1685–95. According to Malcolm Kimber, formerly of Necropolis Ltd, a small number of coffins were removed from the crypt in the 1970s, but the rest are presumably still there.

[*] ST ANDREW UNDERSHAFT, LEADENHALL STREET

First mentioned as St Andrew, Cornhill in 1147, its present name refers to a large maypole erected each year here in the fifteenth century. The rebuilt church of 1520 escaped the Great Fire. In the 1840s the graveyard, which stood 2ft above the pavement, was 265sq.yds. In 1842 curate Henry Knapp occupied the rectory, and told the Select Committee he could not open the windows in summer because of the stench. In the burial ground there was an 'accumulated mass of bodies and matter decomposed and in a putrescent state with abominable exhalations … When performing a funeral

I stood at some distance from the grave because of the exhalations.' A great stench also came from a vault in church, so an entrance was made from outside where the churchyard is 3 or 4ft above the level of the church. He assured the committee that 10 tons of lead had been removed from the vaults, and that bones from there had been buried in a charnel house.[281] A plan of 1853[282] shows a vault under the south-east of the building, and other coffins presumably remain under the church.

[*] ST ANNE AND ST AGNES, GRESHAM STREET

First mentioned in 1137, the church was rebuilt in 1548, and Wren rebuilt it again after the Great Fire. In 1718 the vestry minutes noted that burial fees would be increased because 'soon there will be no room for interments'.[283] In 1763 the fee for burial beneath the altar or in Sir John Drag's vault was £5 (£840), but in the poor ground it was 3s 6d. Badly damaged in 1940, it was rebuilt by Braddock and Martin-Smith, 1963–68. It is now the Gresham Centre, home of the vocal ensemble Voices 8.

[*] ST BARTHOLOMEW-THE-LESS, WEST SMITHFIELD

This has been a parish church and chaplaincy of St Bartholomew's Hospital since c.1184. A plan of the precincts dated 1617 has a 'church-yarde for ye poore', where the present west wing stands,[284] and part is now below the paved courtyard. Ogilby and Morgan's map of 1677 shows a churchyard adjacent to the church now tarmacked over, and also four burial grounds.

In 1966 some human remains were discovered in the hospital grounds halfway between King Edward Street and Giltspur Street, close to the boundary with the post office. This had been the burial ground of Christ Church, Greyfriars, Newgate Street, which was bought by the hospital from the governors of Christ's Hospital in 1902. The remains were taken to Brookwood Cemetery by Necropolis Ltd.[285] The church was practically rebuilt by Thomas Hardwick in 1823. After being damaged in the Second World War, it reopened in 1956. Very little is known about the vaults.

[*] ST BENET, PAUL'S WHARF, UPPER THAMES STREET

The early twelfth-century building was destroyed in the Great Fire and Wren's dark red-brick replacement of 1677–83 can still be seen. In 1801 there were 620 parishioners but in 1811 the two vaults under the church were insufficient for the parish needs, so two new vaults were constructed – one in the churchyard and one under the building. At intervals of ten years these were cleared 'of thoroughly decayed portions of their contents', but by 1837 the churchyard vault was considered 'dangerous to the health of the inhabitants of the neighbourhood'. The entrance to it was always opened the night before an interment 'to permit the escape of the pestilential vapours therein'. On 26 November 1846 the vestry decided to ask counsel for legal advice as to whether they could close the vaults.[286] On 3 December Dr J. Lee's opinion was received, doubting that the human remains could be moved and advising that the rector, who was out of town, must be consulted as the freeholder. He could object to closure if there was 'no public nuisance', but it would be wise if incumbent and vestry could act together in the interests of public health.

The building was scheduled for demolition under the Union of City Benefices Act of 1860, but nineteen years later became the Metropolitan Welsh Church in London, which it remains.

[*] ST CLEMENT EASTCHEAP, CLEMENT'S LANE

The medieval St Clement's, first mentioned in 1067, was repaired in 1632 but destroyed in the Great Fire. The parishioners were so pleased by Wren's rebuilding, 1683–87, that they sent him a third of a hogshead of wine. Between February 1813 and 1853 there were 484 interments in St Clement and St Martin Orgar, eighty-five of which were in St Clement's vaults, which included the Little, Rector's, North and that under the vestry.[287] Damaged in the Blitz, the church is today 'a modest little church which, from its unpretentiousness, is just the sort of place that gets destroyed by administrators'.[288]

[*] ST EDMUND THE KING, LOMBARD STREET

First mentioned in the twelfth century, it was destroyed in the Great Fire and rebuilt by Wren and Robert Hooke. Most interments were in the churchyard, but there were twenty-six burials in the chancel vault between 1805 and the closure in 1851. Among them in 1835 was Susan Horne, aged 15, daughter of the rector. He later obtained a faculty to move her in a new outside coffin to Nunhead Cemetery, where his wife was interred.[289]

[*] ST ETHELBURGA WITHIN BISHOPSGATE

The smallest of the City churches, this medieval building was reduced to a shell in 1993 by a massive IRA bomb, but the paved churchyard garden survived. In 1849 the rector noted that 'Nearly all interments were in the tiny churchyard but occasionally some were interred in the vaults'. Two years later the register records: 'John Jones aged 39 of Bishopsgate died of the cholera on 23 August 1849 as did several other parishioners and residents in the immediate neighbourhood. It was decided advisable that the churchyard be closed. John Rodwell Rector, Sept 4 1849.'[290] The church is now a Centre for Reconciliation and Peace.

[*] ST KATHERINE CREE, LEADENHALL STREET

In early records this is frequently referred to as the 'church or chapel of St Katherine' within the churchyard of Holy Trinity which, founded in 1107, was one of the most important religious houses in England. Its Augustinian canons allowed parishioners to worship in their huge church, but confusion over service times led the laity to build their own church of St Katherine on the cemetery in 1280, and only attend the priory on special occasions. The church was rebuilt in 1504 and the priory was dissolved

St Katharine Cree. An investigation of the south-east corner of the crypt in 2011 revealed these coffins and passages.

and destroyed in 1531, although an arch and wall survive in an office block at the corner of Leadenhall and Mitre streets. St Katherine's was rebuilt in 1630 and consecrated by Archbishop Laud the following year.

The vaults below the church, which are reached through a trapdoor at the south-east of the building, are still full of coffins and there are no plans to remove them. In 2004 John Ewington, the organist, reported that there are a lot of lead coffins which are stacked in threes. The three nearest to the entrance have somehow fallen on each other and it would be tricky to put a ladder down without causing them to topple over. Halfway down the length of the building it is bricked up floor to ceiling.

In October 2011 HMDW Architects Ltd investigated the crypt and suggested that under the north aisle there may be usable space except for the north-west corner where coffins may be found, and under the south aisle there seems also to be usable space of at least three metres in height except for a crypt at the south-east corner containing coffins. No investigation has been undertaken under the nave or sanctuary, the largest area of the floor plan.

[*] ST MARGARET LOTHBURY

First mentioned in 1197, the church was rebuilt in 1440. The Great Fire destroyed it and Wren's rebuilding took place 1686–90. In 1781 by an Act of Parliament the Bank of England purchased the site of the demolished St Christopher le Stocks on condition that they would provide a new burial place when needed. The parish was united with St Margaret and its parishioners were buried in St Margaret's churchyard. By 1825 this churchyard was overcrowded, so on 17 May the vestry asked the bank to buy 'an ancient messuage' belonging to St Margaret adjoining their churchyard on the north-east corner. This building stood in Tokenhouse Yard on the site of the old vestry room, and could be 'converted into a vault' or 'mausoleum'. After negotiations the bank agreed to pay £760 (£70,657) for it, and the Bishop of London consecrated the new vault on 29 May 1829.[291]

[*] ST MARGARET PATTENS, ROOD LANE

First mentioned in 1216, the church was rebuilt in 1530 and repaired in 1614. It was destroyed in the Great Fire and rebuilt by Wren 1684-87. Between 1710 and 1719 there were 160 interments, 103 of which were in the church and twelve with no position given. The registers mention the vaults of Sir Joshua Martin and Sir Peter Delme.

[*] ST MARY ABCHURCH, ABCHURCH YARD

This tiny church, hidden away behind King William Street, is a delight as it has hardly changed since Wren built it with a central dome in 1681–86. At the end of the

Second World War a large flagstone which had been dislodged in the churchyard to the south was lifted, and two vaults were discovered underneath. One, which is domed, is under the pews and has a tablet dated 1690. This is connected by an arch now bricked up to another vault, possibly fourteenth century, which is under the churchyard close to the building. This outer vault, about 12ft square and 10ft high, is reached by lifting a grill in the south aisle under which is a narrow stone staircase. The vault is empty, but a wall plaque directs that only lead coffins may be interred, so almost certainly there are other vaults beneath the church.

[*] ST MARY ALDERMARY, QUEEN VICTORIA STREET

Perhaps the name means that it is an older church than the nearby St Mary Bow. Founded in the eleventh century, the church was restored by Wren after the Great Fire. The vaults beneath the church extend from north to south for the entire breadth and are under the porch and the chancel. In 1813 the chancel vault cost £17 5s 6d (£998) but most funerals cost around £1 10s 0d (£86) with the minister receiving 4s.[292]

After burials ended the churchwardens were instructed in November 1858 by the Burial Act Office to put all the coffins in the vaults on the floor and cover them with 18in of soil and 6in of powdered charcoal. The ventilation openings were to be bricked up and replaced by a tube to the roof. They replied that this was impracticable as the coffins were piled up to the ceiling, but had to comply as best they could following an Order in Council.[293]

[*] ST MICHAEL CORNHILL

On the south side of Cornhill, the church was first mentioned in 1055. The building, except for the fifteenth-century tower, was burnt in the Great Fire and rebuilt by Wren. The church vaults are sealed.

[*] ST MICHAEL PATERNOSTER ROYAL, COLLEGE HILL

First mentioned in 1219, royal is a corruption of Reole, a local street inhabited by wine merchants. Richard Whittington rebuilt the church at his expense in 1409, and when he died in 1423 Stow says that he was buried there 'under a fair monument', but in the reign of Edward VI the parson, 'thinking some great riches to be buried with him', dug him up. He was reburied, but disturbed twice more before being allowed to rest. In 1949 an unsuccessful attempt was made to find his tomb, but only a mummified cat was discovered. The building was burnt down in the Great Fire and rebuilt by Wren in 1689–94. There is a small basement area used as a kitchen, lavatories and store beneath the tower and west end of the building, and presumably the rest of the vaults still contain coffins.[294]

[*] ST NICHOLAS COLE ABBEY, QUEEN VICTORIA STREET

Never an abbey, its title derives from the medieval 'coldharbour', a shelter for travellers. On the south side of Knightrider Street, it was first mentioned in 1144 and the first mass of Queen Mary's reign was held here. It is recorded that the priest, who would now have to be celibate, sold his wife to a butcher and was pelted with eggs as a result.[295] According to Strype, it was the first church to be rebuilt by Wren after the Great Fire and was completed in 1677. The church lost most of its burial ground to the south of the church when Queen Victoria Street was laid out in 1868, and the human remains were taken to the Great Northern London Cemetery. On 11 May 1941 the building was gutted by fire bombs, but it was restored to Wren's design in 1962. There are vaults, but it is thought that they are filled with rubble. The church is now a national centre for Religious Education, and the Culham Institute is based here.

[*] ST PETER, CORNHILL

On the south side of Cornhill, it was first mentioned in 1040, although it was allegedly founded on the site of the Roman basilica by Lucius, the first Christian King of Britain in AD 179.[296] The building was destroyed in the Great Fire and rebuilt by Wren in 1677–78. When a new support base was installed for the nave floor in 1990 the architect reported 'a large number of burials', but these were not disturbed.

[*] ST SEPULCHRE-WITHOUT-NEWGATE, HOLBORN VIADUCT

Founded by Rahere in 1137, it received its name because knights set out from here for the Crusades. It became the largest parish church in the City when it was rebuilt in 1450. The church was 'much damnified' but not destroyed by the Great Fire, which stopped at Pie Corner, a few yards to the north of the building. Wren's master mason, Joshua Marshall, was employed to rebuild it. An 1858 plan[297] of the vaults shows only the one beneath the church – at the south-east corner measuring 20ft by 15ft. It 'was said to be full'.

Today it is known as the National Musicians' Church and there is a thriving musical life.

12

NORTH WESTMINSTER

The Westminster churches with crypts, past and present, described in the next three chapters are in the archdeaconry of Charing Cross.

CHRIST CHURCH, COSWAY STREET

Built in 1822–24 and designed by Philip Hardwick, the building had vaults which were cleared after the war, but no churchyard. The burial register lists forty-seven interments between December 1826 and February 1853 when the vaults were closed. The building was closed in about 1973 and is now offices. About 100 coffins were moved from the crypt according to Malcolm Kimber, formerly of Necropolis Ltd.

HOLY TRINITY, MARYLEBONE

Built in 1824–28 and designed by Sir John Soane, the building closed in about 1942. There were only eighty-one interments in the vaults between 1832 and 1853, of which ten were in 1839. The vaults were cleared after the war. The building was used as an SPCK bookshop until 2004, and is now rented by the diocese as an art gallery and reception venue.

[*] ST JOHN, ST JOHN'S WOOD

In the early nineteenth century more burial land was needed for St Marylebone parish, so in 1808 6 acres of leafy St John's Wood were purchased by the vestry from Mr Samuel Eyre, and the total cost including building a chapel came to £13,901 (£1,039,968). Five years later Thomas Hardwick designed a chapel of ease, with houses for the minister and sexton. It had been a plague pit but was now surrounded by elegant new houses along the banks of the Regent's Canal.[298] The Bishop of

London consecrated the church and burial ground on 24 May 1814. During 1823 interments numbered 1,260, and this annual figure had nearly doubled by 1841 when the population of Marylebone totalled 136,164. The burial ground was used from 1814 to 1855 when the St Marylebone Cemetery at East Finchley was opened. There are thought to be 50,000 graves here.[299] Nearly all the undercroft has been cleared of coffins but two vaults remain. The rest of the space is used by the Crypt Club, a charity for young people. St John's chapel became a parish church in 1952.

[*] ST GEORGE, HANOVER SQUARE AND GROSVENOR CHAPEL, SOUTH AUDLEY STREET

Queen Anne's High Church piety led to the building of this church in the fields north of Piccadilly, where woodcock and snipe could still be shot in the early eighteenth century. John James, the architect, had a very restricted site to work on, which explains why there has never been a churchyard. The building was consecrated by the Bishop of London on 23 March 1724, and no other church could boast such an aristocratic congregation. Resident in the parish were nine dukes, two marquesses, twenty-two earls, six viscounts, twelve barons, one archbishop and two bishops. Until recently it was known as a venue for fashionable weddings – 'Hymen's classic Temple.'[300]

However, fashionable funerals were rare, probably because the noble families were interred not in town but on their country estates in their private mausolea. The crypt, which has four tunnels running east-west, has never contained coffins, because this was forbidden by an Act of Parliament that only applied to the 1711 churches.[301] Occasionally a coffin would be slid through the south-east door into the crypt, but its stay was only temporary. Over the years the vaults have been let to various local firms for storage, and early in the nineteenth century wine was laid down in them until the bishop objected. In 1956 Edward Arnold (Publishers) Ltd stored their books, in 1969 Chappell and Co. Ltd their music, and today a prestigious auction house has a lease to keep their records and documents there. The boiler room is at the eastern end of the crypt, reached by climbing down a rickety wooden ladder from an entrance in Maddox Street.

Sir Richard Grosvenor sold 1½ acres to the south of Mount Street in 1723 for a cemetery. The cost was £300, and seven years later he leased land on its western boundary to a building syndicate of four men led by Benjamin Timbrell to erect a chapel. The Grosvenor Chapel, originally known as the Audley Chapel, was finished in 1731, and the proprietors hired a priest, clerk, organist, organ blower, beadle and six pew-openers. These were paid by pew rents, which were around £1,000 p.a. (£187,764), and by burial fees which ranged from a few shillings for a plot in the cemetery to £6 (£1,126) for a place in the open vaults. A private vault cost £150 (£28,164).[302] The first rector of St George's, the Revd Andrew Trebeck, paid £500 (£93,882) for the freehold of the vaults; the entrance to which was at the north-east of the church. The local undertakers, whose shop was in the cul-de-sac to the north of the chapel, began to do a brisk trade.

When the ninety-nine-year lease on the chapel expired in 1829, St George's purchased the freehold of the building itself, and two years later it became a chapel of ease by Act of Parliament. On 14 June 1849 St George's vestry noted a 'want of room' in the chapel vaults, with twenty-two coffins standing at the entrance. It was decided to end burials there and make catacombs to contain twenty-two coffins.[303] On 7 December 1858 the Medical Officer of Health, Dr C.J. Aldis, told the vestry that he had visited the vaults, which were halfway under the chapel, 'and so completely filled with coffins that it was quite impossible to ascertain their condition'. If any coffin burst it would be impossible to find which it was. 'The catacombs contain a great many coffins and are situated near the passage leading to the school.'[304] The vaults were closed the following year.

The burial ground to the east of the chapel, which still exists as a garden, was well used, so it was full by 1763. Another churchyard was needed, so 4¾ acres off Bayswater Road north of Hyde Park were purchased by the vestry[305] and consecrated on 30 March 1765. Double walls were erected, allowing the ground to be patrolled with dogs. As Professor Curl has pointed out, two walls made a fast escape by bodysnatchers difficult; a sacked-up body would have been a serious impediment to a gang attacked by dogs and armed watchmen.[306] The cemetery lay to the east of Albion Street and had a chapel, caretaker's house and vestry with vaults beneath on Bayswater Road. It is approximately 1¼ miles by road from St George's. The parish was large, and by 1801 had 38,440 inhabitants. Burials ceased in 1854, and four years later Dr Aldis reported that there were 1,121 coffins in the cemetery chapel vaults 'in tiers of six or seven'. There was 'a slight unpleasant smell and many coffins were hidden from the light'.[307]

In 1968 the Revd Bill Atkins, who remained rector for forty-five years until 2000, and his wardens sold the Bayswater Cemetery. The non-profit-making Utopian Housing Society (Group One) Ltd purchased the land for £950,000 (£14 million), which was shared with the Diocese of London, and 300 dwellings were erected on the 7 acre site, from which 11,114 bodies were removed to the South London Crematorium. Only fifty-six were identifiable, the earliest of which was that of Laurence Sterne, author of *Tristram Shandy*, who was buried here on 22 March 1768. Popular belief says that his body was stolen from its grave on the evening of the burial and taken to the University of Cambridge to be sold for use in anatomy classes. However, a friend recognised the corpse when it was being dissected, and the body was returned to London.

In 1969 his skull, some of which had been sawn off and replaced (so perhaps the bodysnatcher story is true), and less than half his skeleton were discovered 10ft down close to the centre of the west wall. Television producer and Sterne enthusiast, the late Kenneth Monkman declared it to be that of Sterne. The skull was found to correspond, in its unusual length and narrowness, with the sculpted head of Sterne that had been made by his contemporary Joseph Nollekens. Under Monkman's direction the body was reburied in the graveyard of St Michael's Church, Coxwold, Yorkshire, where Sterne had been perpetual curate. His tombstone and footstone were also taken there.

The St George's Burial Board had been embarrassed by complaints about the nauseating smells emanating from the Bayswater Cemetery,[308] so when it closed in 1854 they purchased a plot of well-drained land in Uxbridge Road, Hanwell. The 12 acres were consecrated by Bishop Blomfield of London on 6 July 1854, with an appropriate ceremony followed by a cold collation and half a pint of sherry for each guest.

[*] ST-GILES-IN-THE-FIELDS, ST GILES HIGH STREET

The churchyard in this parish of 'immigration and transience' contains parishioners, Lollards, lepers and Roman Catholic martyrs. Today it has few gravestones and provides an acre of open space for business people, tourists and the homeless. Tombs snuggle against the church walls on all sides, and coffins interred in the east end of the crypt share the vaults with the heating apparatus in the centre and an unused area at the west end.

In 1101 Queen Matilda founded on this site a leper hospital dedicated to St Giles, the patron saint of outcasts, and its chapel soon began to serve local people. When the hospital was closed by Henry VIII in 1539 it continued in this role, and a rector was appointed. In 1623 a new church was built and the churchyard was greatly used at the time of the Great Plague, when 1,391 burials were recorded in one month. By 1730 'Filth and various adventitious matter' had raised the churchyard 8ft above the building's floor, and the foundations had suffered so much damage from graves being dug that a new church was needed. Designed by Henry Flitcroft, this was opened in 1734.

Dr G.A. Walker visited St Giles while he was researching his *Gatherings from Graveyards* (1839), and thought that although the church vaults were 'crowded with dead; they are better ventilated than many others'. He was not, however, impressed by the churchyard and its 'bone-houses'. He saw smashed coffins, bodies with flesh on them and drunken gravediggers hacking through coffins of recently buried children.[309]

In the 1840s St Giles had a population of 37,311. The rector, James Endell Tyler, in his evidence to the Select Committee of 1842, said that there were only six to eight interments each year in the church vaults, and the churchyard, which was 4,958sq.yds, was closed in 1805 but reopened in 1822. 'Only dry bones are there, the windows of three schools open on to it and there is no effluvia – it is a decidedly healthy spot.' In 1841 it had received 469 burials.

In 1972 the parish was transferred to the Westminster deanery and today the church serves a residential population of 4,600, providing an oasis of quiet in a busy commercial district.

ST MARK, NORTH AUDLEY STREET

Built in 1825–28 as a chapel of ease for St George Hanover Square, the church was given vaults by the architect J.P. Gandy-Deering. The burial registers record the interment of 158 coffins here until an Order in Council closed the crypt on 8 August 1853. It appears that the eastern area was filled first, then the sexton worked westwards, bay by bay. The easternmost bay, occupied at one time by a baronet who was the Governor of St Helena when Napoleon was imprisoned there, was probably bricked up in 1852.[310] The coffins were placed in the public vault, private vaults or the catacombs. In 1858 Dr Aldis, the Medical Officer of Health, reported to the vestry that there were 160 coffins in the crypt; most were on the floor, and six years earlier one had burst 'and occasioned a very offensive smell'. It was agreed to cover them with earth.[311]

The Home Office was asked for its permission to remove the coffins on 10 December 1987, because the building had been made redundant the year before; it was now vested in the London Diocesan Fund, who wanted to let it. The 1,500sq.ft space had already been let to a recording company in 1965, but they obviously could not use the sealed eastern chamber which contained coffins. These were removed to the East London Cemetery by Necropolis Ltd in June 1988, when bore holes revealed a lead coffin only 2ft beneath the floor. No other part of the floor was explored, so perhaps other coffins or remains are still there. No list of coffins removed has yet been found.[312]

Coffin cages, grilled and gated enclosures still remain at the east end of the crypt. They are rare examples of mort safes[313] and, as Dr Litten has pointed out, their construction is simple: a long side and a front gate set against the corner of the vault, its neighbour being also a long side and front gate bolted on to the original. In this way ranks were added as and when a new mort safe was required. There are four single-width and one double-width mort safe on the north side of the easternmost burial chamber, and four single-width and one double-width on the south side of the same chamber

A catafalque dating from the earliest days of the church is in a room off the north-west angle of the nave, which means that the coffin had to be taken out of the building at the end of the funeral and placed in this room; then it would descend to the crypt. It is a hand-operated mechanism, the descending platform guided by iron rollers set within the four grooved upright wooden beams at the corner of the rectangular shaft; the pulley for the rope survives. The only other catafalque in a London church was operated at St George Bloomsbury, and was more appropriately sited in front of the chancel steps. The mortuary chapel was created in a portion of the vaults in 1874 so that it could 'be used to deposit the Dead until the day of the funeral'. It has its own entrance and mourners were given a key. The cost of £200 (£19,152) was quickly raised by wealthy parishioners. The walls are covered with Parian cement and Minton tiles 'to prevent the possibility of any effluvia arising therefrom'. Most of its wall plaques record post-1852 deaths.[314] Dr Litten doubts if this chapel had much use, because by the late 1870s undertakers were providing chapels on their own premises.[315]

Gandy-Deering gave the church two entrances: the poor arrived from Balderton Street, and the wealthy through the portico, where they entered a large narrow narthex which served as a meeting place for 'The fashionable belles who embellish it at the conclusion of their devotions'.[316] It became a separate parish in 1863, and Sir Arthur Blomfield transformed the building in 1878 by creating a chancel.

The church was made redundant on 1 June 1974. The crypt can be accessed from Balderton Street at the rear of the building so could be treated separately. In July 2009 the Church Commissioners gave the go-ahead for the building to be leased to George Hammer, honouring a decision they first made in 2006. In September 2010 Robert Plant, 'one of today's rock aristocracy', and his new Band of Joy played at a 'secret gig' in the church. The *Daily Express* said that the deconsecrated church was 'still a fittingly spiritual setting for a set peppered with Gospel influenced tracks'. In 2010, despite much opposition, the building was sold on a long lease to Hammer Holdings for a rumoured £1 million, at a rumoured rent of £60,000 a year, for use as a venue.

MAYFAIR CHAPEL, CURZON STREET

Erected in 1730 in the parish of St George, this chapel had a very unconventional minister, Alexander Keith, who had moved to London from Scotland because of his belief in episcopacy. He specialised in irregular and unlicensed 'Fleet' weddings, often 6,000 each year, and the registers of St George contain around 7,000 of these, conducted by Keith and his assistants. He also officiated at many burials, and when he was excommunicated in October 1742 he excommunicated the Bishop of London and the rector of St George's in turn, saying 'I'll buy 2 or 3 acres of ground and by God I'll *underbury* them all.'[317]

While in prison, Keith seems to have had a keen eye to business. During his incarceration his wife died, and he kept her corpse embalmed and unburied for many months, and by that means advertised his trade. On 30 January 1750 the *Daily Advertiser* reported that the previous November her corpse 'was removed from her husband's house to an apothecary's in South Audley Street, where she lies in a room hung with mourning, and is to continue there till Mr. Keith can attend the funeral'. Then follows the announcement that 'marriages are still carried on as usual by another regular clergyman'.[318] The chapel closed in 1754, and Keith died a prisoner in the Fleet Prison four years later. The building was demolished in 1898.

[*] ST JOHN THE EVANGELIST, HYDE PARK CRESCENT

Charles Fowler built the church with vaults in 1832. They closed in about 1853.

[*] ST MARY, PADDINGTON GREEN

The building was erected in 1788–91 on the site of two earlier churches. In 1831 there were 451 burials including forty-three paupers, and a note records that between 1798 and 1821 there were four coffins interred in the north vault without lead.[319] The burial fees received by the wardens in 1831 were £665 6s 9d (£58,222), of which nearly a third was for gravestones and monuments.

In the early 1960s the Marylebone Flyover of the A40 was constructed and a slice of the churchyard at the south-west corner had to be compulsorily purchased. Exhumation work by Wilments Bros lasted from 9 May until 25 August 1966, the workmen digging to a depth of 15ft to remove the human remains of 708 deceased parishioners; forty-one of these from ten family vaults were reburied in the churchyard,[320] and the other 667 were taken to Mill Hill Cemetery, Milespit Hill (167 of these were identified).[321]

In 1972 the rector, John Foster, had tea with a 92-year-old parishioner who told him that Paddington Town Hall, which had stood next to the church until it was demolished, was on the site of an unused graveyard consecrated in the 1840s. The vacant land was reclaimed by the church and sold for a large sum.[322] In 1972–73 a restoration of the building by Raymond Firth and Quinlan Terry included stacking the coffins in the vaults more compactly,[323] and today the space is used as a columbarium.

13

CENTRAL WESTMINSTER

[*] ALL SOULS, LANGHAM PLACE

The church was designed by John Nash in 1822–24 and restored in the 1950s. Its crypt has never been used for interments.

HANOVER CHAPEL, REGENT STREET

Built by C.R. Cockerell under Nash's supervision, the building was consecrated on 20 June 1825. Its fine Ionic portico faced Regent Street (west side). The vaults were closed in 1858 when there were twenty-four coffins, all but two uncovered.[324] It was demolished in 1897 when Regent Street was remodelled, and the human remains were taken to plot 85 at Brookwood. A headstone in good order in 2011 records the burial. No. 235/241 Regent Street is now on the site of the church.

HOLY TRINITY, KINGSWAY

The first church, designed by Francis Bedford 1829–31, was demolished in 1909 because its foundations were undermined by the construction of the Piccadilly Line, and a dangerous structure order was served by the LCC. The crypt, which had three tunnels running east-west containing a boys' club, workshop and rifle range, only had four bricked-up vaults.[325] The human remains from these were taken to plot 85 at St George the Martyr Avenue in Brookwood, and a memorial was erected (see page 126). The new church by Belcher and Joass 1909–11 closed in 1991, and eight years later was demolished except for the façade, behind which there are now offices.

[*] ST ANNE, DEAN STREET, SOHO

After the bombing of the Admiral Duncan pub in Old Compton Street on 30 April 1999 the rector of St Anne's, Clare Herbert, invited mourners to hold a service in the church gardens which are normally used as a place to eat sandwiches and relax. Few of the large congregation realised that the lawns have thousands of former parishioners buried beneath them, which is why they are raised 6ft above Wardour Street. In 1851 it was said that during the previous twenty years there had been 13,788 burials in this ¾ acre burial ground.[326] At this time churchwarden Joseph George, a leather manufacturer in Dean Street, in opposition to his incumbent Nugent Wade, wanted to close the churchyard because of its 'reeking abominations', which probably refers to the revelations reported at the Select Committee of 1842. Bartholomew Lyons, one time gravedigger at St Anne, gave evidence 'against practices that would disgrace, if not disgust, a cannibal', such as playing games of skittles and nine-pins with bones and skulls.[327] Walker, in his lectures published five years later, mentions that Lyons had died in the meantime, and describes him as 'a miserable half putrid, walking nuisance during his life-time. After he gave his evidence he was hunted like a wild beast from graveyard to graveyard where he sought to obtain employment in his filthy avocation.'

Another former gravedigger, E.C. Copeland, related the doings of the notorious sexton, Mr Fox, who sold handles he removed from coffins. After only three weeks it was 'a common occurrence' to cut a coffin in half – 'I have seen them chopped up', said Copeland, 'before they were a quarter decayed. I felt a sort of stoppage in my throat like chewing a penny piece … I was obliged to go out and get a drop of spirits now and then.'[328]

In the early nineteenth century the parish had a large resident population, 15,600 in 1831. The three funeral day books of the parish, 1814–24, reveal that nearly half of the 8,039 burials were those of children less than 5 years of age. These figures mean that approximately 500 bodies a year had to be crammed into the churchyard. It was in everyone's interest that decomposition should be swift, so that bones could be removed and placed in the bone-house to make more room. A note appeared in one of the three books: 'NO, No Corpse suffered to be interred in the Church and Vaults, unless enclosed in a Leaden Coffin, and no Corpse allowed in either of the Church Yards in any but a Wooden Coffin.'[329] The three books show that 'convulsions' and 'inflammation' caused a quarter of the deaths, as did 'decline', which was probably consumption; ninety-seven women died from childbirth during the period.

Carved out of the parish of St Martin-in-the-Fields, St Anne's was consecrated on 21 March 1685/6. The building had a basilican plan and the architect might have been Sir Christopher Wren or William Talman, who probably added the spire in 1714. A new watchhouse with a first-floor vestry room was erected in 1801, having a frontage of 36ft on Dean Street, with a cellar containing three vaults; northern and central for burials and southern for storing fuel. A fire engine house stood next door. By 1856 the watch house was occupied by the police, but the Secretary of State for the Home Department reluctantly agreed that it could be the first mortuary in London, so the police handed over the keys that March. An additional small building was erected on 3 April at the rear of the watch house in the churchyard, also to lodge dead bodies. In 1892 rector Cardwell suggested to his parishioners in his magazine that if they had no space at home when a death occurred they could bring the corpse to the mortuary, whence it could be taken as soon as possible to 'The porous soil at Brookwood'. To avoid expense he considered that it would be a good idea to order 'a readily perishable inexpensive coffin of hardened pulp', which could be obtained from the Necropolis Company.

On 25 August vestry members wrote to Lord Palmerston congratulating him that the 1852 Act discontinued 'The burying of the dead in the midst of the living', and on 9 February 1854 they talked to various cemetery companies telling them they would need 325 interments each year, including forty-nine paupers. Kensal Green asked for 600 guineas per acre, Victoria Park Cemetery offered a portion costing £15,000 (£1.4 million) for exclusive use, and Brookwood said only fees would be charged, the land being free.[330] The new St Anne's Burial Board, the first in London and appointed by the vestry on 22 June, met on 20 July 1854. The members not surprisingly decided the following February to purchase two plots at Brookwood, 1 acre in the Nonconformist area, and 2 acres in the Anglican area. Today they are neglected and forgotten. As a consequence of the 1975 Brookwood Cemetery Act part of plot 1 is now used by the Said family.

On 14 May 1909 the rector was given permission by the chancellor to clear the remains from the vault under the south aisle of the church so that the space could be used for a boys' club and other parochial purposes. Presumably the bones were taken to the parish plot at Brookwood. Only the tower survived two horrendous air raids in September and October 1940, so the congregation now had to worship in the chapel of the Upper Room on the first floor of St Anne's House, Dean Street, which survived the raids. In the 1970s the diocese of London was anxious to sell the valuable site and use the monies to build new churches in the suburbs, but the provisions of the 1965 St Anne Soho Act demanded that the churchwardens should agree. Fortunately Mr Tim Miller and Mr Bryan Burrough were not willing to give their consent, so after prolonged negotiations between the congregation, the diocese, the Soho Society and the Soho Housing Association a new development of church, rectory, community centre, shops and offices was built, being opened on 26 July 1991. The complex, which also contains twenty flats, was by the Westwood Partnership (Jan Piet and Julian Luckett).

For forty-three years the site of the church and the yards to the east of the tower had been derelict. Beneath the church was the empty south vault, together with the north vault and the chancel vault, both of which had been crushed by landmines and seriously affected by water seepage. In 1974 part of the roof of the north vault collapsed, and Necropolis Ltd, having found bones, suggested that coffins might lie beneath. A polythene membrane was placed above the remains for their protection and the void was backfilled with hardcore, which meant the area could be leased as a car park. When a faculty was issued on 18 June 1985[331] to exhume the remains, it was uncertain whether Necropolis Ltd should enter from above or attempt to find a door to enter from the side. It soon became obvious that the only possible entry could be from above, through the concrete car park floor. It was found that all the coffins were squashed together but 178 still had their breastplates. Exhumation began on 27 November 1987 and ended on 19 March 1988, during which 152 deteriorated lead coffins, twenty-six dilapidated wood coffins and around 4,500 skeletons were removed to the City of London Cemetery. Brookwood could not be used, because the authorities there were under the impression that St Anne's no longer needed their plots and were using them for Muslim burial. They offered plots Nos 86 or 87, but it was decided to move the remains to Ilford where they were placed in one large pit.

In early February Dr Litten was shown a pile of some fifty breast plates 'of the standard type, being either undecorated lead (presumably inner coffin plates) or of a loose rococo design or the flying angels with attendant figures style ... I noticed two fine brass plates, one to a lady named Britannia, whose inner coffin lead plate was also on the pile.' There were also two very small children's plates, of brass for Augusta Webb who died aged 4 in 1825, and two of lead belonging to Cassandra Gylby aged 2 weeks (1823) and Edward Stone, 4 months (1818). When Dr Litten returned two weeks later a third of them had vanished.[332]

The human remains came from the north vault, the chancel vault and the area outside and around the building. There was only earth below the nave floor and no coffins were found in the small crypt below the tower, which is entered from the south. Nearby were piles of bones all neatly stacked beneath the surface, which suggests that a sexton used this area to reinter the bodies he had dug up to make more space. Some skeletons were partly under the foundations of the next-door houses, so not all the bones could be removed. A workman, having been unable to remove the legs of one corpse for this reason, asked what would happen to the person at the Resurrection. The vault floors were excavated and the wooden coffins and their contents there were also removed, but those in the western graveyard remained *in situ*, and today its garden is maintained by Westminster City Council. The entrance to the north and south vaults was found on the western wall of the church beneath ground level, and a chute had obviously been used by the sexton to get the coffins into the crypt.

Some of the interments under the former chancel were in narrow brick-lined graves. As one would expect, three of these were clergy, including a former rector,

John Pelling, who died on 30 March 1750. There was much press publicity before the project began due to the possibility of finding the remains of the eccentric Lord Camelford, a young Regency rake who had died in a duel. He had been interred in the north vault on 17 March 1804, but no trace of him was found.[333] However, the descendants of Sir John Macpherson did find his coffin, which had been placed in the north vault in 1821 and removed his bones to the family grave in Sleat churchyard on the Isle of Skye. He had succeeded Warren Hastings as Governor of India and his memorial tablet in St Anne's had been destroyed in 1940.

Today this cosmopolitan parish of restaurants, theatres, shops and striptease nightclubs has a resident population of 5,000, and the congregation still has a strong social conscience.

[*] ST BARNABAS PIMLICO, ST BARNABAS STREET

The church was built in 1846–49 and designed by Thomas Cundy. The crypt, which was fitted up by G.F. Bodley in 1887, has never contained coffins.

[*] ST JAMES, PICCADILLY

The fields belonging to Saint James's Palace began to be built on in the late seventeenth century and the Earl of Saint Albans, Henry Jermyn – after whom the street is named – was given permission by King Charles II to develop the area. In 1674 he appointed his friend, Christopher Wren, to be the architect who would design a church for the new neighbourhood. He found an entirely new site and the foundation stone was laid in 1676. After eight years and £8,000 it was consecrated by Henry Compton, Bishop of London, on 13 July 1684 to serve parishioners in the western part of St Martin's parish, but the following year it became a separate parish with Dr Tenison, later Archbishop of Canterbury, as vicar – holding it in plurality with St Martin's.

Obviously the churchyard had always been too small, because on 13 October 1693 the vestry bought a sublease then the freehold of ½ acre for £80 at the north end of Pawlett's Garden, to the west of Poland Street. A shed was erected 'to shelter the Minister from the bad weather in Winter'. A complaint was made in 1711 about the 'noysome and offenceive' smoke coming from the gravedigger's chimney, which was caused by him burning rotting coffin wood. Five years later the ground was over-full, so more land was rented in Pesthouse Close. It was reckoned that it would hold 12,000 bodies, 'which rot so fast that 800 may annually be buried in it'.[334]

By an Act of Parliament, in 1784 St James acquired a new 4 acre burial ground on the east side of Hampstead Road, NW1, and its chapel of St James was consecrated and clergy house opened in 1791. From 1836 until his death in 1883 the resident priest was the Revd Henry Stebbing, author and friend of Southey, Scott and Dickens.[335] He claimed to have conducted more than 18,000 funerals, which may not be an exaggeration as the parish was populous; and by 1800 St James Piccadilly had 34,462 inhabitants. It was reckoned that 50,000 bodies were interred in the Hampstead Road Cemetery. St James's vaults, churchyard and this cemetery closed by an Order in Council of 8 August 1853.

On 24 October 1821 John How, sexton's assistant at St James, was sentenced at the Old Bailey to one year's imprisonment for stealing eleven coffin plates, dated between 1798 and 1817, and 58lb of lead together valued at 9s (which would be £45 today) from the north vault under the church. Benjamin White, the watchman, saw him on two occasions on 13 October at 8 p.m. take bundles to Forder's old iron shop and apprehended him. The vault was visited by Thomas Gook, the watch-house keeper, who said: 'I found eleven inscription plates taken off the coffins, three appeared distinctly to be forced off – In another vault, a great many were gone; some of the coffins are placed one on another, and some are much decayed.'[336] The prisoner said that he thought the coffin plates were of no value.

In July 1923 Necropolis Ltd removed ninety-two coffins from the crypt to the City of Westminster Cemetery, Hanwell. Five of these were from the Lubbock vault – Sir John, who died in 1816, his son Sir John William, 1840, and Mary his wife, 1845; Master Hugh, who was only aged 6 months when he died in 1817, and Anne, who died in 1822. The vaults were under the St James vestry Hall and it is unclear why they were moved. Three dated from the eighteenth century and the rest were interments up to 1849. The names and inscriptions are at the WCA.[337]

On the night of 14 October 1940 the church and vicarage were severely damaged by high explosives and incendiaries. Fortunately all the work by Gibbons had been removed to Hardwick Hall in Derbyshire, and worship continued in the south aisle until the restoration work by Sir Albert Richardson was completed in 1954.

[*] ST PAUL, COVENT GARDEN

Francis, 4th Earl of Bedford, asked Inigo Jones to be the architect of a church on the former convent land but not to spend too much – it should be 'not much better than a barn'. 'My Lord, you shall have the finest barn in England,' said Jones. The cost amounted to £5,000, and the second Anglican church since the Reformation was consecrated on 27 September 1638.[338]

The vaults under the church were used for burial, but few parishioners took this option. In the period from the first burial on 27 October 1653 to 25 March 1658 there were 506 interments, only forty-two under the church. There were 1,335 interments from 1750 to 1754, and only fourteen beneath the church. A popular vault was under the Charity Boys' schoolroom.[339] In 1717 Marmaduke Conwaye died aged 108 and was buried in the church. He had attended the coronation of Charles I and was 'sensible to the last moment'.

By 1735 the members of the vestry were concerned that the level of the yard was rising, mainly because it was being 'filled with the remains of multitudes of Paupers', so an overspill burial ground was opened in Cleveland Street in the parish of St Pancras in 1774.

Burials ceased on 15 August 1853 when there had been fifty-four interments that year. The vestry decided on 28 September 1854 to lay flat the head and foot stones,[340] and the churchyard was lowered and levelled. An attempt was made to remedy 'a soakage from the graves into the houses. Some displaced bodies were put in a vault under the church and the rest were removed and reinterred at Brookwood.'[341] On 29 December *The Times* reported that a few days earlier 'eight double loads of the consecrated ground full of human remains, were wheeled from the Covent Garden churchyard, where a brick grave had been dug, to Church Place'. It stayed there until carts took it away, but 'various bones were played with by boys including jaw bones with the teeth perfect'.

Today St Paul's is the 'Actors' Church', because David Garrick worshipped here, and the building is surrounded by theatres. Its walls are covered with memorial plaques to members of the profession, and many memorial services are held each year.

[*] ST PAUL, KNIGHTSBRIDGE, WILTON PLACE

Designed by Thomas Cundy II in 1840–43, this has a small crypt space at the south-east of the building, which is used as a columbarium.

[*] ST STEPHEN, ROCHESTER ROW

Built in 1847–50, it has vaults, and was designed by Benjamin Ferrey. Burials were forbidden in 1853 by an Order in Council, but an exception was made for Baroness Coutts (see Introduction).

14

SOUTH

WESTMINSTER

[*] ST CLEMENT DANES, STRAND

The name of this church probably derives from the Danes, who married English women during the time of Alfred the Great and were allowed to settle in this part of London. Stow says that Harold, a Danish king, was buried here. Around AD 1000 a stone building replaced a wooden one, which in 1189 was transferred to the Order of the Knights Templar then the Austin Friars.[342] It escaped the Great Fire, but was in such a parlous condition that Wren agreed to rebuild it in 1678. The south side of the building is more ornate because on the north side buildings pressed close against the church wall. The medieval churchyard of St Clements lay to the east and west of the building, but today less than an acre of these is left and it is paved. The parish was populous in 1710 with 11,004 inhabitants, but by 1801 there were only 8,857. Part of the churchyard was compulsorily purchased in 1802 to improve the Strand and the entrance to the City at Temple Bar.[343] A detached burial ground on the south side of Portugal Street had been purchased in 1604 and extended in 1638.

On 17 December 1766 two gravediggers, Charles Dennet and Samuel Newcomb, appeared at the Old Bailey charged with stealing 10lb of brass nails, valued at 5s (£38). On the orders of the churchwardens an undertaker, Mr Tupper, had searched St Clement's crypt and found that a coffin buried four months earlier had three rows of nails missing. Another coffin 'had a great many nails taken out'. Elizabeth Shelcroft testified that she had seen 'a great quantity of nails' in Newcomb's house. Despite this they were both acquitted.

In the 1840s burial fees brought the church a considerable income as the best vault near the altar cost £6 12s 4d (£530), and in the churchyard the dues were £1 17s 2d for an adult and £1 10s 2d for a child.[344] The nearby Enon Chapel (see below) only charged 15s (£63), so no doubt many parishioners went there.

Brookwood. St Clement Danes. Celtic cross, 1900 and enclosure (containing c.4,000 corpses). In the background is the Aberdeen granite obelisk, 1902, of St George, Botolph Lane.

In 1899 the London County Council decided to widen the Strand[345] and compulsorily purchase most of the two churchyards there. This would maroon St Clement's and St Mary le Strand on islands, but despite spirited opposition by both vestries the plan went ahead, and both lost large portions of land. In 1901, 4,000 bodies were taken to Brookwood, and a Celtic cross, erected in 1909, is still in good order.

In 1839 Dr Walker reported that the church vaults were entered by descending through an entrance in the aisle near the communion table. When opened, evil-smelling gas came up into the church: 'a diluted poison is given in exchange from the dead to the living'. The other vaults were also crowded, and he says that fifty years earlier a fire had broken out, which 'continued burning for some days, and many bodies were destroyed'.

The Great Vault beneath the church measured 33ft east to west, 52ft north to south and was 9ft 6in high. The entrance was in the northern part of the church porch. In April 1840 Rear Admiral John Sykes who lived in Arundel Street, Strand, was given permission to build a family vault with an iron gate in the north-east corner of this.[346] The Select Committee of 1842 was told that there was often 'The sound of breaking up coffins', and that Edwards, the bell ringer, 'burnt nothing but coffin wood from St Clement's vaults'.

In 1941 churchwarden E.A. Young visited the crypt and described it: 'The roof is of groined vaulting, carried on brick piers and stone columns. It is very massive, yet the columns standing under the nave, in rows of three, seem to give the crypt an architectural value. The floor I could not see as it was covered with a layer of earth (probably containing human remains).' This obviously is correct, because he tells us that in the 1850s the overseers had enclosed the best of the coffins in a newly formed chamber and covered the floor to a depth of 30in with earth and quicklime.[347]

In December 1941 the church was bombed: the tower, steeple and walls remained intact but the interior was gutted. It was not until November 1953 that discussions began with the Royal Air Force, who wished to make St Clement's their spiritual home. The architect of the Air Ministry, W.A.S. Lloyd, asked that the lead coffins and bones be removed to create a crypt chapel and a marshalling area for processions to the church above. In 1954 the chancellor was told that 'The crypt is some four layers deep in coffins surrounded by lime. Some of these coffins have collapsed. Dry rot is active in one corner.'[348] A faculty was granted, and in 1956 the vaults were emptied of coffins so that a chapel, which lies north-south and is approximately 30ft across, could be created at the west end. It has four aisled bays with a pointed groined vault on cylindrical pillars. The human remains were cremated and the ashes are now interred below the south stairs. Many of the breastplates from the coffins are displayed on the chapel walls, although most of their wording

St Clement. West end of crypt c.1956 after the clearance of the coffins and debris.

is indecipherable. The centre area is empty and bricked up, but a door in the chapel wall would provide access. The costs of this work were defrayed by St Clement's quaintly named Amicable Society.

After the clearance £150,000 (£3.1 million) was donated by the RAF to reconstruct the church to its present splendour. Sadly one of the casualties of the Blitz was the memorial to the Revd William Pennington-Bickford, rector 1910–41, and his wife Louie, who died three months after him and had been churchwarden for seventeen years. Unfortunately when she placed her husband's ashes in a cinerary urn under the altar she forgot to obtain a faculty, so when her executor asked to inter her ashes there he had to apologise to the chancellor for 'an unintentional breach of ecclesiastical law'. Their ashes are now

St Clement. The crypt chapel today; some of the depositum plates removed from the coffins decorate the wall.

St Clement. The western crypt cleared and ready to become the chapel.

beneath the altar in a semi-circular crypt together with thirteen other persons, including Sir Archibald McIndoe and Sir Douglas Bader. Access is difficult because two small flagstones in the sanctuary have to be lifted; if a door could be inserted in the crypt below it would enable ashes of RAF members to be placed there.

St Clement. Sunlight, the first in the crypt for centuries.

In the parish was the infamous Enon Chapel, which opened in 1822, and stood in St Clement's Lane. It was built by a baptist minister as a speculation, the ground floor being used for worship and the cellar, 60ft by 29ft, for burials. In 1851 Charles Knight reckoned that by that date 12,000 bodies had been interred there.[349] Mr William Burn, a master carman, told the 1842 Select Committee that he had taken sixty loads of bones and rubbish from there to tip into a hole near Waterloo Bridge where a pathway was being laid.[350] A cabinet maker who worshipped at the chapel also testified: 'The smell was most abominable and very injurious ... also there were insects, something similar to a bug in shape and appearance, only with wings, about the size of a small bug; I have

St Clement. The uncovered entrance to the old crypt.

seen them in the summer time hundreds of them flying about the chapel.' After it was closed in 1842 the new owners covered the existing wooden floor with a single brick floor, in turn covered in a new wooden floor, and opened the premises as a 'low dancing-saloon'. A publicity leaflet was issued:

Enon Chapel. Dancing on the Dead.
Admission Threepence.
No one admitted without shoes and stockings.[351]

In 1837 Dr George Walker opened a surgery at No. 101 Drury Lane, and two years later in his book *Gatherings from Grave Yards* he had described the horror of the cellar: 'numbers of coffins were piled in confusion – large quantities of bones were mixed with the earth and lying upon the floor of this cellar lids of coffins might be trodden upon at almost every step'.[352] In 1848 he paid £100 (£10,080) for the building and reinterred the human remains in one pit at Norwood Cemetery. The coffin wood was burnt. The site is now beneath the London School of Economics.

ST JOHN SMITH SQUARE

This church, 'a great turbulence of architecture, playing for astonishment and thus fully baroque',[353] has had a chequered history. Some thought that it began to sink while it was being built between 1714 and 1727, to a design of Thomas Archer, who put on four towers 'that the whole might sink equally'.[354] When this new parish was carved out of St Margaret Westminster its population was estimated at 4,250, but this had risen to 34,295 by 1851. In 1742 the building was rebuilt after a fire, and in 1812 it had to be propped up with huge timbers which were removed for William Inwood's new Grecian design. The building was bombed and burnt out in 1941, and for twenty years it stood as an empty shell until it was sold in 1964 for £50,000 (£858,064) to the Friends of St John Trust. Today, thanks to the architect Marshall Sisson, St John's is a magnificent concert hall with first-rate acoustics. Its crypt's southern area is a restaurant, The Footstool,[355] to the north of which is a small caretaker's flat.

There have never been interments in the crypt because this church was one of three built in Westminster by commissioners who hoped to build fifty new churches in the metropolis. Their 1711 Act forbade burials, but several attempts were made over the next 100 years to do so. In 1731 the vaults were let to one of the churchwardens, Sir Thomas Crosse, for the storage of coal used in his brewery close by, but three years later it was reported that the vaults had become 'a receptacle for vagrants and beggars'. The vestry's solution was to move a family in to live there, on the condition that they kept clean the pavement round the church. In 1736 a proposal that burials be allowed was rejected because the owners of nearby houses objected, so a carpenter in Tufton Street leased the vaults for £12 p.a. (£2,253) Another attempt to allow burials failed in 1741, which is surprising as the income from this would have been considerably greater than the £15 p.a. (£3,100) received from the new tenant, Charles Grosse, who used the space for his brewery.

In 1781 the incumbent, Dr John Blair, claimed that the vaults were part of his freehold and the case was heard in court on 29 May 1781. The parishioners won, and two years later the vestry let the space under the steps for £16 p.a. (£2,128) to store wine and beer. In 1813 and 1821 further attempts to allow interments were made, a churchwarden suggesting that 2,500 coffins could be stored there.

St John Smith Square. Today's crypt restaurant.

Fees charged for the parish would have been at least £6 (£491) for each interment, so much income was lost. The last recorded tenant was another brewer, Messrs Starkey, who in 1822 paid £50 p.a. (£5,379) for the space for several years.[356] The burial registers record that there were 529 interments that year in the parish burial ground purchased in Horseferry Road in 1729, some of whom would have been in the vaults if they were available.

[*] ST MARGARET, WESTMINSTER

Founded by the Abbot of Westminster towards the middle of the twelfth century the church was rebuilt in 1486–1523. In 1614 the Commons made it their church.[357] The churchyard was 2¼ acres, and it is still large. In about 1745 the young William Cowper, while he was at Westminster School, took a short cut across it one night: 'Just as I arrived at the spot a grave digger, who was at work by the light of his lanthorn, threw up a skull which struck me upon the leg. This little incident was an alarm to my conscience.'[358]

The nearby Broadway burial ground is an old burial site established in about 1627 with its chapel of ease. On 26 August 1680 Colonel Thomas Blood, who had attempted to steal the Crown Jewels in 1671,[359] was buried there. People thought this was another trick of his, so the coroner ordered the body to be dug up. There was some difficulty in identification, but then someone remembered that the thumb of his left hand was twice its proper size. The jury saw that this was true, so he was reinterred. The chapel was replaced by Christ Church, Victoria Street, the 7,000sq.yds churchyard of which is now a park.

In 1758 the House of Commons voted £4,000 (£608,000) 'for the purposes of new pewing and decorating the Church', and some of this was used to build a vault the whole length of the building.[360] It was subdivided into separate chambers – in the registers there are references to the great vault, the pulpit vault, the new and inner vaults and that under the chancel. In 1840 there were 689 burials, and two years later the rector, the Revd H.H. Milman, told the Select Committee that few could afford the fee for a vault interment and the churchyard should be closed because digging graves always revealed other coffins or bones.[361] In 1853 interments ended, and bones from the churchyard were transferred to the vaults. Some went to the new Brookwood Cemetery two years later.

[*] ST MARY-LE-STRAND

The more observant passenger in a bus passing this small Baroque church will notice several vault numbers etched in the stones above the pavement. Are there bodies behind them? Not originally, but there are now, because when the Strand was widened at the beginning of the twentieth century the London County Council compulsorily purchased the tiny strip of land to the south of the building. It contained coffins because the vaults were outside the walls. These were taken inside, and today in the church's three tunnel vaults, which lay east-west, 220 coffins covered with earth and charcoal are stored. It is not a pleasant place to visit. One of the vaults is known as the rector's vault but this is not, as in other places, below the chancel.

The present building, designed by James Gibbs, is the first of the fifty proposed new churches. It was erected in 1714–17 when the parish population was around 1,500. The previous church, dedicated to the Nativity of Our Lady and the Innocents, was demolished in 1549 by Protector Somerset, who built a great house named after himself between the Strand and the Thames.[362]

The building was consecrated on 1 January 1723/4, and on 31 July the vestry fixed the burial fees 'for the Pavement Inclosed within Iron Pallisades about the new Church in the Strand', while on 7 October they decided that there should be no 'raised Tombs' in this churchyard but vaults would be allowed at a cost of £10 (£1,877) for the ground and £5 for the brickwork.

The *London Evening Post* for 1 April 1736 records that 'Thursday night about Ten o'Clock the corpse of Jacob Tonson Esq; one of His Majesty's Justices of the Peace for the County of Hereford … was carry'd from his Great Nephew's Dwellinghouse in the Strand, and interr'd in a vault in St Mary Le Strand, in a very handsome Manner …'

The church had no burial space apart from this small churchyard and the vaults, so in 1726 the rector and churchwardens paid £150 for a cemetery in nearby Russell Court, and on 12 January 1726/7 Edmund Gibson, Bishop of London, standing under a resplendent tent consecrated it and the chapel. Bones were dug up after a while and thrown into the charnel houses so that the land could be reused. Completely enclosed by buildings, it was probably the scene of Charles Dickens's Tom-all-Alones in *Bleak House*. Nearly 10,000 bodies were interred in Russell Court over the next fifty years.

By 1801 the parish population was 1,704, and as in other places it was probably the less well-off parishioners who were buried in the cemetery; the wealthy were placed in the vaults. In 1824 the churchwardens made a ground plan of these showing their measurements, inside and outside the church walls. The two rector's vaults are at the south-east corner of the building next to the engine house.[363] Today the vaults are inaccessible, and there is no plan to clear them.

[*] ST PETER, EATON SQUARE

Soon after the Greek revival building designed by Henry Hakewill was consecrated in 1827 interments began in the crypt, and these continued until 1859 when an Order in Council banned them. Dr C. Aldis, the Medical Officer of Health, visited the crypt on 7 December 1858 and reported that he had found 350 coffins of which '50 are uncovered and the rest closed with brickwork. A safe plan would be to embed the coffins in soil covered with charcoal.'[364] This was presumably done.

When Prebendary Kirk, the priest in charge during the 1950s, visited the vaults in 1951 accompanied by Dr Shinnie, the Westminster Medical Officer of Health, he was horrified to find 'that the coffins had been tampered with and moved many times from one part of the crypt to another, and a large number had been transferred from some other place'. He and his Parochial Church Council decided to clear the vaults. Five corridors ran east-west under the church; the three central ones were divided by walls, but the north and south vaults ran the length of the building. Five vaults each about 25ft by 16ft and 7½ft high were found to be filled with 400 coffins up to about 6½ft. All were lead encased in wood, but many of the cases were broken. A faculty was granted and the remains were taken to Brookwood in 1951 by Necropolis Ltd, and a memorial stone was erected there. Cecil Brown, the church architect, drew up a plan for the conversion of the crypt and this was done, costing £7,000 plus £3,900 to remove the remains, a total of £10,900 (£289,940).

However, the following January Colonel Codrington, whose great-grandfather Admiral Sir Edward Codrington, had been interred 'in a family vault on 2 May 1851', wrote to the registrar complaining that the project had been carried out 'in an impetuous and cavalier manner'. He had once been a vicar's warden and asked if the burial registers, which were in a bank, had been consulted. The memorial in church would have alerted the incumbent to his ancestor being buried beneath. Prebendary Kirk assured the registrar that there were no burial registers and he, being a busy man, had not inspected the memorials nor had the chancellor instructed him to do so. The only coffin plates found had illegible inscriptions. 'I visited the crypt during the time of the operations and I can say that from the stench and other disagreeable aspects connected with the work it was not a pleasant task.' The colonel had to accept that his ancestor had gone to Brookwood and it was agreed to say this on a plaque beneath the memorial in church.[365] Today it seems incredible that there were no burial registers and even more incredible that the 400 coffins could not be identified. The crypt was obviously in good order when interments ceased, because on 8 March 1850 the coffins of William Profit and Jane Longueville, who died in 1835 and 1842 respectively, were identified and removed after faculty to Norwood.[366] The church but not the crypt suffered from incendiary bombs in 1941, so when and how were the coffins damaged so irreparably?

In 1987 the building was gutted by fire, and when it was rebuilt four flats were placed in the roof space. The building now contains a parish hall on the second floor, a meeting room on the ground floor, and the crypt, approximately 968sq.ft, is suitable for practical activities like fitness classes, craft groups, children's parties, discos, etc. It has recently been fitted with acoustic panelling so that it is now also suitable for meetings, lectures, etc. There is lift access, good cloakroom facilities, and a kitchen suitable for preparing hot and cold food.

Maps and Tables

1 CITY OF LONDON CHURCHES WITH CRYPTS DEMOLISHED SINCE 1666 AND PRICES OF SALE

Church	Demolition date	Sale price of site; 2012 value in brackets[367]	Remains to
All Hallows Lombard Street	1937	£265,000 (£15,286,987)	Ilford
All-Hallows-the-Great	1893	£13,129 (£1,428,673)	Brookwood
All Hallows Staining	1870	£12,418 (£1,251,734)	Ilford
Christ Church Newgate	1962	£514,000 (£9,286,913)	Coffins below ground
Holy Trinity Minories	1959		?
St Alban Wood Street	1955		Ilford
St Alphege	1923		Ilford
St Andrew Hubbard	1883		?
St Antholin	1875	£44,990 (£4,396,165)	Ilford and Brookwood

St Bartholomew by the Exchange	1840		Coffins went to St Margaret Lothbury
St Benet Fink	1842	£5,000 (£478,800)	?
St Benet Gracechurch	1867	£24,000 (£2,275,485)	Ilford
St Christopher le Stocks	1782	£4,462 (£637,733)	Nunhead in 1930s
St Dionis Backchurch	1878		Ilford
St Dunstan in the East	1957	with St Mary Aldermanbury: £600,000 (£9,838,356)	Ilford
St Katharine Coleman Street	1925	£18,000 (£926,709)	Crypt never used
St Martin Orgar	1825		Vault in churchyard
St Martin Outwich	1874		Ilford
St Mary Aldermanbury	1965	with St Dunstan in the East: £600,000 (£9,838,356)	Ilford
St Mary Somerset	1867	£10,200 (£967,081)	Ilford
St Mary Magdalene Old Fish Street	1886		Great Northern London Cemetery
St Matthew Friday Street	1883	£22,005 (£2,265,805)	Ilford
St Michael Bassishaw	1882	£36,000 (£3,667,404)	Great Northern London Cemetery
St Michael Crooked Lane	1831		St Michael Orgar, St Peter Cornhill, St Clement Eastcheap
St Michael Queenhythe	1876		Churchyard vault

St Michael Wood Street	1894			Brookwood
St Mildred Bread Street	1898			Brookwood
St Mildred Poultry	1872	£50,200 (£4,807,152)		Ilford
St Olave Old Jewry	1888	£22,400 (£2,465,544)		Ilford
St Peter le Poer	1907	£96,000 (£9,779,744)		Ilford
St Stephen Coleman Street	1955			?
St Swithin	1958			Brookwood

2 TODAY'S CITY OF LONDON CHURCHES WITH CRYPTS

Church	Crypt emptied?	Date	Present use	Coffins removed to
All Hallows by Tower	Yes	c.1950	Chapel, museum, office	?
All Hallows London Wall	No			
St Andrew by the Wardrobe	No			
St Andrew Holborn	Yes	2001	Venue for theatre, meetings, etc	Ilford
St Andrew Undershaft	No			
St Anne/ Agnes	No			
St Bartholomew -the-Great	No		Part used as a chapel	
St Bartholomew -the-Less	No			

St Benet Paul's Wharf	No			
St Botolph Aldersgate	Yes	1892	Crypt now empty	Brookwood
St Botolph Aldgate	Yes	1891 and 1989	Crypt now empty, but coffins are below the crypt floor	Ilford East London Cemetery
St Botolph Bishopsgate	Yes		Coffins are below floor	
St Bride Fleet Street	Yes	1953	Chapel, museum and offices	In crypt
St Clement Eastcheap	No			
St Dunstan in the West	Yes	1987	Crypt now empty	East London Cemetery
St Edmund the King	No			
St Ethelburga Bishopsgate	No			
St Giles Cripplegate	No			
St Helen Bishopsgate	Part	1891	May be unusable	Ilford
St James Garlickhythe	No			
St Katharine Cree	No			
St Lawrence Jewry	Yes	1954 and 2000	Crypt now empty but may be unusable	Ilford East London Cemetery
St Magnus the Martyr	Yes	1893	Parish room and store	Brookwood
St Margaret Lothbury	No			

St Margaret Pattens	No			
St Mary Aldermary	No			
St Mary-at-Hill	Yes	1892 and 1991	Vaults filled with soil	Norwood East London Cemetery
St Mary-le-Bow	Yes	1954	Chapel, Court of Arches and restaurant	Ashes under crypt floor
St Mary Woolnoth	Yes	1893	Probably unusable	Ilford
St Michael Cornhill	No			
St Michael Paternoster Royal	Part	1967	Kitchen, lavatories and store	?
St Nicholas Cole Abbey	No		Rubble probably in crypt today	
St Olave Hart Street	Part	1934	Small chapel	
St Peter Cornhill	No			None
St Sepulchre	No			
St Stephen Walbrook	Part	1953	Meeting room, offices, kitchen and lavatories	?
St Vedast	Yes	1881	Probably unusable	Ilford

3 CITY OF WESTMINSTER CHURCHES WITH CRYPTS DEMOLISHED OR SOLD SINCE 1666

Church	Date of sale/ rent/demolition	Sale price	Remains to
Hanover Chapel Regent Street	1897	£45,000 (£4,953,103)	Brookwood
Holy Trinity Kingsway	1909 1991 (new church)	£7.9m (£14,363,090)	Brookwood

Holy Trinity Marylebone	c.1950	Building rented	?
Christ Church Cosway Street	1973	Building rented	
St John Smith Square	Sold 1963	£50,000 (£886,666)	Crypt not used for interments
St Mark North Audley Street	Cleared 1988	Building rented	East London Cemetery

Forty-five church buildings without crypts have also been demolished in Westminster, all except six in the twentieth century.

4 CITY OF WESTMINSTER CHURCHES WITH CRYPTS 1666–2010

* Church still in use

Church	Date	Crypt cleared?	Clearance date; remains taken to; use today
*All Souls Langham Place	1824		Never used for burials, the crypt is a hall today
Christ Church Cosway Street	1822	Yes	Cleared, closed and leased in 1973 as offices
*Grosvenor Chapel	1731	No	
Hanover Chapel Regent Street	1825	Yes	Demolished in 1897 and human remains went to Brookwood
Holy Trinity Kingsway	1831	Yes	Demolished in 1909 and remains went to Brookwood; new church sold and closed in 1991
Holy Trinity Marylebone	1824	Yes	Cleared post-war and church now unconsecrated, owned by diocese. Retail venue, art gallery
*St Anne Soho	1686	Yes	Exhumation in 1909 and 1987. New church centre opened in 1991
*St Barnabas Pimlico	1849		Never used for burials. Now a chapel

*St Clement Danes	1678	Yes	Cleared 1956. Part of crypt now used as a chapel
*St George Hanover Square	1724		Crypt never used for burials. Today it is a store
*St Giles-in-the-Fields	1734	No	
*St James, Piccadilly	1684	No	
St John Smith Square	1727		Never used for burials. Sold in about 1964, and is now a restaurant for the concert hall
*St John, St John's Wood	1813	Partly	Two vaults remain. The rest of the space is used by the Crypt Club, a charity for young people
*St John Hyde Park Crescent	1832	No	
*St Margaret Westminster	1523	No	
St Mark North Audley Street	1828	Yes	1988 human remains removed to East London Cemetery. Church and crypt soon to be leased
*St Martin-in-the-Fields	1726	Yes	Cleared 1859 and 1938. Now a homeless centre, restaurant, Chinese club and bookshop
*St Marylebone	1817	Yes	Cleared 1982–83. Now the Marylebone Counselling and Healing Centre. Half the crypt is rented to the Marylebone Health Centre
*St Mary Bourne Street	1873		Never used for burials. Now a columbarium
*St Mary le Strand	1717	No	
*St Mary Paddington Green	1791	Yes	Cleared c.1995. The crypt is used as a columbarium
*St Paul Covent Garden	1638	No	
*St Peter Eaton Square	1827	Yes	In 1951 the human remains went to Brookwood, and the crypt is now a hall
*St Stephen, Rochester Row	1850	No	

MAP OF THE CITY OF LONDON PARISHES.

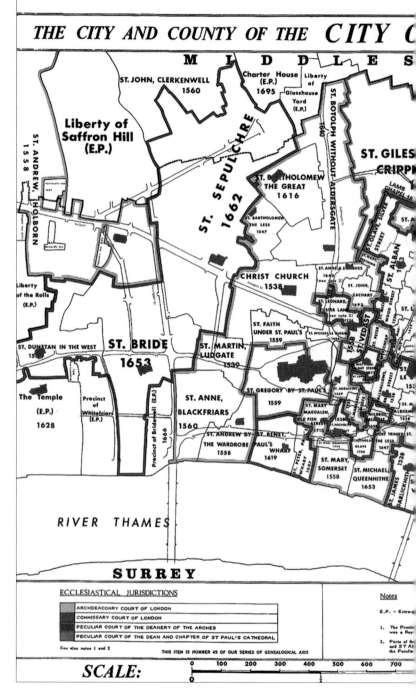

THE CITY AND COUNTY OF THE *CITY O*

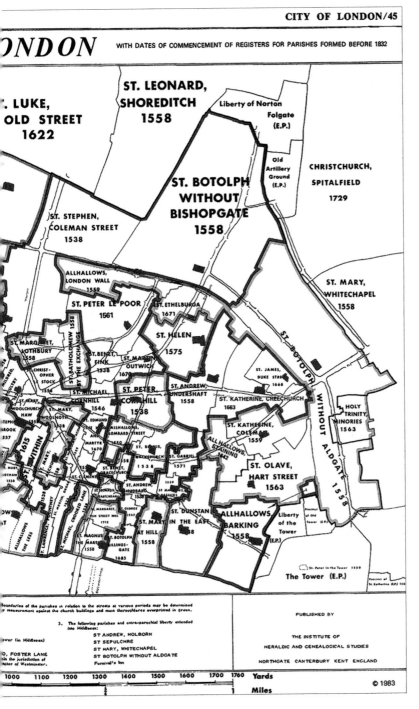

ONDON WITH DATES OF COMMENCEMENT OF REGISTERS FOR PARISHES FORMED BEFORE 1832

ST. LEONARD, SHOREDITCH 1558

Liberty of Norton Folgate (E.P.)

. LUKE, OLD STREET 1622

Old Artillery Ground (E.P.)

CHRISTCHURCH, SPITALFIELD 1729

ST. BOTOLPH WITHOUT BISHOPGATE 1558

ST. STEPHEN, COLEMAN STREET 1538

ALLHALLOWS, LONDON WALL 1559

ST. MARY, WHITECHAPEL 1558

ST. PETER LE POOR 1561

ST. ETHELBURGA 1671

ST. HELEN 1575

ST. MARGARET, LOTHBURY 1558

ST. BARTHOLOMEW 1558 BY THE EXCHANGE

ST. BENET, FINK 1538

ST. MARY OUTWICH 1670

ST. CHRIST-OPHER STOCK

ST. JAMES, DUKE STREET 1668

ST. MICHAEL CORNHILL 1546

ST. PETER CORNHILL 1538

ST. ANDREW, UNDERSHAFT 1558

ST. KATHERINE, CREECHURCH 1663

HOLY TRINITY MINORIES 1563

ST. MARY WOOLCHURCH HAW

ST. MARY WOOLNOTH

ST. EDMUND

ALLHALLOWS, LOMBARD STREET

ST. DENIS

ST. KATHERINE, COLEMAN 1559

ST. WITHIN 1615

ST. MARY ARTYR 1670

GRACECHURCH

ST. GABRIEL 1571

ALLHALLOWS STAINING 1642

ST. OLAVE, HART STREET 1563

ST. BENET, GRACECHURCH 1538

ST. CLEMENTS

ST. ANDREW, HUBBARD 1538

ALLHALLOWS THE LESS

ST. LAWRENCE

ST. MICHAEL CROOKED LANE

ST. MARGARET, FISH STREET HILL 1712

ST. GEORGE 1547

ST. DUNSTAN IN THE EAST

ST. MARY IN THE EAST HILL 1558

ALLHALLOWS BARKING 1558

Liberty of the Tower (E.P.)

ST. MAGNUS THE MARTYR 1558

ST. BOTOLPH BILLINGS-GATE 1683

St. Peter in the Tower 1550

The Tower (E.P.)

Boundaries of the parishes in relation to the streets at various periods may be determined by measurement against the church buildings and main thoroughfares overprinted in green.

3. The following parishes and extra-parochial liberty extended into Middlesex:

ST ANDREW, HOLBORN
ST SEPULCHRE
ST MARY, WHITECHAPEL
ST BOTOLPH WITHOUT ALDGATE
Furnival's Inn

PUBLISHED BY

THE INSTITUTE OF

HERALDIC AND GENEALOGICAL STUDIES

NORTHGATE CANTERBURY KENT ENGLAND

1000   1100   1200   1300   1400   1500   1600   1700   1760   Yards

Miles

© 1983

NOTES

N.B. Unless otherwise stated the place of publication is London

1   Carol Davidson Cragoe, 'Fabric, Tombs and Precinct 1087–1540' chapter II,
    in Derek Keene, Arthur Burns and Andrew Saint (eds), *St Paul's. The Cathedral
    Church of London 604–2004* (Yale University Press, 2004), p.140.

2   Frank Buckland, *Curiosities of Natural History Third Series*, two vols (1862), ii, p.159.

3   Julian Litten, *The English Way of Death* (Robert Hale, 1991), pp.195–226.

4   Julian Litten, 'Post-Reformation vault burial in English Churches 1550–1850'
    (Cardiff University PhD thesis, 2001), p.310.

5   *Ibid.*, pp.4, 56.

6   Henry VIII and Charles I are buried at St George's Chapel, Windsor.

7   See R. Watt, *Bibliotheca Britannica* (1996), p.954.

8   The Revd W. Watson, *The Clergy-Man's Law* (H. Lintot, 1747), p.387.

9   In addition two completely new churches were built which did not have a crypt
    – All Saints Skinner Street (1830) and Holy Trinity Gough Square (1838).

10 Vestries, meetings of parish ratepayers who were responsible for local
    administration such as the care of the poor, wre often, but not always, presided
    over by the incumbent; they had secular as well as sacred duties and elected the
    churchwardens, set the parish rate, maintained highways, etc. From 1837 the care
    of the poor was given to elected boards of guardians.

11 Quoted in G.A. Walker, *Gatherings from Graveyards* (Longman, 1839), p.209.

12 *Life and Works of Sir Christopher Wren, From the Parentalia or Memoirs of his son
    Christopher* (1750) ed. E.J. Enthoven (1903), pp.193–94.

13 Kerry Downes, *Vanbrugh* (Sidgwick and Jackson, 1987), pp.257–58.

14 In the Minutes of the Commissioners, 23 March 1714/15 the clerk is instructed
    to write to the incumbent and wardens of St Alfege Greenwich telling them
    that a report of 'several burials' in the crypt 'contrary to the Acts' had been
    received and that this must end. However, interments there continued. Lambeth
    Palace Library (hereafter LPL) Commission for the Building of Fifty New
    Churches (The Queen Anne Churches) 1711–59, Ms.2690.

15 Vanessa Harding, 'And One More May Be Laid There. The location of Burials in Early Modern London', *London Journal*, vol. 14, no. 2 (1989), pp.116–18.

16 George Crabbe (1754–1832), 'The Pauper's Funeral' in *The Village* Book 1 (1783).

17 Catharine Arnold lists these pits in *Necropolis, London and its Dead* (Simon and Schuster, 2006), pp.64–67.

18 See James Stevens Curl (ed.), *Kensal Green Cemetery* (Phillimore, 2001).

19 In Paris large new cemeteries were opened and the old ones were cleared and disinfected between December 1785 and October 1787. The Cimetière du Père-Lachaise opened in 1804. Philippe Aries, *The Hour of our Death* (Knopf New York, 1981), pp.90-96.

20 *Hansard* 3rd ser. xxiv (13 May 1830), cols 680–82. Carden also condemned the state of two churchyards – St Mary Abchurch and St Giles-in-the-Fields, which was 'a nuisance from time immemorial'.

21 Norwood 1837, Brompton 1837, Highgate 1839, Nunhead 1840, Abney Park, Stoke Newington 1840, Tower Hamlets 1841, and Victoria Park, Bethnal Green 1845.

22 Chadwick (1800–90) was called to the Bar in 1830 but never practised.

23 'Sanitary' and 'sanitation' today have a cloacal connotation, but to the Victorians they meant the conditions that affect public health, especially with regard to dirt and infection.

24 WCA, m/f St Anne, vol. 162, St Anne Soho vestry minutes, 9 February 1854.

25 For a full account of these negotiations see S.E. Finer, *The Life and Times of Sir Edwin Chadwick* (Methuen, 1952), pp.412–20.

26 William Hale, 'Charge to the Clergy of the Archdeaconry of London' (1855), and 'Intramural burial in England not injurious to the public health: its abolition injurious to religion and morals' (1855).

27 Dr Brown married Hannah Meredith on 19 December 1844 and they lived at the home of Baroness Burdett Coutts, No. 1 Stratton Street, until his death. Charles Dickens made the funeral arrangements, which included constructing a new vault under the chancel because the one prepared under the altar by the baroness was too near the heating. Brown was interred in the crypt on 7 November 1855, two years after burials had ceased there. Hannah died on 21 December 1878 and was interred in St Stephen's six days later.

28 Edna Healey, *Lady Unknown* (Sidgwick and Jackson, 1978), p.225.

29 Forty-five church buildings without a crypt or churchyard have also been sold in Westminster (all except six demolished in the twentieth century), but despite research at LDF it has not been possible to find the proceeds of sale.

30 Email to the author from the archivist at the Church of England Record Centre Customer Services, 10 February 2009.

31 LMA, Ms. 24777. Diocese of London correspondence on use of churches/ churchyards as air-raid shelters 1940–48.

32 The Spitalfields Project vol. 1, *Across the Styx*, Jez Reeve and Max Adams (Council for British Archaeology (CBA), 1993), pp.127–28.

33 I am grateful to Mr Andrew Lodge of Lodge Bros, Undertakers, Feltham, for this information.

34 Warwick Rodwell, *Church Archaeology* (1989), pp.160–64 discusses this more fully.

35 E.K. Barnard, *From Parish church to Portsmouth Cathedral 1900–39*, Portsmouth Papers No. 52 (June 1988), pp.3–4.

36 Email to author from Dr Litten, 21 February 2005.

37 Chadwick to Blomfield undated: Chadwick Papers, Copy Book 2181.

38 The service was not reinstated after the Second World War, but the entrance to the terminus still stands at No. 121 Westminster Bridge Road.

39 J.M. Clarke, *Brookwood Necropolis Railway* (1988), p.15. The bishop was making a general point, not criticising the Necropolis plan.

40 *Ibid.*, p.74.

41 J.M. Clarke, *London's Necropolis. A Guide to Brookwood Cemetery* (Sutton, 2004), p.204.

42 Clarke, *Brookwood Necropolis Railway*, (Oakwood Press, 2006), p.91.

43 In June 2009 the cemetery was designated as a Grade I Historic Park and Garden by English Heritage.

44 Sir John Simon, 'Introductory Report Suggesting the Outline Of A Scheme For Extramural Interment' (1853).

45 See David McCarthy, *The City of London Cemetery and Crematorium* (2004), Heritage Brochure.

46 *The Standard*, 7 February 1983.

47 B. Weinreb and C. Hibbert (eds), *The London Encyclopaedia* (Book Club Associates, 1983), p.747.

48 Harvey Hackman, *Wates Book of London Churchyards* (Collins, 1981), p.106.

49 St John, St John's Wood, Holy Trinity Marylebone and Christ Church Marylebone.

50 Julian Litten, *The English Way of Death*, p.33.

51 Notes made by Dr Litten in January/February 1983 and shown to the author.

52 'Annual Report and Financial Statements Marylebone Parish Church' (December 2009), p.28. I am grateful to Michael Bithell, PCC secretary, for his help.

53 T.R. Forbes, *Burial Records for the Parish of St Anne Soho* (1974). LMA Pam 13200.

54 PP 1843 [509] Chadwick, A Supplementary Report on the Results of a Special Inquiry into the Practice of Interment in Towns (1843), p.99.

55 *The Sunday Times*, 12 June 1831.

56 WCA. St Martin-in-the-Fields Parish Records F 6102.

57 John McMaster, *A short history of the Royal Parish of St Martin-in-the-Fields* (G. Holder, 1916), pp. 1–2.

58 Stephen Smith, *Underground London* (Hachette Digital, 2004), p.120.

59 George Gater and Walter Godfrey, *LCC Survey of London*, vol. 10 (1940), pp.30–54.

60 John McMaster, *op. cit.*, pp.64–68 and pp.119–33.

61 *St Martin's Review*, June 1933, p.277.

62 *Ibid.*, pp.62–67, 169–76.

63 Malcolm Johnson, *St Martin-in-the-Fields* (Phillimore, 2005), pp. 62–67.

64 Malcolm Johnson, *op. cit.*, pp.91–92.

65 Malcolm Johnson, *op. cit.*, pp.96–97.

66 John Betjeman, *City of London Churches* (Pitkin, 1974), p.22.

67 Gerald Cobb, *The Old Churches of London* (Batsford, 1942), p.60.

68 Proceedings of the Old Bailey Ref. t17320114-1.

69 LMA, Ms. 10918. St Mary Bow vestry minutes, 1859–1902, pp.25–26.

70 *Ibid.*, LMA, Ms. 18319/182.

71 Mrs Robert Henrey, *The Virgin of Aldermanbury* (Jim Dent, 1958), pp.60–67.

72 *The Spitalfields Project Vol. 1 Across the Styx*, Jez Reeve and Max Adams (Council for British Archaeology, 1993), p.6.

73 *Ibid.*, pp.7–13.

74 Edwin Chadwick, *A Supplementary Report* (1843), p.83.

75 LMA Ms. 18319/109.

76 *The Spitalfields Project*, vol. 1 see above and vol. 2, *The Middling Sort*, Theya Molleson and Margaret Cox (CBA, 1993).

77 *Ibid.*, vol. 1, pp.17–19.

78 *The Spitalfields Project*, vol. 2, pp.189–90.

79 *Ibid.*, p.23.

80 *Ibid.*, p.123.

81 *Ibid.*, p.99.

82 *Ibid.*, p.205.

83 Margaret Cox (ed.), *Grave Concerns* (1998), p.18.

84 *The Spitalfields Project*, vol. 1, pp.78–83, 97–98.

85 *Ibid.*, p.67.

86 *Ibid.*, Appendix B, p.134.

87 Jez Reeve, *Grave Concerns* (1998), p.223.

88 Christopher Courtauld, 'Proceedings of the Huguenot Society', vol. 17 (5) (CBA, 2002), pp.731–33.

89 I am grateful to Leah Elsey for this information.

90 Professor Grimes studied many London bomb sites from 1946 to 1962, and at St Bride's worked under the auspices of the Roman and Medieval London Excavation Council. His interim report on St Bride's was published in 1968, but he died twenty years later without completing a final report.

91 In the 1820s the burial registers mention some of these vaults – Dockters, South-west, vestry and New.

92 LMA Ms. 18319/124.

93 Gustav Milne, 'St Bride's Church London. Archaeological Research, 1952–60 and 1992–5' (1997), p.93.

94 W. Redpath, 'The Bones at St Bride's', *West London Medical Journal* (1955), 60.3, p.139. Redpath could tell a good story: he was chairman of the publicity committee and London editor of Provincial Newspapers.

95 J.L. Scheuer and S.M. Black, *The St Bride's Documented Skeletal Collection* (University of Glasgow, 1995).

96 Gustav Milne, *op. cit.*, pp.81–95.

97 *Current Archaeology*, no. 190 (February 2004), pp.440–41.

98 *The Times*, 21 April 1841.

99 Louise Scheuer, 'Age at death and cause of death of the people buried in St Bride's church, Fleet St, London' in *Grave Concerns* (ed.) Margaret Cox (1998), p.100.

100 LMA, m/f 1952130 (7), All Hallows by the Tower burial registers.

101 AOC Archaeology Group, *A Post-excavation Assessment of All Hallows by the Tower* (October 2000).

102 Michael Stancliffe, 'The Reign of Dean Stanley' in *A House of Kings* (John Baker, 1966), p.302.

103 Peter Ackroyd, *Dickens* (Sinclair-Stevenson, 1990), p.xiii.

104 In this chapter I have used the convention of ecclesiastical architects who regard the altar end of the building as the east. As the Abbey is built north-south with the altar at the geographical south, this means that in the text the liturgical west is the geographical north, and so on.

105 Julian Litten, *The English Way of Death*, p.202.

106 Nikolaus Pevsner, *The Buildings of England*, London, vol. 1 (Penguin), p.366.

107 The hands have subsequently been lost so this is no longer apparent.

108 Arthur Stanley, 'On an Examination of the tombs of Richard II and Henry III in Westminster Abbey', *Archaeologia*, vol. 45 (1880), pp.309–22.

109 Samuel Pepys, *Diary*, iv (Bell and Hyman, 24 February 1669), p.253.

110 Arthur Stanley, *Historical Memorials* (John Murray), p.148.

111 *Ibid.*, p.161.

112 Julian Litten, *The English Way of Death*, pp.42–43.

113 A. Tindal Hart, 'The Reformation and its Aftermath' in *A House of Kings* (1966), p.146.

114 *Ibid.*, p.168.

115 Antonia Fraser, *Cromwell* (Phoenix, 1973), pp.853–54.

116 *Ibid.*, p.867.

117 John Brooke, *King George III* (Constable, 1972), pp.9–25.

118 Thomas Cocke in *Westminster Abbey. The Lady Chapel of Henry VII*, pp.321–24.

119 Prince Edward, Duke of York and Albany (1739–67), was an albino and died in Monaco. His body was re-cased on his repatriation.

120 Prince William Augustus, Duke of Cumberland (1721–65), has, according to Dr Litten, an exceptionally large coffin and a viscera chest decaying, its lead shell 'diseased'.

121 Stanley, *Historical Memorials*, p.544.

122 Rowland Prothero, *The Life and Correspondence of Arthur Penrhyn Stanley* (1894), vol. 2 (John Murray, 1894), p.286.

123 *Ibid.*, pp.473–75.

124 For a detailed list and description of the courtiers and famous people buried or commemorated in the Abbey in the sixteenth to nineteenth centuries see Stanley, *Memorials*, p.194 onwards.

125 E.F. Carpenter (ed.), *A House of Kings* (1966), p.245.

126 Richard Jenkyns, *Westminster Abbey* (Profile Books, 2004), pp.83, 247–48.

127 *Ibid.*, p. 85.

128 Derek Keene, Arthur Burns, and Andrew Saint (eds), *St Paul's. The Cathedral Church of London 604–2004* (2004).

129 *Ibid.*, pp.53, 140, 432.

130 Ben Weinreb and Christopher Hibbert (eds), *The London Encyclopaedia* (1983), p.758.

131 Julian Litten, *The English Way of Death* (1991), pp.52–53.

132 Keene, Burns and Saint, *St Paul's*, pp.271–72.

133 *Ibid.*, p.269.

134 *Ibid.*, pp.284–85.

135 G.L. Prestige, *St Pauls in its Glory 1831–1911* (SPCK, 1955), pp.70–71.

136 Peter Burman, *St Paul's Cathedral* (Bell and Hyman, 1987), p.124. This book also contains a list of memorials in the crypt, pp.127–52.

137 The model suggests what Wren would have liked to build if the dean and chapter had agreed.

138 The Broadgate Development now covers the site.

139 Parliamentary Papers (PP) 1831–32 (199), 'The General Report to the King's Most Excellent Majesty in his High Court of Chancery' (Ecclesiastical Courts Commission, 1832), p.62 suggested that it be repealed.

140 Only the tower remains today. It is incorporated into the cathedral's choir school.

141 LMA, Ms. 0613. St Augustine Watling Street vestry minutes, vol. 1 (1744–81), pp.41–174.

142 *Life and Works of Sir Christopher Wren. From the Parentalia or Memoirs of his son Christopher* (1750), p.124.

143 Ben Weinreb and Christopher Hibbert (eds), *The London Encyclopaedia* (1983), p.711.

144 The statue of Queen Anne is on the site.

145 LMA, PR. 221/FAI shows a plan of the churchyard and vault in 1753.

146 LMA, Ms. 1336. St Gregory-by-Pauls vestry minutes, vol. 2, p.67.

147 LMA, Ms. 18319/24. Diocese of London Faculty papers.

148 Elizabeth and Wayland Young, London's Churches (Grafton, 1986).

149 LMA, Ms. 23947. St Lawrence Jewry.

150 John Schofield and Cath Maloney (eds), *Archaeology in the City of London* 1907–97.

151 LMA, Ms. 18319/142. Removal of human remains. Diocese of London Faculty papers.

152 *The Times*, 10 September 1846.

153 LMA, Ms. 2897. St Matthew Friday Street, List of coffins removed, 1883.

154 J.P. Malcolm, *Londinium Redivivum*, 4 vols (Nichols, 1802–05), vol. 2, p.116.

155 H.B. Wheatley, *London Past and Present* (John Murray, 1891), vol. 2, p.491.

156 *The Newgate Calendar*, 1778, vol. 4, pp.128–29.

157 LMA, 3592/2. St Mary Aldermanbury burial fees, 1834.

158 Stephen Porter, 'Death and Burial in a London Parish: St Mary Woolnoth 1653–99', *London Journal*, vol. 8, no. 1 (1982).

159 This is probably referred to in the burial registers as 'The Great Vault' and the others are the 'Outer Vault'.

160 LMA, Ms. 18319/34. Diocese of London Faculty papers.

161 Elizabeth and Wayland Young, *op. cit.*, pp.167–70.

162 P. Fitzgerald, *Picturesque London* (Nabu Press, 1890), p.238.

163 LMA, Ms. 18319/6. Diocese of London Faculty papers.

164 LMA, Ms. 21545/57. Faculty papers for City of London parishes.

165 LMA, Ms. 3469. St Mildred Bread Street vestry minutes, vol. 4., 1897.

166 LMA, Ms. 18319/10 and 18319/16. Diocese of London Faculty papers.

167 J.M. Clarke, *London's Necropolis. A Guide to Brookwood Cemetery*, p.59. Originally the remains were to have gone to Ilford, but the City of London's charges were higher.

168 LMA, Ms. 2345. St Mildred Bread Street. Costs incurred for removal of remains, 1896.

169 Gerald Cobb, *The Old Churches of London* (1942), pp.50–52.

170 Author's conversation with Prebendary Varah, 2000.

171 Malcolm Johnson, *Outside the Gate* (Stepney Books, 1994), p.19.

172 LMA, COL/PL/01/103/A 34-76. Z1 76 54.

173 LMA, v901194x and 1876 w/c v90128ix. 1800, pen and ink.

174 Edward Tomlinson, *A History of the Minories* (Murray, 1922), pp.293, 295.

175 Malcolm Johnson, *op. cit.*, pp.47–51, 115.

176 Kevin McDonnell, East London Papers, July 1965.

177 Roberta Gilchrist and Jez Reeve, St Botolph Without Bishopsgate. Research Design and Project Design for Proposed Crypt Clearance, Unpublished Paper (1991), University of East Anglia/Norfolk Archaeological Unit, p.31.

178 *Ibid.*, p.9.

179 *Ibid.*, p.13.

180 *The Builder*, 24 July 1858.

181 LMA, Ms. 11274/1. St Dionis Backchurch Register of coffins, 1878.

182 B. Weinreb and C. Hibbert, *op. cit.*, p.703.

183 T.B. Murray, *Chronicle of a City Church* (1859), p.20. Strype quotes Machyn's Diary.

184 Elizabeth and Wayland Young, *op. cit.*, pp.106–07.

185 Revd J.E. Cox (ed.), *The Annals of St Helen's Bishopsgate, London* (1876), p.100.

186 W.B. Bannerman (ed.), *The registers of St Helen Bishopsgate 1575–1837* (Harleian Society, xxxi, 1904), pp.311–417.

187 LMA, Ms. 18319/128. Diocese of London Faculty papers.

188 David McCarthy, *The City of London Cemetery and Crematorium* (2004), p.48.

189 LMA, Ms. 6884. *Removal of Human Remains from St Helen's to Ilford Cemetery*, May–September 1892.

190 J.P. Malcolm, *Londinium Redivivum*, 4 vols (1802–05), 1802, vol. 3, p.553.

191 LMA, 297/HEL. An 1808 sketch of the coffin.

192 Elizabeth and Wayland Young, *op. cit.*, p.108.

193 Charles Dickens, *Uncommercial Traveller* (1860), Oxford illustrated edition, p.233.

194 LMA, Ms. 18319/80. Diocese of London Faculty papers.

195 The gruesome circumstances of this felony are explicitly described in an anonymous, undated pamphlet published by W. Price near the Sessions House of the Old Bailey, price 3d, in the possession of the church.

196 Proceedings of the Old Bailey Ref. 17471014–11.

197 Pamphlet, pp.10–11.

198 LMA, Ms. 6678. St Andrew Holborn, Sexton's burial book, 1812–15.

199 Stephen Smith, Underground London (2004), p.189.

200 LMA, Ms. 3858/2 and 3858/3. St Botolph Aldersgate burial registers.

201 LMA, Ms. 18626. St Botolph Aldersgate, list of coffins removed, 1893.

202 Elizabeth and Wayland Young, *op. cit.*, pp.102–03.

203 The Complete Newgate Calendar (1711), vol. 2, pp.221–22.

204 *Burial Grounds. Supplementary Returns … to the House of Commons* (1834), p.356.

205 LMA, Pam. 879. Philip Neve, 'A Narrative of the Disinterment of Milton's Coffin' (1790).

206 J.J. Baddeley, *St Giles without Cripplegate* (Baddeley, 1888), pp.193–94.

207 Edwin Chadwick, *A Supplementary Report …* (1843), pp.273–74.

208 Minutes of London Diocesan Fund (1964), 29441/376/1.

209 *Ibid.*, 12 August 1996.
210 St Luke's Old St Church Conservation Plan (Purcell Miller Tritton, 2000), p.41.
211 The Church of St Luke Islington London EC1. Post Excavation Assessment and Updated Project Design, Oxford Archaeology, 11 March 2002. I am grateful to Alison Law of LSO St Luke's for her help with this chapter.
212 B. Weinreb and C. Hibbert, *op. cit.*, p.155.
213 J.P. Malcolm, *Londinium Redivivum* (1802), vol. 3, p.340.
214 *Penny Magazine*, 2 August 1834, p.298.
215 O.L. Dick, *Aubrey's Brief Lives* (1949), pp.274–75.
216 J. Litten, *The English Way of Death*, p.217.
217 LMA, Ms. 18677. St Dunstan in the West, Papers re. closure of vaults, 1857–58.
218 LMA, Ms. 21545/32. Faculty papers for City of London parishes.
219 Details of the names on the coffins are kept in the parish office.
220 LMA, Ms. 22844. St James Garlickhythe, various papers.
221 Adrian Miles, Report from the Museum of London Archaeological Service (1993). Site code JA 591.
222 LMA, Ms. 36857/39.
223 Professor Don Brothwell, York University, Dr White, Curator of bio-archaeology at the Museum of London, and Professor Kenneth Pye, Royal Holloway College, University of London.
224 2005 Report by Atlantic Productions, Charecroft Way, London, W14 0EH.
225 Conversation with the rector, Dr Alan Griffin, March 2007.
226 I am very grateful to Mr Ellis Charles Pike, whose booklet *Jimmy Garlick* (July 2005) is available for more details.
227 It was discovered during the work of 1893.
228 The northern part of this was bricked up in 1849 and contained forty wooden coffins.
229 LMA, COL/pl/01/103/A 34–76. Z1 27 69 – a detailed plan of this made in 1858.
230 LMA, Ms. 18319/6.
231 LMA, Ms 35949. St Magnus the Martyr, Papers relating to the removal of human remains 1893-95.
232 *Ibid.*
233 LMA, Ms. 18319/81. Diocese of London Faculty papers.
234 LMA, Ms.23908 St Martin Ludgate which also contains a plan of the vaults and the ten catacombs.
235 *Select Committee on improvement of the health of towns* (1842) Report, pp.87–89.
236 LMA, Ms. 1326. St Martin Ludgate burial register.
237 LMA, Ms. 18319/6. Diocese of London Faculty papers.
238 LMA, Ms. 23906 vol. 1 and 2, St Martin Ludgate. Register of coffins removed (1893).
239 *The Times*, 27 September 1841.
240 W. Lewis, *Report of a general scheme for extra mural sepulture* (HMSO, 1850), p.29.
241 LMA, Ms. 18319/34. Faculty Papers Diocese of London.
242 Paul Jeffery, *St Mary at Hill* (Hambledon Press, 1996), pp.53, 65–67 (Appendix A by Bruce Watson).
243 LMA, Ms. 09311. All-Hallows-the-Great, list of names on coffins (1894).
244 LMA, Ms 20457. All Hallows Lombard Street, sale of churchyard.

245 Report dated 16 October 1939. LMA Pam. 436. The Church Commissioners state that seventy-seven coffins were found, together with sixty-nine unattached coffin plates.

246 Church of England Record Centre File ECE/7/1/28540A/5 1940–59.

247 B. Weinreb and C. Hibbert, *op. cit.*, p.17.

248 LMA, Ms. 19225/11. St Alban Wood St Diocese of London Files of parish papers, etc.

249 Mrs Robert Henrey, *The Virgin of Aldermanbury* (1958), p.38.

250 David McCarthy, *The City of London Cemetery and Crematorium* (2004), p.50.

251 It is not known when this was emptied.

252 *The Times*, 13 December 1955. It is not known where the remains were reinterred.

253 LMA, Ms. 17611A. St Benet Gracechurch, Minutes of a meeting to discuss removal of human remains, 1867.

254 John M. Clarke, *London's Necropolis* (2004), p.60.

255 B. Weinreb and C. Hibbert, *op. cit.*, p.727.

256 Church of England Record Centre file ECE/7/1/65311/1 1877–1921.

257 *Ibid.*, Part 3.

258 This community of French Protestants was established in *c.*1686 and was based at a number of addresses in the City, including Jewin Street and in Buckingham House, College Hill, before taking the lease of St Martin in 1699.

259 J.E. Cox, *Annals of St Helens Bishopsgate London* (1876), p.435.

260 LMA, Ms 6840A. St Martin Outwich, list of bodies exhumed.

261 J.P. Malcolm, *op. cit.* (1802), vol. 4, p.415.

262 H.B. Wheatley, *London Past and Present*, vol. 2 (John Murray), p.505.

263 Thomas Milbourn, *London and Middlesex Archaeological Society 3* (1870) p.267.

264 LMA, Ms. 18319/84. Diocese of London Faculty papers.

265 LMA, Ms. 959. St Martin Orgar vestry minutes, vol. 5, 1834.

266 LMA, Ms. 22891/2. St Michael Queenhithe, List of persons buried in the church, *c.*1689–1850, compiled 1876.

267 H.B. Wheatley, vol. 2, p.540.

268 LMA, Ms. 18319/211. Diocese of London faculty papers.

269 LMA, Ms.4396 vol. 1. St Martin Pomeroy vestry minute books.

270 In 1888 medieval masonry and two coffin-shaped pits were discovered 10ft below the surface near the western doorway. John Emslie sketched the scene: LMA, Pr.445/OLA.

271 J.P. Malcolm, vol. 4, p.567.

272 LMA, Ms. 29100. St Peter le Poer, names of bodies removed to Ilford, 1907. The Ecclesiastical Commissioners granted £10 towards a private removal.

273 *Select Committee on improvement of the health* …, p.103.

274 LMA, Ms. 4396, vol. 1. St Olave Jewry vestry minutes.

275 John Hearsey, Bridge, Church and Palace (1961), p.77.

276 Gerald Cobb, *op. cit.*, p.33.

277 LPL AA/V/H/40/18. 1724.

278 *The Times*, Letters to the Editor, 30 April 1850.

279 LMA, Ms. 18319/4. Diocese of London Faculty papers.

280 Gerald Cobb, *op. cit.*, p. 28.

281 *Report of Select Comm.* (1842), pp.46 and 89–92.

282 LMA, COL/pl/01/103/A/01-33. Z1 27 8.

283 LMA, Pam 20440, p.56, A City Church Chronicle.

284 Mrs B. Holmes, *The London Burial Grounds* (Macmillan, 1896), p.173.

285 LMA, Ms. 21545/22. Faculty papers for City of London parishes.

286 The register mentions an inner vault and one under the vestry.

287 LMA, Ms.4786. St Clement Eastcheap burial registers.

288 John Betjeman, *op. cit.*, p.12.

289 LMA, Ms. 11442A. St Edmund the King, Parish Clerk's list of burials.

290 LMA, Ms. 4240. St Ethelburga Bishopsgate, Burials 1813–49.

291 LMA, Ms. 8862. St Margaret Lothbury, papers relating to purchase of vault by the Bank of England 1824–29.

292 LMA, Ms. 4866, St Mary Aldermary burial fees account book.

293 LMA, Ms. 4866, St Mary Aldermary vestry minutes.

294 LMA, Ms. 9325, St Michael Paternoster Royal – the faculty to remove a coffin from a vault underneath St Michael's.

295 B. Weinreb and C. Hibbert, *op. cit.*, p.751.

296 B. Weinreb and C. Hibbert, *op. cit.*, p.764.

297 LMA, COL/pl/01/087/B/17.

298 B. Weinreb and C. Hibbert, *op. cit.*, p.726.

299 A transcription of the still legible tombstones was made in 1962 and may be consulted in the Westminster City Archives.

300 I am grateful to Reginald Colby's splendid *Mayfair, a Town within London* (1966) for this information.

301 10 Anne. c. XI. Section 31. 1711.

302 Ann Callender, *Godly Mayfair* (Grosvenor Chapel, 1980), pp.1, 2.

303 St George Hanover Square vestry minutes WCA m/f 538.

304 *Ibid.* Minutes of vestry committee appointed to close vaults, etc., WCA m/f 562.

305 It was purchased by Act 3 Geo. III *c*.50 1762/3 and made part of St George's parish.

306 James Stephens Curl, *Kensal Green Cemetery* (2001), p.25.

307 St George Hanover Square, Minutes of a committee appointed to close vaults etc., WCA m/f 562.

308 Hugh Meller, *London Cemeteries* (1981), p.291.

309 G. Walker, *Gatherings from Graveyards* (1839), p.177.

310 Dr Julian Litten kindly showed me the correspondence concerning his visit to the vaults in January 2001.

311 St George Hanover Square, Minutes of the committee appointed to close the crypts, etc., WCA m/f 562.

312 Diocese of London Faculty papers, LMA Ms. 29441/394.

313 The mortsafe was invented in about 1816 to protect the bodies of the dead from disturbance. These were iron or iron and stone devices of great weight, in many different designs. Often they were complex heavy iron contraptions of rods and plates, padlocked together. Sometimes a church bought them and hired them out. Societies were also formed to purchase them and control their use, with annual membership fees, and charges made to non-members.

314 Diocese of London Faculty papers, LMA Ms. 18319/89.
315 Dr Litten also tells me there are mortuary chapels at Holy Redeemer Clerkenwell and St Augustine Stepney, now the library of the Royal London Hospital.
316 *The Gentleman's Magazine*, vol. 99, November 1829, p.393.
317 H.B. Wheatley, *op. cit.*, vol. 2, p.516.
318 E. Walford, *Old and New London* (1878), vol. 4, p.345.
319 LMA P87/MRY/129.
320 The ten families were Balmain and Chew, Chandless, Haines, Raggett, Gaddes and Holland, Johnstone, Oliver, Thrupp, Darkes and Thornton. Their monuments moved with them. Two cremation urns were also reinterred.
321 Approximately half in lead and half in wood coffins, they are listed in WCA 1438/7.
322 *Evening Standard*, 5 July 1972.
323 Paddington Churches, *A History of the County of Middlesex*, vol. 9, pp.252–59.
324 St George Hanover Square, Minutes of a committee appointed to close churchyards, etc., WCA m/f 562.
325 Diocese of London Faculty Papers LMA Ms. 18319/131.
326 *The Builder*, 12 July 1851, p.440.
327 *Select Committee on Improvement of The Health of Towns* (1842), p.252.
328 *Ibid.*, p.7.
329 T.R. Forbes, 'Burial Records for the Parish of St Anne Soho London in 1814–1828', *Yale Journal of Biology and Medicine*, 47 (1974), pp.93–100. LMA Pam. 13200.
330 St Anne Soho vestry minutes, WCA St Anne m/f 162.
331 The Faculty had to be extended as work did not finish until 12 September 1989.
332 Dr Litten to Mr B. Burrough, 5 and 19 February 1988.
333 The biography of Thomas Pitt, Baron Camelford, The Half Mad Lord, was written by Nikolai Tolstoy, who took a very close interest in the exhumation.
334 Survey of London St James Westminster, vol. xxxi, pp.209–18.
335 *Oxford Dictionary of National Biography*, pp.2004–06.
336 The Proceedings of the Old Bailey Ref: 18211024–127.
337 WCA f 929.3.
338 The first was St Katharine Cree in the City of London.
339 St Paul Covent Garden burial registers. Harleian Society, vol. 36.
340 Diocese of London Faculty Papers, LMA Ms. 18319/137. The faculty was granted on 31 May 1855.
341 Diocese of London Vicar General's books, LMA Ms. 9532/15.
342 B. Weinreb and C. Hibbert, *op. cit.*, p. 701.
343 The deputy registrar of the London diocese in Burial Grounds. Supplementary Returns 1834, p.2, states that the City gave to the parish land equal to that acquired but it is not known where this was.
344 J. Diprose, *Some Account of the Parish of St Clement Danes* (1868), p.80.
345 LCC (Improvements) Act 1899, 62 and 63 Vict. c.266, section 50.
346 LMA Ms 19224, file 216.
347 William Kent, *Lost Treasures of London* (1947).
348 LMA Ms. 18319/131.
349 Charles Knight (ed.), *London* (1841, 1851 edn), vol. 4, p.164.

350 PP 1842 (327), *Report from the Select Committee on Improvement of The Health of Towns together with the Minutes of Evidence. Effect of Interment of Bodies in Towns*, pp.13–14.

351 John McMaster, St Martin in the Fields, pp.98–99.

352 George Walker, *Gatherings from Graveyards*, p.157.

353 Elizabeth and Wayland Young, *op. cit.*, pp.124–26.

354 H. Chamberlain, *A New and Compleat History and Survey of the Cities of London and Westminster* (1770), vol. 2, p.590.

355 There is a legend that the architect Thomas Archer consulted Queen Anne on the design of the new church. In reply the monarch petulantly kicked over her footstool and snapped 'Like that!' Thus the four towers are said to give the building the semblance of an upturned footstool.

356 J.E. Smith, St John the Evangelist Westminster (1892), pp.67–69.

357 Ben Weinreb and Christopher Hibbert, *op. cit.*, p.732.

358 William Cowper (1731–1800), *Memoir of My Early Life*, quoted in H.B.Wheatley, *London Past and Present* vol. 2, p.469.

359 Disguised as a parson, Blood got to know Talbot Edwards, Keeper of the Jewels. On 9 May he and others arrived at 7 a.m. and Edwards took them to see the jewels. Blood hit him with a mallet, removed the grille but was arrested as he tried to escape. He was not charged, and died in 1680, aged 62.

360 Philip Holland, St Margaret's Westminster (1993), p.68.

361 *Select Committee on Improvement of The Health of Towns 1842*, p.166.

362 F. Harcourt Hillerson, *St Mary le Strand London* (1938), p.11.

363 WCA St Mary le Strand m/f vol. 16.

364 St George Hanover Square, Minutes of a vestry committee appointed to close the churchyard etc. WCA m/f 562.

365 Diocese of London Faculty Papers, LMA Ms. 18319/118.

366 Diocese of London Faculty Papers for Middlesex parishes, LMA Ms. 21544/584.

367 Bank of England inflation calculator 1750–2010.

 # BIBLIOGRAPHY

N.B. Unless otherwise stated the place of publication is London

Books and Pamphlets

A Magistrate, *A Few Words upon Intramural Burials suggesting a Remedy* (F. Warr, 1849)

Ackroyd, Peter, *London. The Biography* (Vintage, 2001)

Allen, F.D., *Documents and Facts showing the Fatal Effects on Interments in Populous Cities* (New York, 1822)

Anon., *Urban Burial* (W. Strange, 1847)

Aries, Philippe, *The Hour of our Death* (Harmondsworth, 1977)

Arnold, Catharine, *Necropolis, London and its Dead* (Simon and Schuster, 2006)

Baddeley, J.J., *St Giles without Cripplegate* (Baddeley, 1888)

Bard, Robert, *Graveyard London* (Historical Publications, 2008)

Bell, W.G., *The Great Plague in London in 1665* (Bodley Head, 1951)

Betjeman, John, *City of London Churches* (Pitkin, 1974)

Boddington, A., Garland, A.N. and Janaway, R.C. (eds), *Death, decay and reconstruction* (Manchester University Press, 1987)

Bradley, Simon and Nikolaus, *London: The City Churches* (Penguin, 1998)

Bradley, Simon and Nikolaus, *The Buildings of England London, 6 Westminster* (Penguin, 2003)

Briggs, Asa, *Public Opinion and Public Health in the Age of Chadwick* (1946)

Brooke, John, *England's 'Prussian Minister': Edwin Chadwick and the Politics of Government Growth 1832–1854* (Pennsylvania State Press, 1988)

Brown, Sir Thomas, *Urne Buriall* (1658) ed. J. Carter (Cambridge University Press, 1958).

Burman, Peter, *St Paul's Cathedral* (Bell and Hyman, 1987)

Byrne, M. and Bush, G.R. (eds), *St Mary-le-Bow. A History* (Wharncliffe, 2007)

Callender, Ann (ed.), *Godly Mayfair* (Grosvenor Chapel, 1980)

Campbell, K.E., *St Katherine Cree Churchyard: historical facts* (1981)

Cardwell, Revd J.H., *Twenty Years in Soho* (Truslove and Hanson, 1911)

Carpenter, Edward (ed.), *A House of Kings* (John Baker, 1966)

Chadwick, Owen, *The Victorian Church Parts 1 and 2* (Adam and Charles Black, 1966–70)

Chamberlain, Henry, *A New and Compleat History and Survey of the Cities of London and Westminster …* (Cooke, 1769)

Clarke, Revd H.W., *The City Churches* (Simpkin, Marshall, Hamilton and Kent, 1898)

Clarke, John M., *London's Necropolis. A Guide to Brookwood Cemetery* (Sutton Publishing, Stroud, 2004)

Clarke, John M., *The Brookwood Necropolis Railway* (Oakwood Press, 1988)

Cobb, Gerald, *The Old Churches of London*, 3rd edn (1989; 1st pub. B.T. Batsford, 1942)

Colby, Reginald, *Mayfair, a Town within London* (Country Life, 1966)

Coleman, Penny, *Corpses, Coffins, and Crypts: A History of Burial* (Henry Holt & Co., New York, 1997)

Cox, J.E. (ed.), *The Annals of St Helen's Bishopsgate, London* (1876)

Cox, Margaret (ed.), *Grave Concerns* (CBA Research Report 113, 1998)

Curl, James Stevens (ed.), *Kensal Green Cemetery* (Phillimore, 2001)

Curl, James Stevens (ed.), *The Victorian Celebration of Death* (Sutton Publishing, Stroud, 2000)

Defoe, Daniel, *A Journal of the Plague Year* (1722), ed. Cynthia Wall (Penguin, 2003)

Downes, Kerry, *Vanbrugh* (Sidgwick and Jackson, 1987)

Diprose, J., *Some Account of the Parish of Saint Clement Danes, past and present* vol. 1 (1868), vol. 2 (Diprose and Bateman, 1876)

Finer, S.E., *The Life and Times of Sir Edwin Chadwick* (Methuen, 1952)

Forbes, T.R., *Burial Records for the Parish of St Anne Soho* (1974)

Fraser, Antonia, *Cromwell* (Phoenix, 1973)

Giesen, Myra (ed.), *Curating Human Remains: caring for the dead in the United Kingdom* (Boydell & Brewer, 2013)

Gittings, C., *Death, Burial and the Individual in Early Modern England* (Croom Helm, Beckenham, 1984)

Gordon, Caroline and Dewhirst, Wilfrid, *The Ward of Cripplegate in the City of London* (Cripplegate Ward Club, 1985)

Gorer, Geoffrey, *Death, Grief and Mourning in Contemporary Britain* (Crescett Press, 1965)

Hale, Archdeacon William, *Charge to the Clergy of the Archdeaconry of London* (Rivington, 1855)

Hale, Archdeacon William, *Intramural burial in England not injurious to the public health: its abolition injurious to religion and morals* (Rivington, 1855)

Hale, Archdeacon William, *A Letter to the Lord Primate on Intramural Burial* (Rivington, 1855)

Harben, Henry, *A Dictionary of London* (Herbert Jenkins, 1918)

Harcourt Hillerson, F., *St Mary le Strand London* (1938)

Harding, Vanessa, 'Burial of the plague dead in early modern London', *Centre for Metropolitan History Working Paper 1* (1993)

Harding, Vanessa, 'And one more may be laid here. The Location of Burials in Early Modern London', *The London Journal*, vol. 14, no. 2 (1989)

Hearsey, John, *Bridge, Church and Palace* (1961)

Henrey, Mrs Robert, *The Virgin of Aldermanbury* (J.M. Dent, 1958)

Henrey, T.S., *St Botolph without Aldersgate* (Henrey, 1895)

Hill, Mark, *Ecclesiastical Law* (Oxford University Press, 2001)

Holland, Philip, *St Margaret's Westminster* (Aidan Ellis, 1993)

Hollis, Leo, *The Phoenix. St Paul's Cathedral and the Man who made Modern London* (Weidenfeld and Nicolson, 2008)

Holmes, Mrs I., *The London Burial Grounds* (Macmillan, 1896)

Honeybourne, M.B., *A short account of the church of St James Garlickhythe* (Thomas and Newman, 1965)

Houlbrooke, R., *Death, Religion and the Family in England 1480-1750* (Oxford University Press, 1998)

Huelin, Gordon, *Vanished Churches of the City of London* (Guildhall Library Publications, 1996)

Hyde, Ralph, *Ward Maps of the City of London* (Topographical Society, 1999)

Inwood, Stephen, *A History of London (*Macmillan, 1998)

Jacob, W.M., *The Clerical Profession in the Long Eighteenth Century 1680–1840* (Oxford University Press, 2007)

Jeffery, Paul, *The City Churches of Sir Christopher Wren* (Hambledon Press, 1996)

Jeffery, Paul, *St Mary-at-Hill* (The Ecclesiological Society, 1996)

Jenkyns, Richard, *Westminster Abbey* (Profile Books, 2004)

Jenner, Mark, 'Death, Decomposition and Dechristianisation? Public Health and Church Burial in Eighteenth-Century England', *English Historical Review*, vol. 120, No. 487 (2005)

Johnson, Malcolm, *Bustling Intermeddler? The Life and Work of Charles James Blomfield* (Gracewing, Leominster, 2001)

Johnson, Malcolm, *Outside the Gate. St Botolph Aldgate.* (Stepney Books, 1994)

Johnson, Malcolm, *St Martin-in-the-Fields* (Phillimore, Chichester, 2005)

Jupp, Peter, *From Dust to Ashes* The Congregational Lecture (CMH Trust, 1990)

Jupp, Peter, *Death in England* (Manchester University Press, 1999)

Keene, Derek, Burns, Arthur and Saint, Andrew (eds), *St Paul's. The Cathedral Church of London 604–2004* (Yale University Press, 2004)

Keene, Derek, and Harding, Vanessa, *Cheapside Gazetteer – All Hallows Honey Lane (*1987)

Kent, William, *Lost Treasures of London* (Phoenix House, 1947)

Knight, Charles, (ed.) *London*, 6 vols, (C. Knight, 1841–44)

Landers, John, *Death and the Metropolis; studies in the demographic history of London* (Cambridge University Press, 1993)

La Parte-Payne, R.M., *A Short History of St Mary Abchurch* (Blades, East and Blades, 1946)

Lewis, R.A., *Edwin Chadwick and the Public Health Movement 1832-1854* (Longmans Green, 1952)

Lewis, Thomas, *Seasonable Considerations on the Indecent and Dangerous Custom of Burying in Churches and Churchyards with Remarkable Observations historical and philosophical. Proving that the Custom is not only contrary to the Practice of the Antients, but fatal in case of INFECTION* (A. Bettesworth, 1721)

Lewis, W., *Report of a general scheme for extramural sepulture* (HMSO, 1850)

Litten, Julian, *The English Way of Death* (Robert Hale, 1991)

Loudon, John Claudius, *On the Laying Out, Planting and Managing of Cemeteries and on the Improvement of Churchyards* (facsimile 1843 edn), intro. James Stevens Curl (Ivelet Books, 1981)

Maitland, William, *History of London* (T. Osborne, 1756)

Malcolm, J.P., *Londinium Redivivum*, 4 vols (Nichols, 1802–05)

McCarthy, David, *The City of London Cemetery and Crematorium* (Heritage Brochure, 2004)

McManners, J., *Death and the Enlightenment: Changing Attitudes to Death among Christians and Unbelievers in Eighteenth-Century France* (Clarendon Press, Oxford, 1981)

McMaster, John, *A Short History of St Martin-in-the-Fields* (G. Holder, 1916)

McMurray, William, *A city church chronicle: being a short history of the united parishes of St. Anne and St. Agnes, Aldersgate, and of St. John Zachary, London* (McMurray, 1914)

Meara, David, *St Bride's Church Fleet Street* (Jarrold, 2004)

Milbourn, Thomas, *History of St Mildred the Virgin Poultry* (J.R. Smith, 1872)

Miles, Adrian and White, William with Tankard, Danae, *Burial at the site of the parish church of St Benet Sherehog before and after the Great Fire* (MOLAS, 2008)

Miles, Adrian, *Archaeological Excavations 75–82 Farringdon St, 20/30 St Bride's St incorporating St Bride's Lower Burial Ground* (MOLAS, 1992)

Milne, Gustav, *St Bride's church, London. Archaeological research 1952–60 and 1992–5* (English Heritage, 1997)

Molleson, Theya and Cox, Margaret, with A.H. Waldron and D.K. Whittaker, *The Spitalfields project vol. 2 The Anthropology The Middling Sort* (CBA, 1993)

Murray, T.B., *Chronicle of a City Church, St Dunstan in the East* (Smith Elder, 1859).

Newcourt, Richard, *Repertorium ecclesiasticum parochiale londinense*, 2 vols. (Bateman, 1708–10)

O'Donaghue, Revd E.G., *History of Bridewell Hospital* (c.1902)

Parsons, Brian, *Committed to the Cleansing Flame. The Development of Cremation in the Nineteenth Century* (Spire, 2005)

Parsons, Brian, *The London Way of Death* (Sutton Publishing, Stroud, 2001)

Peel, M.J., *Bishop Tait and the City Churches 1856–1868* (The Ecclesiological Society, 1992)

Peggs, James, *A Cry from the Tombs: or Facts and Observations on the Impropriety of Burying the Dead among the Living* (John Snow, 1840)

Pepys, Samuel, *The Diaries of Samuel Pepys; A New and Complete Transcription*, eds Latham, R. and Matthews, W. (Bell and Hyman, 1970–83)

Port, Michael (ed.), *The Commissions for Building Fifty New Churches.* (London Record Society, 1986)

Porter, Stephen, *The Great Plague* (Sutton Publishing, Stroud, 1999)

Prestige, G.L., *St Pauls in its Glory 1831–1911* (SPCK, 1955)

Prothero, Rowland, with Bradley, G.G., *The Life and Correspondence of Arthur Penrhyn Stanley*, 2 vols (John Murray, 1894)

Reeve, Jez and Adams, Max, *The Spitalfields Project vol. 1 The Archaeology Across the Styx* (CBA, 1993)

Redpath, W., *Fleet Street Church Restored* (Guild of St Bride, 1957)

Richardson, R., *Death, Dissection and the Destitute* (Routledge & Kegan Paul, 1988)

Rodwell, W.J., *Church Archaeology* (Batsford, 1989)

Rugg, J. and Hussein, I. 'Burying London's dead: a study of strategic failure',
  Mortality, 8 (2003)

Scheuer, J.L. and Black, S.M., *The St Bride's Documented Skeletal Collection* (University
  of Glasgow, 1995)

Schofield, John and Maloney, Cath (eds), *Archaeology in the City of London 1907–91*
  (Museum of London, 1998)

Smith, E., *The Church of St Mary Abchurch* (Ecclesiological Society, 1959)

Smith, J.E., *St John the Evangelist Westminster* (Wightman, 1892)

Smith, Stephen, *Underground London* (Little Brown, 2004)

Stanley, Arthur, *Historical Memorials of Westminster Abbey* (John Murray, 1876)

Strange, Julie-Marie, *Death, Grief and Poverty 1870–1914* (Cambridge University Press, 2005)

Strange, Julie-Marie, 'Only a Pauper Whom Nobody Owns: Reassessing the Pauper
  Grave *c.* 1880–1914', *Past and Present*, No. 178 (Feb. 2003)

Stone, Revd William, *The Present Interment Act. Its unjust, inefficient and mischievous
  character. A Letter addressed to the Rt Hon Lord Viscount Palmerston* (Rivington, 1853)

Stow, John, *Survey of London 1598* (John Windet, 1603)

Strype, John, *A Survey of the Cities of London and Westminster* (1720)

Tatton-Brown, Tim and Mortimer, Richard (eds) *Westminster Abbey. The Lady Chapel
  of Henry VII* (Boydell Press, 2003)

Tomlinson, Edward, *A History of the Minories* (Murray, 1922)

Turner, J., *Burial Fees of the Principal Churches, Chapels and New Burial Grounds in
  London and its Environs; with List of Searchers, Hours of Burial, Early Dues &c.,
  and all Necessary Information for Undertakers* (Cunningham and Salmon, 1838)

Walcott, M.E.C., *History of the parish of St Margaret Westminster* (W. Blanchard, 1847)

Walker, G.A., *Gatherings from Graveyards* (Longman, 1839)

Walker, G.A., *Interment and Disinterment* (Longman, 1843)

Watson, Revd W., *The Clergy-Man's Law* (H. Lintot, 1747)

Webb, E.A., *The Records of St Bartholomew Smithfield*, 2 vols (Oxford University Press, 1921)

Weinreb, Ben and Hibbert, Christopher (eds), *The London Encyclopaedia* (Book Club
  Associates, 1983)

Westlake, H.F., *St Margaret Westminster* (Smith Elder, 1914)

Wheatley, H.B., *London Past and Present*, 3 vols (John Murray, 1891)

Wheatley, H.B., *Stow's Survey of London* (Dent, 1956)

Wooldridge, Kevin, *An Evaluation and Assessment of Archaeological Resources for
  the proposed development of 75–83 Farringdon St, 20–30 Shoe Lane London EC4
  incorporating the St Bride's Lower Burial Ground* (MOLAS, 1991)

Wren, Christopher, *Life and Works of Sir Christopher Wren. From the Parentalia or
  Memoirs of his son Christopher (1750),* ed. E.J. Enthoven (E. Arnold, 1903)

Young, Elizabeth and Wayland, *London's Churches* (Grafton Books, 1986)

Survey of London

(All published by the LCC or GLC)

Vol. 5, Riley, W.E. and Gomme, L., *St Giles in the Fields* (1914)

Vol. 9, Reddan, M. and Clapham, A., *St Helen Bishopsgate* (1924)

Vol. 10, Cox, M.H. and Norman, P., *St Margaret Westminster* (1926)

Vol. 12, Redstone, E.J., *All Hallows Barking* (1929)

Vols 18–20, Gater, G.H. and Hiorns, F.R., *St Martin-in-the-Fields* (1940)

Vols 29–30, Sheppard, F.H.W., *St James Piccadilly* (1963).

Vols 33–34, Sheppard, F.H.W., *St Anne Soho* (1966)

Vol. 36, Sheppard, F.H.W., *St Paul Covent Garden* (1970)

Reports and Surveys

PP 1831–32 (199) *The General Report to the King's Most Excellent Majesty in his High Court of Chancery* (Ecclesiastical Courts Commission, 1832)

Burial Grounds. Supplementary Returns to an Address of the Honourable The House of Commons. 22 March 1834. A Return of the several sums expended by the Parishes of the Diocese of London, Compiled by Joseph Shephard Deputy Registrar of the Bishop of London's Registry

PP 1842 (327) *Report from the Select Committee on Improvement of The Health of Towns together with the Minutes of Evidence. Effect of Interment of Bodies in Towns*

PP 1843 [509] Chadwick, *A Supplementary Report on the Results of a Special Inquiry into the Practice of Interment in Towns* (W. Clowes for HMSO, 1843)

The 1851 Census of Great Britain. Report and Tables on Religious Worship in England and Wales (Eyre and Spottiswoode, 1853)

Dawson T., Reports to Commissioners of Sewers 1853–56 Report re the number of burials in City of London parishes 1849–52 (1853)

Simon, Sir John, *Introductory Report Suggesting the Outline Of A Scheme For Extramural Interment* (1853)

PP 1858 (387) *Report of the Select Committee of the House of Lords appointed to inquire into the deficiency of means of spiritual instruction and places of divine worship in the Metropolis, and in other populous districts in England and Wales, especially in the mining and manufacturing districts*

The Religious Census of London reprinted from *The British Weekly* (Hodder and Stoughton, 1888)

London County Council, Proposed Demolition of Nineteen Churches: A Report by the Clerk of the Council and the Architect of the Council (1920)

A Post-excavation Assessment of All Hallows by the Tower (AOC Archaeology Group, 2000)

The Church of St Luke Islington London EC1. Post Excavation Assessment and Updated Project Design (Oxford Archaeology, 2002)

'Home Office, Burial Law and Policy in the 21st Century: The need for a sensitive and sustainable approach' (2004)

Dept for Culture, Media and Sport, *Guidance for the Care of Human Remains in Museums* (2004)

'Church of England, English Heritage, Guidance for best practice for treatment of
    human remains excavated from Christian burial grounds in England' (2005)
'Ministry of Justice, Burial Law and Policy in the 21st Century: The Way Forward' (2007)

Newspapers and periodicals/serial publications

The Builder	*The Penny Magazine*
Chronicles of Convocation	*Quarterly Review*
The City Press	*The Record*
The Complete Newgate Calendar	*St Martin's Review*
Current Archaeology	*The Standard*
The Gentleman's Magazine	*The Times*
Hansard	*The Weekly Dispatch*

INDEX